W9-AAZ-793

A Rabbi Looks at Jesus' Parables

A Rabbi Looks at Jesus' Parables

Frank Stern

ROWMAN & LITTLEFIELD PUBLISHERS, INC.
Lanham • Boulder • New York • Toronto • Oxford

ROWMAN & LITTLEFIELD PUBLISHERS, INC.

Published in the United States of America
by Rowman & Littlefield Publishers, Inc.
A wholly owned subsidiary of The Rowman & Littlefield Publishing Group, Inc.
4501 Forbes Boulevard, Suite 200, Lanham, Maryland 20706
www.rowmanlittlefield.com

PO Box 317
Oxford
OX2 9RU, UK

Copyright © 2006 by Rowman & Littlefield Publishers, Inc.

All rights reserved. No part of this publication may be reproduced,
stored in a retrieval system, or transmitted in any form or by any
means, electronic, mechanical, photocopying, recording, or otherwise,
without the prior permission of the publisher.

British Library Cataloguing in Publication Information Available

Library of Congress Cataloging-in-Publication Data

Stern, Frank, 1936-
  A rabbi looks at Jesus' parables / Frank Stern.
    p.   cm.
  Includes bibliographical references and index.
  ISBN 0-7425-4270-X (cloth : alk. paper)—ISBN 0-7425-4271-8 (pbk. : alk.
  paper)   1. Jesus Christ—Parables.   2. Jesus Christ—Jewish interpretations.   I.
  Title.
  BT375.3.S73   2006
  226.8'06—dc22   2005020327

Printed in the United States of America

∞ ™ The paper used in this publication meets the minimum requirements of American
National Standard for Information Sciences—Permanence of Paper for Printed Library
Materials, ANSI/NISO Z39.48–1992.

Contents

Acknowledgments

At the Hebrew Union College in Cincinnati, I studied under Samuel Sandmel, Ellis Rivkin, and Julius Guttmann. A brilliant teacher, Sandmel was one of the few Jews then in academia devoted to New Testament and intertestamental scholarship. I've devoured most of his books: *Herod, Profile of a Tyrant; The Genius of Paul; Judaism and Christian Beginnings; A Jewish Understanding of the New Testament;* and *The First Christian Century in Judaism and Christianity.*

A creative scholar, Rivkin explored the birth of rabbinic Judaism in *A Hidden Revolution* and Jesus' crucifixion in *What Crucified Jesus?*

Guttmann taught Talmud and provided wonderful insights into the early development of rabbinic tradition in *Rabbinic Judaism in the Making.*

Though I didn't study with them personally, the writings of Solomon Zeitlin, Emil Schürer, and Joseph Klausner significantly influenced my understanding of New Testament traditions.

Among contemporary historians, I'm particularly grateful to Michael Grant: *The Jews in the Roman World; Jesus: An Historian's Review of the Gospels; The Roman Emperors;* and *Herod the Great.*

Jacob Neusner's books on Mishnah and Midrash have been very insightful.

Among books published recently on the life and teachings of Jesus, I found these books particularly helpful: James Charlesworth, *Jesus' Jewishness* and *Jesus Within Judaism;* Alan Segal, *Rebecca's Children: Judaism and Christianity in the Roman World;* John Dominic Crossan, *The Essential Jesus* and *Jesus: A Revolutionary Biography;* John Dominic Crossan and Jonathan Reed, *Excavating Jesus;* A. N. Wilson, *Jesus: A Life;* Richard Horsley, *Bandits, Prophets and Messiahs: Popular Movements at the Time of Jesus;* Philip Yancey, *The Jesus I Never Knew;* E. P. Sanders, *The Historical Figure of Jesus;* David Flusser,

Jesus; Donald Spoto, *The Hidden Jesus*; Bruce Chilton, *Rabbi Jesus*; and John Shelby Spong, *Liberating the Gospels: Reading the Bible with Jewish Eyes.*

I respond positively to those scholars who see Jesus' Jewishness not as incidental but as essential to his life and teachings and who assert that we cannot fully understand Jesus' teachings without understanding the context in which they were offered. *A Rabbi Looks at Jesus' Parables* tries to strip away twenty-one centuries of interpretation and analysis to discover how listeners in Jesus' audiences might have understood his stories.

I want to acknowledge the assistance provided me by Brian Romer and Marian Haggard at Rowman & Littlefield Publishers, and I thank my friends, and particularly my wife, for their encouragement and support. Though the ideas are my own, their comments improved the quality of my book.

This book is dedicated with love to Joyce, our children and grandchildren.

CHAPTER ONE

Introduction

Most Jews fear to read the New Testament, and most Christians read the New Testament unaware it is permeated with Jewish ideas and images. As a consequence, both Christians and Jews miss an opportunity to share a common treasure.

Jesus spoke primarily to Jews. His parables reflected and expanded the Jewish experiences of his audiences. Cleared of centuries of Christian interpretations and presented within their Jewish context, these parables can be a mine of information for Jews about Judaism in the first century—about how Jews behaved then, what Jews believed, and why some Jews responded to but most rejected Jesus' teachings.

The parables are among the most memorable aspects of Christian instruction. Ministers still preach about the Great Supper, the Ten Maidens, and the Good Shepherd. Sunday school classes still study the Good Samaritan and the Prodigal Son. But what the parables mean today is different from what they meant to the Jews who first heard them twenty-one centuries ago.

The people in the synagogues where Jesus preached, on the mountain in Galilee and along the shore of Lake Ginesseret, were Jews. Jesus' words triggered Jewish images in their minds. Jesus' healings reinforced Jewish understandings and Jewish beliefs. Seen in their original context as an outgrowth of Jewish experiences in the first century, Jesus' parables provide enormous insight to Christians about Jesus' first followers and their initial understandings of his message.

While the parables do not contain all of Jesus' experiences, they provide a wonderful introduction to his teachings. Almost one-third of all the words Jesus spoke are in these stories. More significantly, Jesus used parables to hide information he alone understood and wanted to convey only to his supporters—dangerous information that contradicted conventional wisdom and irritated the leaders of the Jewish people. By uncovering the secrets hidden within his parables, we come to understand why some Jews were attracted to his teachings but many Jews were shocked and appalled by them. In the process, we also explore the dynamics of Jewish life in first-century Palestine.

Each chapter attempts to accomplish the same two objectives: to uncover the message(s) hidden within each parable, and to relate each parable to its first-century religious and historical context. Every parable Jesus spoke is explored.

Presentation

There is no set order to Jesus' parables. They occur in different places throughout the gospels. Some writers present them as they occur from gospel to gospel—all the parables in Matthew first, then all the parables in Mark, until the gospels have been covered. This gets a little confusing when some parables from Matthew are repeated in Mark and Luke. I explore all similar parables in the same chapter.

Some writers presume each parable has a particular and unique message, and they organize the parables theologically, grouping Jesus' teachings about the Kingdom of God in one section and his comments about faith in another. I disagree. I believe some parables have multiple meanings. Jesus kept the referents vague deliberately to encourage listeners to uncover layers of meaning.

Some writers give a theological twist to their titles. Titles like the "Parable of the Unrighteous Steward" and the "Parable of the Wicked Vineyard Owner" convey to the reader the writer's conclusions about the meaning of the story. Even a title like the "Parable of the Prodigal Son" focuses on the son when just as much attention ought to be paid to the father. I try to use neutral language and to avoid titles that push the reader in one direction or another.

Translations

Jesus prayed in Hebrew and taught in Aramaic, but we have no ancient Hebrew or Aramaic versions of the New Testament. The oldest record we have of Jesus' speeches is in Greek. From Greek the texts were translated into Latin, French, German, Russian, Icelandic, and several hundred other languages.

Most of us acquired our knowledge of the New Testament in English. But

English translations often differ significantly in their understandings of the original Greek. For example, on the birth of Jesus in the opening chapter of Matthew, the King James Bible translates verse 18 as "Mary was espoused to Joseph," but the *Twentieth Century New Testament* translates the same verse as "Mary was engaged to Joseph." Those are very different images. In the first version, Mary was Joseph's wife. In the second, Mary was his fiancée.

The same is true of the next verse. The Revised Standard Version translates verse 19 as "her husband Joseph," while *The New Testament: A New Translation* provides "Joseph, her husband-to-be." In the first, Mary and Joseph were married. In the second, they were not yet married.

Every English translation distorts the Greek text. That was as true of the Tyndale Bible and the King James Bible as it is of the modern translations produced by William Beck, James Moffatt, Edgar Goodspeed, and the Jewish Publications Society.

For example, the translation of the Hebrew word *rakhameem* as "mercy" or "compassion" falls short of the intense emotions involved. A *rekhem* is a womb, and *rakhameem* are the emotions a mother and father feel for their newborn child.

Two Greek words—*agape* and *eros*—in the New Testament are translated by the same English word, "love." The same word cannot indicate the differences between the two Greek terms. "Friendship" (*agape*) and "romance" (*eros*) don't convey the complex emotions involved.

Nonetheless, I had to provide an English translation. Otherwise, most readers would have no access to the text. For the New Testament, I chose the *Revised Standard Version of the Bible*, published in 1946 by the Division of Christian Education of the National Council of the Churches of Christ in the United States of America. The Revised Standard Version is grounded in Christian scholarship, widely accepted, provides an English version of the gospels that reads smoothly, and preserves the integrity of the Greek.[1]

For the Old Testament, I chose *Tanakh: A New Translation of the Holy Scriptures according to the Traditional Hebrew Text*, published in 1985 by the Jewish Publications Society. Tanakh is America's most widely read English translation of the original Hebrew.[2]

Jesus deliberately couched his teachings in parables because they sometimes contained dangerous secrets. Rather than state them directly, he spoke about them metaphorically. The initiated understood. Others were intrigued, confused, or annoyed. This book will reveal these hidden and dangerous secrets.

What Is a Parable?

Scholars have tried to distinguish the differences between metaphors, similes, allegories, riddles, and parables, to no avail. Some metaphors are riddles, and some riddles are parables. They slip and slide over one another. Especially in the case of Jesus' teachings, it's best to understand that his parables encompassed all these forms—and often contained multiple meanings.

None of these forms was unique to Jesus. Just the opposite. Because his listeners were used to hearing instructions presented metaphorically, they felt comfortable with his way of teaching and could quickly apprehend the ideas he was conveying. If I wrote this sentence in French or Greek, many readers would have difficulty understanding it. The form interferes with the message. So too in the first century. The language Jesus spoke, the forms he used to convey his teachings, and even the symbols he employed were effective in part because they were familiar to his audiences. The form didn't interfere with the message. It was Jewish.

The Hebrew word for parable is *mashal*. Jeremias provides examples of *m'shalim* in post-biblical Judaism. They include "parable, similitude, allegory, fable, proverb, apocalyptic revelation, riddle, symbol, pseudonym, fictitious person, example, theme, argument, apology, refutation, [and] jest."[3] First-century Jewish literature was rife with *m'shalim*. Here are two examples:

The sages offered a parable about women.

[When is a woman like] an unripe fruit, a ripening fig, or a fully ripe fig? "An unripe fruit"—while she is still a child [up to twelve years]; "a ripening fig"—these are the days of her girlhood [between twelve and 12.5 years]; . . . and "a fully ripe fig"— after she is past her girlhood, when her father has no more rights over her.[4]

A king had a delightful park in which were fine rare figs. He put two keepers in it, one lame and the other blind. The lame man said to the blind man, "I see fine rare figs in the park. Let me mount on your back and we'll get them to eat." So the lame man climbed on the blind man's back and they got them and ate them. After a while the owner of the park came and asked, "Where are the fine rare figs?" The lame man said, "Have I legs to walk about?" The blind man said, "Have I eyes to see?" What did the king do? He made the lame man get on the back of the blind man and punished the pair together.[5]

The parable was popular in Jesus' day, thoroughly Jewish, and familiar to Jesus' audiences as a format in which teachers conveyed their ideas.

What Is Midrash?

Books did not exist in the first century. Jews read scrolls. The *archisynagogos*[6] was charged with protecting the sacred scrolls owned by the community, and he provided the scrolls used during worship in the synagogue.

Scrolls were hand-written and very expensive. Only the most dedicated scholars and the rich could afford to spend their hard-earned assets on scrolls. Ordinary Jews did not own scrolls. They saw scrolls in the synagogue and heard them read at Sabbath and holiday services. On rare occasions, they may have paid a scribe to record on a scroll a business transaction, marriage contract, or divorce decree.

As children they were told biblical stories. Each Sabbath in their synagogues they heard a section of the Torah—the first five books of the Hebrew Bible—and a section of one of the prophets. On holidays other sacred scrolls were read to them. Over years they acquired a fairly extensive knowledge of the Hebrew Bible—but it was all by rote.

According to their belief, God had revealed all knowledge to Moses on Mount Sinai; and Moses transmitted all that knowledge to the Jewish people in the five scrolls that bore his name. All that God created in the universe, all that God was, all that would happen in the future, and all that God wanted us to do was contained in the revelation Moses received, recorded, and transmitted. But it was abbreviated and buried in the text.

Anyone hearing a quotation from the Hebrew Bible could give his own opinion on what the text meant, but his guess was likely to be far-fetched and have little to do with what God intended. To bring to light what God actually meant involved knowledge and skills beyond the abilities of most ordinary Jews. So there emerged in the centuries just before Jesus sages adept at teasing from sacred scripture the hidden meanings of the text—the actual revelations God made to Moses on Sinai.

The method they used was Midrash.

The Hebrew verb-root *d-r-sh* means "to search," and Midrash was the process of interpretation by which teachers extracted their understandings of God's will from biblical texts. The same text could convey many meanings. There could be differences of opinion. But the foundation of first-century Jewish teaching was Midrash. In their synagogues, preachers expounded the Law using Midrash. Teachers instructed their students using Midrash. Scholars discussed, probed, and challenged using Midrash. The ideas they extracted and the rules they articulated became the basis for Jewish life.

Neusner records a discussion on this verse in the Song of Songs: "I have come back to my garden, my sister, my bride."[7] Initially a parable was presented: Rabbi Azariah in the name of Rabbi Simon said, "[The matter may be compared to the case of] a king who became angry at a noble woman and expelled her from his palace. After some time he wanted to bring her back. She said, 'Let him renew in my behalf the earlier state of affairs, and then he may bring me back.'"[8] In other words, it was not enough that the king regretted his behavior. He had to undo the harm he had created.

Later in the discussion Rabbi Hanina said, "The Torah teaches you proper conduct, specifically that a groom should not go into the marriage canopy [should not have intercourse with his wife] until the bride gives him permission to do so." Rabbi Hanina used the verse immediately preceding to prove his point: "Let my beloved come into his garden and enjoy its luscious fruit."[9]

Parable, notions about repentance, and moral instruction all in one discussion—that's Midrash. And that's what Jesus, his disciples, and the people in his audiences were used to.

Assumptions

There are scholars who contend that Jesus never lived, that the words and actions attributed to him were fabrications, and that Paul or someone else (or some other group) invented Jesus. I disagree. This book assumes that Jesus was a historical figure who lived and taught in the first century and who began the movement we now call Christianity.

There are scholars who contend that Jesus never spoke large sections of the parables attributed to him. They claim they were embellishments of the early Christian community or inventions of the gospel writers. I disagree. This book assumes that the parables written in the gospels reflect Jesus' teachings—though elaborations and interpretations may have been added to them by succeeding generations of early Christians.

This work is a study of Jesus' parables. As a consequence, most of the discussion focuses on the gospels. Large parts of the New Testament are not explored, especially the experiences and teachings of Paul and others who lived in the centuries after Jesus. Little of the writings of the Church Fathers and later Christian theologians are considered. Using the gospel parables, my goal is to uncover what Jesus said to his contemporaries and how they might have understood his words.

With considerable variety, each chapter will include a brief introduction, the parable, clarifications of key words and phrases, some discussion of its message(s), an exploration of comparable concerns in Jewish literature, a review of the secrets uncovered, and a clear articulation of where Jesus differed from Jewish tradition.

The words *son* and *spirit* are not capitalized, since they were not capitalized when they were spoken. For additional discussion and scholarly explorations, the reader is encouraged to consult the bibliography.

Notes

1. To make a specific point, occasionally I provide a different translation.

2. Occasionally I provide my own translation.

3. Joachim Jeremias, *The Parables of Jesus*, revised edition (New York: Charles Scribner's Sons, 1963), 20.

4. M. Niddah 5:7.

5. Mekhilta de-R. Simeon ben Yokhai, as presented in George Foot Moore, *Judaism in the First Centuries of the Christian Era* (Cambridge, Mass.: Harvard University Press, 1927), vol. 1, 487–88.

6. A Greek term meaning "chief of the synagogue," *archisynagogos* referred to the highest-ranking official of the synagogue.

7. Song of Songs 5:1.

8. *Pesiqta deRav Kahana*, as presented in Jacob Neusner, *The Midrash: An Introduction*, (Northvale, N.J.: Jason Aronson Inc., 1989), 8–9.

9. Song of Songs 4:16.

CHAPTER TWO

The Search for Paradise

Singer Peggy Lee's haunting refrain "Is that all there is?" was echoed two thousand years ago in the discussions of Jewish sages about God's justice and mercy. How is it fair, they asked, that the innocent suffer and the wicked prosper? How is the death of young children or the spread of infectious diseases or oppression by foreign governments compatible with God's love and concern? Their affirmations provided an ideological framework within which Jews found answers to their most perplexing problems.

Prophets and sages alike declared without qualification that God was fair. Ultimately, every soul would receive its just desserts. Sometimes God's justice manifested itself while people were still alive. More often justice prevailed after a person died—when his soul was brought to judgment.

By the time of Jesus, most Jews shared a common set of beliefs about life after death:

- At death, the soul separated from the body. The body decomposed, but the soul remained intact and alive.
- God reviewed the life of each human being and determined the fate of every soul.
- As a result of His evaluation, God assigned to every soul its portion in the world beyond death.

In this world beyond death, God governed and divine justice prevailed. The righteous received their proper reward. The wicked suffered appropriate punishment.

This afterlife was called by many names in Jewish literature: Paradise, the World to Come, and the Kingdom of God.

Everyone wanted to get in, so teachers arose who offered pathways to paradise—different paths for different teachers:

- The path of reason.
- The path of Jewish mysticism.
- The path offered by the Dead Sea community.
- The path the sages taught.
- The path that Jesus taught.

The Path of Reason

Philo Judeaus equated soul with mind, suggesting that a man's mind operated in and on his body the way God's presence operated in and on the universe. Love of wisdom could sweep the human soul beyond this world to comprehend the grand images in the mind of God. For Philo, to think like God was be in God's presence and to apprehend the world from God's point of view. At that point, the human soul merged with God and entered Paradise.

Simeon ben Joshua ben Eleazar ben Sirakh introduced each of the eight sections of his collection with a poem extolling wisdom. Wisdom was Torah, the true basis of divine thought and human comprehension. Ben Sirakh invited the untutored to his school and instructed each student to devote his whole mind to the pursuit of wisdom and to concentrate his thoughts on the Law of the Most High. "If he lives he will leave a greater name than the multitude; and when he rests from his labors [dies], it will be greater still."[1]

The Path of Jewish Mysticism

The first chapter of Genesis gave rise to speculations about how God created the world and what the universe was like before Creation, and the visions of Ezekiel encouraged vivid imaginings about God's throne and God's appearance. These speculations were considered by traditional authorities improper and dangerous. Nonetheless, some sages determined to explore the mysteries of Jewish mysticism. Much more than a study of texts and traditions, the mystical quest to experience the divine directly demanded journeys into Paradise induced by mystic rapture. Their visions were believed to be real ascents into heaven.

Four of the most eminent sages of the early second century—Rabbi Simeon ben Azzai, Rabbi Simeon ben Zoma, Rabbi Elisha ben Abuya, and Rabbi Akiba—practiced mystical rites in order to apprehend the mysteries of God and Creation. All were overwhelmed by their experiences: Ben Azzai died, Ben Zoma lost his mind, and Ben Abuya became an apostate. Only Akiba survived.[2]

The Path Offered by the Dead Sea Community

One of the earliest examples of Jewish mysticism was found in Cave 4 at Qumran. Though just a fragment of a larger hymn, it conveyed dazzling images of life in God's presence with such phrases as "the seat of Your honor and the footstools of the feet of Your glory," "the chariots of Your glory with their multitudes and wheel-angels," "foundations of fire," "fires of lights and miraculous brilliances," "fountain of discovery and counsel of holiness and secret truth," "dwelling places of uprightness," and "congregation of goodness and pious ones of truth and eternal merciful ones and miraculous mysteries."[3]

In this glorious future time, all secrets would stand revealed. The members of the Qumran fellowship (both alive and dead) would experience the splendor and glory of God's Presence. And the wicked would vanish from the earth.

The pathway to these Final Days was suggested in the text declaring that those who observed "the weeks of Holiness in their rightful order and monthly flags in their seasons and festivals of Glory in their times" would be welcomed into Paradise. All others would be rejected and perish.

Another Dead Sea document reinforced this image. It described a feast in which all Israel would participate during the Last Days. "As they arrive, all the newcomers shall be assembled—women and children included—and read all the statutes of the Covenant. They shall be indoctrinated in all of their laws, for fear that otherwise they may sin accidentally."[4]

The Path the Sages Taught

The disciples of Rabbi Eliezer gathered about him as he lay sick in bed and asked him, "Master, teach us the ways of life that by them we may attain life in the World to Come." He replied, "Take care to honor your fellowman, restrain your sons from reading [the Bible on their own, without traditional commentaries and explanations], set them between the knees of scholars, and when you pray, know before whom you stand. Thus will you attain life in the World to Come."[5]

The disciples of Hillel and Shammai agreed that Daniel 12:2 referred to the wholly righteous and the wholly wicked. The wholly righteous were destined for "eternal life"; the wholly wicked would suffer "everlasting abhorrence." But they differed on the question of what would happen to the majority of people in between, who were neither totally righteous nor totally wicked.

The School of Shammai held that those who had done more evil than good or in whom good and evil were equally balanced would go down to Gehenna, spend some time there, arise from there healed, and enter heaven.[6] For them, the fires of Gehenna were purgatory. Like gold and silver, these souls would emerge refined and pure.

The School of Hillel agreed that those who had committed more evil than good would go to hell and be purged, but it maintained that in the case of those in whom good and evil were equally balanced, God would incline the balance to the side of mercy and not send them down to Gehenna at all.[7]

Rabbi Eleazer of Modiim asserted that any person who profaned the sacred offerings, despised the festivals, shamed another in public, nullified the covenant of Abraham,[8] or disclosed meanings in the Law that were not according to Jewish legal tradition committed a heinous sin. No matter how much learning and good works he possessed, he had no share in the World to Come.[9]

It says in Leviticus 18:5 concerning the commandments of the Torah: "If a man do them, he shall live." That means he shall live in the World to Come, for in this world a man's end is that he dies.[10]

These are examples of the kind of discourse to which Jews of the first century were exposed. Sadducees, Pharisees, and Essenes taught in the outer courtyard of the Temple and in cities and villages across the land. Prophets, preachers, and priests journeyed from town to town, excoriating, warning, instructing, and enlightening the Jews they encountered. Stoics and Epicureans dined in the homes of wealthy Jews and lectured in stoa and academies throughout Palestine. Scrolls containing the wisdom of Enoch, Esdras, Ben Sirakh, Baruch, and Solomon, and the philosophies of Plato, Democritus, Zeno, Aristotle, and Philo were available to Jews who could afford to buy them. Into this dynamic cultural and religious discourse Jesus inserted his own teachings.

The Path That Jesus Taught

In Jerusalem at the close of the Last Supper, Jesus declared he was leaving his fellowship of followers to prepare a place for them in heaven. One of the disciples, Thomas, asked poignantly, "Lord, we do not know where you are going. How can we then know the way?" And Jesus responded, "I am the way. . . . No one comes to the Father except by me."[11]

Jesus rejected the other paths—including the path prescribed by the sages—and he expected his followers to do the same. The only way to Paradise was through Jesus. By obeying his teachings and devoting themselves to his ideas, true believers would experience the presence of God. "If you had known me, you would have known my Father also."[12]

There was also a general consensus among Jews on the future of human civilization. According to most teachers, civilization would experience the same cycle of life, death, and afterlife. Just as individual human beings died, so would society as it was presently constituted. In the course of that collapse, all people then alive would be arraigned for judgment. Some would survive the devastation and live on in a glorious New World. Most would die and disappear.

In Jewish literature, this splendid New World was called by the same names: Paradise, the World to Come, and the Kingdom of God.

Images of the Conflagration in Daniel

Daniel depicted the ultimate triumph of God and Israel in vivid and graphic detail:

> Four mighty beasts, different from each other, emerged from the sea. The first was like a lion but had eagles' wings. . . . A second beast was like a bear, but raised on one side, with three fangs in its mouth among its teeth. . . . Another one was like a leopard, and on its back it had four wings. . . . (and) four heads. . . . There was a fourth beast—fearsome, dreadful and very powerful—with great iron teeth that devoured and crushed and stamped the remains with its feet. . . . The beast was killed as I looked on. Its body was destroyed and consigned to the flames. The dominion of the other beasts was taken away. . . . I asked the true meaning of all this. . . . Four kingdoms will arise out of the earth. Then the holy one of the Most High will receive the kingdom and will possess the kingdom forever. (Daniel 7:3–18)

By the time of Jesus, Jewish tradition had identified the first three beasts as Babylonia, Persia, and the Greeks—with the three horns in the third beast representing the breakup of Alexander's empire into three regions. The fourth beast—Rome—was the most terrifying of all. Yet even this empire, which devoured all the others, would succumb to God's will. Roman rule would be overthrown. The Jews would be free of foreign domination and oppression and live forever under God's providence.

Images of the Apocalypse in the Dead Sea Scrolls

In the Last Days, Jews would experience the final showdown between Light and Darkness, Righteousness and Evil. A series of scroll fragments from Cave 1 at Qumran outlined battle formations and depicted battle scenes in which the members of the *Yahad* (the fellowship of believers), led by the authentic High Priest, would vanquish the armies of the Devil (Belial, the King of Darkness). One fragment opened with the following description:

> The Rule of War. The first attack of the Sons of Light shall be against the forces of the Sons of Darkness, the army of Belial . . . the troops of Edom, Moab and the sons of Ammon and . . . the Philistines and against the Kittim of Assyria and their allies those who violated the Covenant:[13] . . . The Sons of Light shall battle the forces of Darkness amid the roar of a great multitude and the clamor of gods and men to (make manifest) God's might. It shall be a day of disaster. . . . It shall be a time of great tribulation for the people. . . . Of all its afflictions none shall be like this, from its sudden beginning until its end in eternal redemption. (1QM)[14]

This worldwide conflagration would result in the defeat and demise of the forces of evil and the establishment of God's kingdom forever on earth.

Images of the Conflagration Jesus Taught

Jesus warned his disciples that a terrible time was coming in which they would be beaten and brought to trial. "Brother will deliver up brother to death, and the father his child, and children will rise against parents and have them put to death."[15] God's Temple in Jerusalem would be desecrated and destroyed.

> For nation will rise against nation, and kingdom against kingdom; there will be earthquakes in various places, there will be famines; this is but the beginning of the birth-pangs. . . . For in those days there will be such tribulation as has not been from the beginning of the creation which God created until now, and never will be. . . . After that tribulation, the sun will be darkened, and the moon will not give its light, and the stars will be falling from heaven, and the powers in the heavens will be shaken. And then they will see the son of man coming in clouds with great power and glory. And then he will send out the angels, and gather his elect from the four winds, from the ends of the earth to the ends of heaven. (Mark 13:8–27)

While Jesus' teachings were unique, they contained images common to Jewish literature in the first century. They had to. Otherwise his listeners wouldn't have understood his allusions.

In this vision of the end of days, Jesus deliberately included the following phrases to connect with images already in the minds of his audience:

- *Earthquakes . . . famines*—A nice bit of alliteration. In both Hebrew and Aramaic the words are *ra'ash* and *ra'av*. The phrase reminded people of the punishments predicted by Isaiah, Jeremiah, Ezekiel, and Zechariah.[16]
- *Birth-pangs*—The phrase often appeared in rabbinic literature as "birth-pangs of the Messiah."[17]
- *Son of man*—The phrase occurred frequently in Hebrew *(ben adam)* and Aramaic *(bar enosh)* literature, where it meant simply "a human being." In Daniel 7:13; Enoch 46:2, 48:2; and Sibylline Oracles 5:414, the phrase exhibited messianic overtones.
- *Angels*—In Jewish literature, angels frequently were depicted as God's messengers. Two angels protected Lot from attack by his neighbors and warned him of the impending destruction of Sodom and Gomorrah; an angel of the Lord slew 185,000 Assyrian soldiers laying siege to Jerusalem; and an angel protected Daniel from being torn and eaten by lions. In Jacob's vision, angels were ascending and descending God's ladder.[18]

Jesus provided one path to paradise. Other teachers suggested different routes. They had one thing in common—each pathway to paradise quoted the Bible, for everything about God, the universe, human life, and salvation was contained in its verses. Jews in the first century accepted as authentic only those notions rooted in the Hebrew Bible.

Each sentence of the Bible contained myriads of information. Peel back one layer of meaning and another emerged—and beneath that another and another. Every text had its simple meaning (called *p'shat* in Hebrew); hinted at additional insights (called *remez* in Hebrew); and included homilies, moral lessons, advice for proper living and inspiration (called *d'rash*), and secret knowledge accessible to the trained reader (called *sod*). By plumbing all these levels, by exploring and comprehending all the nuances of meaning of even one biblical verse, a person entered paradise (*pardeys* in Aramaic—an acronym made up of the first letter of *p'shat*, *remez*, *drash* and *sod* = P̲aR̲- D̲eyS̲).

Every Sabbath morning and on every major holiday—year in and year out—Jews would hear sections of the Bible read and explained in the course of their communal worship. Though few were scholars, most Jews in Jesus' time were familiar with biblical images, insights, injunctions, and allusions. Most of their spiritual, moral, and religious education as adults came from the explanations of biblical verses offered by local scholars and itinerant teachers.

Jesus' preaching fit this pattern. He taught often in synagogues, sprinkled his sermons with biblical quotes and allusions, and warned about the coming conflagration.

Therefore, we begin our survey of Jesus' parables in his hometown synagogue, with an amazing story told by Luke.

Notes

1. Ben Sirakh 39:11.

2. Hagigah 14b.

3. 4Q286–87 Manuscript A Fragment 1, as presented in Robert Eisenman and Michael O. Wise, *The Dead Sea Scrolls Uncovered* (New York: Penguin Books, 1993), 226ff.

4. 1QSa, 1Q28a, as presented in Michael Wise, Martin Abegg, and Edward Cook, *The Dead Sea Scrolls: A New Translation*(San Francisco: HarperSanFrancisco, 1996), 144f.

5. Berakhot 28b.

6. They used Zech 13:9 and 1 Sam 2:6 as their proof texts.

7. They used Exodus 34:6–7 to indicate God's mercy and Psalm 116 as their proof text. See Tosefta Sanhedrin 13:3, Rosh Hashana 16b–17a.

8. By surgically reversing his circumcision.

9. M. Abot 3:12.

10. Sifra 85d.

11. John 14:2–6.

12. John 14:7.

13. Edom, Moab, and Ammon were kingdoms the Jews defeated in the original Exodus (Ex 15:15; Num 21:11, 24; Joshua 12:12; 24:9). Like the Exodus from Egypt, the war between the Sons of Light and the Sons of Darkness would last forty years. David defeated the Philistines to secure the Land of Israel (1 Sam 17:51–53). Assyria conquered the northern kingdom and transported ten tribes of Israel into exile (2 Kings 15:29, 17:44). Kittim is often used in the Dead Sea scrolls to refer to the Romans. "Those who violated the Covenant" refers to Jews who have spurned the message of the *Yahad*.

14. As published in Wise, Abegg, and Cook, *The Dead Sea Scrolls: A New Translation*, 151–52.

15. Mark 13:12–13.

16. For example, Isaiah 29:5–6; Jeremiah 14:12, 15:2–3, 29:17–18; Ezekiel 5:12, 15–17; 38:19–20; Zechariah 14:4–5.

17. The birthpangs of the Messiah were the sufferings either he or the people of Israel would endure until the Messianic era began. For examples, see Claude G. Montefiore and H. Loewe, *A Rabbinic Anthology* (London: Macmillan, 1938), 551, item 1545; 583, items 1616 and 1617; and especially 584–86, item 1618.

18. Genesis 19:1–19, Isaiah 37:36, Daniel 6:22, and Genesis 28:12.

CHAPTER THREE

Jesus Teaches in His Hometown Synagogue

Jews in Palestine worked six days a week and took time off only on holidays. On Sabbaths and festivals, they gathered for worship and instruction. In their synagogues, Jewish farmers, merchants, carpenters, masons, and laborers heard and evaluated the teachings of sages who passed through their communities.

Jesus spoke in various synagogues throughout Galilee. The disciples taught in synagogues in and around Palestine. Paul traveled to and preached in synagogues across the Mediterranean. Synagogues played a seminal role in the development and spread of early Christianity.[1]

Some time after he began teaching and healing in the towns of Galilee, Jesus returned to his hometown:[2]

> And he came to Nazareth, where he had been brought up; and he went to the synagogue, as his custom was, on the Sabbath day. And he stood up to read; and there was given to him the book of the prophet Isaiah. He opened the book and found the place where it was written, "The Spirit of the Lord is upon me, because he has anointed me to preach good news to the poor. He has sent me to proclaim release to the captives and recovering of sight to the blind, to set at liberty those who are oppressed, to proclaim the acceptable year of the Lord." And he closed the book, and gave it back to the attendant, and sat down; and the eyes of all in the synagogue were fixed on him. And he began to say to them, "Today this scripture has been fulfilled in your hearing." And all spoke well of him, and wondered at the gracious words which proceeded out of his mouth. (Luke 4:16–22a)

Jesus normally went to synagogue on the Sabbath. On this Sabbath he went to his hometown synagogue, where in the course of the worship service he was invited to read from the scroll of Isaiah. Luke quotes two verses, but Jesus probably read more—possibly the entire chapter of Isaiah 61. Following the reading, Jesus returned the scroll, sat down, and began preaching. He based his sermon on the passage from Isaiah he had just read, and his former neighbors and friends spoke well of him and his remarks.

Then the reaction of the townspeople changed dramatically, to the point that Jesus' life was endangered.

> And he said to them, "Doubtless you will quote to me this proverb, 'Physician, heal yourself; what we have heard you did at Capernaum, do here also in your own country.'" And he said, "Truly, I say to you, no prophet is acceptable in his own country. But in truth, I tell you, there were many widows in Israel in the days of Elijah, when the heaven was shut up three years and six months, when there came a great famine over all the land; and Elijah was sent to none of them but only to Zarephath, in the land of Sidon, to a woman who was a widow. And there were many lepers in Israel in the time of the prophet Elisha; and none of them was cleansed, but only Naaman the Syrian." When they heard this, all in the synagogue were filled with wrath. And they rose up and put him out of the city, and led him to the brow of the hill on which their city was built, that they might throw him down headlong. (Luke 4:23–29)

What got them so angry, angry enough nearly to throw Jesus off the nearest cliff?

Was it that he, a local, presumed to teach them the meaning of Isaiah 61? Or was it the particular Isaiah passage he read? Was it that he said "this scripture has been fulfilled"? Or was it his assertion that he, Jesus, was the "anointed one"—the fulfillment of that scripture?

Jesus probably did not choose Isaiah 61 to read on that Sabbath morning. It was the passage he was given.

By the first century, a portion of the Torah and a selection from one of the prophets were read in the synagogue at every Sabbath morning service. On one Sabbath the reading was from Hosea, on another from Micah, on a third from Zephaniah. Sections of the larger scrolls—Isaiah, Jeremiah, and Ezekiel—were read frequently during the year. On the morning Jesus joined in synagogue worship, Isaiah 61 was the assigned portion. So congregants weren't angry because he read that particular passage. It was what they expected to hear.

Nor were they upset at the messianic images he drew from the text. "Strangers"[3] did confiscate their flocks; "foreigners" did siphon off the produce of their fields and vines. Just as Isaiah accurately described their current suffering as vassals of the Romans, they believed he accurately predicted their ultimate future. They would "eat of the wealth of the nations and revel in their splendor."[4] Some day the nations of the world would recognize them as "a people whom the Lord has blessed."[5] When Jesus read "the Lord has anointed me,"[6] his fellow worshippers understood it to refer not only to Isaiah but also to the Anointed One they awaited—the Messiah.

They were not even shocked when Jesus applied those verses to himself, for they had already heard about his healings and teachings in other parts of the Galilee.

What enraged the population was something far more disturbing. Having asserted he was the fulfillment of Isaiah's prophecy, Jesus was challenged to do what Isaiah said: "give sight to the blind," as the reports said he had done in Capernaum. He refused to do it.

So he was branded a false prophet, a braggart, and a liar, bringing shame on himself and his family. "Is this not Joseph's son?"[7]

Jesus tried to explain. He couldn't cure everyone who was afflicted. He had to pick and choose. Like the prophets Elijah and Elisha, he healed only particular individuals.

These excuses further infuriated the townspeople. The Redeemer they were expecting would free them from Roman oppression, deliver them from economic hardship, end their sufferings, and heal their illnesses. He wouldn't make excuses about why he couldn't deliver, and he wouldn't affirm there was no person in Nazareth worthy of being healed. No wonder they were ready to kill him!

Jesus escaped. "Passing through the midst of them he went away."[8]

A Similar Incident in Matthew
Matthew reported a similar incident in which Jesus returned to Nazareth and was rejected:

> And when Jesus had finished these parables, he went away from there, and coming to his own country he taught them in their synagogue, so that they were astonished, and said, "Where did this man get this wisdom and these mighty works? Is not this the carpenter's son? Is not his mother called Mary? And are not his brothers James and Joseph and Simon and Judas? And are not all his sisters with us? Where then did this man get all this?" And they took offense at him. But Jesus said to them, "A prophet is not without honor except in his own country and in his own house." And he did not do many mighty works there, because of their unbelief. (Matthew 13:53–58)

In Luke, Jesus' visited the synagogue in Nazareth early in his ministry, soon after he left John the Baptist in the Judean wilderness. In Matthew, his visit occurred much later, after Jesus spoke in many other communities and after John the Baptist had been imprisoned. Was this a second visit? Or was it just Matthew's version of the incident reported in Luke?

Jesus often preached in the same community on different occasions. Just as he spoke frequently along the shore of the Sea of Galilee and in the village of Capernaum, he might have returned to Nazareth on several visits. His family and friends lived there.

However, I believe both gospels described the same incident. Jesus returned to Nazareth, read from the scroll of Isaiah, and shared his understandings of the text. He was favorably received at first, but his comments eventually enraged his former neighbors to the point they wanted to cast him off the nearest cliff.

After incurring such enmity, Jesus would not have been allowed to preach again in the synagogue.[9]

There are interesting differences in the two Gospel texts.

Matthew provided biographical information not mentioned in Luke—that Jesus had brothers and sisters. Jesus' mother and brothers were indicated by name: Mary, James, Joseph, Simon, and Judas. The names and number of his sisters were not indicated. The brothers were presented in chronological order. James was the oldest, Judas the youngest. Jesus' father was a carpenter.

In Luke, Jesus himself explained why he performed no healings when he was requested to do so. In Matthew, the editor explained; they were not Jesus' words.

In Luke, Jesus stated that, like the prophets Elijah and Elisha, he only healed selected individuals. The townspeople assumed the choice was his to make and he deliberately refused to heal any of the ill people in Nazareth. In Matthew, it was not Jesus' fault he could not heal. He tried to heal and failed, because the people were so lacking in faith. In order to be healed, people had to believe.

In Luke, initially Jesus' words were favorably received. In Matthew, Jesus' childhood friends and neighbors were amazed at his teaching and at the reports of his healing because they had never heard or seen him do them before! If he had displayed the same behavior growing up, people would have noticed and remembered and not been *astonished.*

And that provides some insight into the question the townspeople asked about Jesus: "Where then did this man get all this?"[10] He didn't learn it in Nazareth!

Why Such Significant Gospel Differences?

How is it possible for two gospels to report the same incident with such significant differences?

Three reasons account for the differences.

The first is straightforward and simple. In the course of his ministry, Jesus told the same stories to different audiences, at different seasons of the year, in different communities and synagogues. He didn't speak from notes. He spoke extemporaneously, often in response to comments and questions from his listeners. He told stories—sometimes the same stories—but never in exactly the same way. So different versions of the story were heard and repeated by his audiences.

For example, in Luke 15:2 the Pharisees and the scribes challenged Jesus, wanting to know why he dined with sinners. The Parable of One Lost Sheep (Luke 15:3–7) was Jesus' response to their questions. In Matthew 18:12–14, the same parable was addressed to his disciples. Jesus told the same parable twice—once to his detractors and again to his disciples.

The second is complex and requires an understanding of how the gospels came to be.

None of the gospel writers were eyewitnesses to the information they conveyed. None lived in Palestine. None had heard Jesus preach.

The earliest gospel, Mark, was written three decades after Jesus' crucifixion, around the year 65.

Matthew lived in Antioch and wrote his gospel almost a decade later, shortly after the conquest of Jerusalem and the destruction of the Temple in 70.

Luke may have accompanied Paul on his journeys. He authored his gospel around 80, in Rome.

John, possibly written as late as 100, was the last gospel produced.

The oldest documents in the New Testament are not the gospels but Paul's letters to fledgling Christian communities in the Mediterranean world, yet the first time Paul claimed to have experienced any personal contact with Jesus was on the road to Damascus several years after Jesus' crucifixion.

The gospel writers lived in different communities in the Roman world. They wrote in different decades, about incidents they never observed. They wrote in Greek, trying to convey words and images Jesus spoke in Galilean Aramaic. Their translations—like all translations—missed some of the nuances and allusions of the original language.

Two illustrations will suffice. The Aramaic word *mishtutha* means both "banquet" and "wedding celebration." This may account for a royal wedding in Matthew and a great banquet in Luke. The Aramaic word *sh'bakha* can be translated as "praise," "honor," or "profit." The Greek in Luke 14:8–11 suggests the parable is about *honor*. A very different image would result if the Greek translator had selected accumulating *profit* as the focus of concern.

Furthermore, the gospel writers often used Hellenistic expressions to translate Galilean images. In Luke 6:48 the builder "digs deep" and lays the foundation of his house on bedrock—but most homes in Palestine were built with dirt floors. They had no basements, crawl spaces, or substructures. Again in 11:33, Luke mentions "a cellar"—not usual in Palestine. In Luke 13:19, the mustard seed is planted in "a garden." In Palestine, sowing mustard in garden beds was forbidden. On the basis of the system used by the Roman military, Mark 13:35 divides the night into four watches. In Jewish tradition, the night had three watches.

In translating from Aramaic into Greek, the gospel authors lost some allusions and changed some images to reflect familiar Hellenistic experiences. These factors alone explain many of the differences in the parables reported in the gospels.

There were systemic factors as well. Mark was composed before the destruction of the Temple. For him Jerusalem was still a vibrant Jewish city, and the Temple was still the focus of Jewish religious life. Matthew, Luke, and John were composed after the year 70—during a period of struggle and change that saw synagogues replace the Temple as the prime locations for Jewish worship, sages replace priests as the religious leaders of the Jewish community, and Roman persecution and Jewish resistance increase. Those changes certainly impacted the way Jews, Jerusalem, and Jewish traditions were perceived in the Roman world.

As a general rule, the later the composition of a gospel, the less Jewish it is, the less it reflects Jewish dietary and life-cycle observances, the less it concerns Jewish holiday rituals and requirements, and the more it conveys the images and experiences of people living in Corinth, Ephesus, and Rome. The gospels were not written for Jesus' followers in Palestine, but specifically for new Christians living in cities scattered around the Mediterranean Sea.

In summary, then, each gospel includes at least four layers of development.

The first is the actual words of Jesus—Aramaic words—as he spoke them aloud to the members of his family, to individuals he healed and comforted, to his disciples and followers, to congregants in the synagogues he attended, to the crowds that gathered about him, and to those who opposed him and tried to punish him.

These eyewitness accounts were repeated and repeated by both his follow-ers and his detractors as they discussed his activities and his teachings. Some were recorded; most were retold orally. This process was accelerated after he died, when all that remained were memories of his teachings. After his death, his followers added what they themselves had experienced.

Peter, Paul, and other disciples brought the story of Jesus and his teachings to communities far beyond the confines of Palestine. They were not alone. Exporters, craftsmen, vacationers, buyers of foreign goods and services, and friends and relatives of Jesus' followers in the course of their travels in other lands shared their remembrances of Jesus.

Those stories were told and retold in distant cities along the Mediterra-nean Sea. Eventually, there emerged accepted traditions about Jesus and his ministry. Corinth had its traditions. Rome had its understandings. Some of these traditions were written down; most were transmitted orally—more often in Greek than Aramaic.

In Rome, Mark recorded the written and oral traditions he had accumu-lated. Matthew (in Antioch), Luke (in Rome), and John (in Ephesus) did the same. Each composed a document in Greek to present the good news to Christians in his region. Each was a unique individual living in a community separated by space and time from other Christian communities, and the gos-pel each composed reflected his own personal understandings of the Jesus traditions he had gathered and recorded.

The gospels we have today are a distillation of this process. They present the stories about Jesus' life and teachings carried orally by Christians moving through the Roman world, gathered together in Antioch, Ephesus, and other cities, and edited through the minds of four authors we call Matthew, Mark, Luke, and John. No wonder they differ from one another!

A Similar Incident in Mark
There is yet a third record of this incident reported in the Gospel of Mark:

> He went away from there and came to his own country; and his disciples followed him. And on the Sabbath he began to teach in the synagogue; and many who heard him were astonished, saying, "Where did this man get all this? What is the wisdom given to him? What mighty works are wrought by his hands! Is not this the carpenter, the son of Mary and brother of James and Joses and Judas and Simon, and are not his sisters with us?" And they took offense at him. And Jesus said to them, "A prophet is not without honor except in his own country, and among his own kin, and in his own house." And he could do no mighty work there, except

that he laid his hands upon a few sick people and healed them. And he marveled because of their unbelief. (Mark 6:1–6)

Again there are some interesting differences:

- Jesus was called a carpenter. Apparently he followed in his father's occupation.
- His mother and brothers were identified by name, but the last two names were reversed: Mary, James, Joses, Judas, and Simon. According to Mark, Simon was the youngest brother.
- Mark added the phrase *and among his own kin* to Jesus' statement about where a prophet receives no honor—to emphasize that even the members of his own family did not honor him and may have been among those offended by him.
- Though there was significant unbelief in Nazareth, Jesus laid his hands on a few people and cured them. Unlike both Luke and Matthew, Mark insisted that Jesus did heal a few people in Nazareth.
- Mark mentioned no violent reaction against Jesus by his former neighbors and friends. Though they were *astonished* by his teachings and *took offense* at him, they did not hurt Jesus or try to throw him off a cliff—perhaps, because in Mark's tradition, Jesus did heal a few people.

Jesus as a Prophet

In all three gospel stories, Jesus compared himself to a *prophet* who does not receive the proper honor, and in Luke he compared himself specifically to Elijah and Elisha. These two prophets were chosen deliberately because they conveyed to Jesus' Jewish listeners images about himself Jesus wanted to reinforce:

- Elijah belonged to no established band of prophets. He was unique and worked alone. Jesus also belonged to no recognized school or group.[11]
- Elijah chose Elisha to be his disciple and successor. Jesus also selected disciples and established their authority to convey his teachings.
- Elijah and Elisha received their messages directly from God and spoke God's word. Jesus implied he also spoke God's word.
- Both Elijah and Elisha revived the dead and healed the infirm. It was a sign of their authenticity as prophets. According to all reports, Jesus also healed the sick.

Jesus presented himself as a *prophet* and built on images of Biblical prophets already in his listeners' minds. Like Elijah, Amos, Hosea, and Isaiah, he claimed he heard God and spoke God's words. As their predictions came true, so would his. This conviction that Jesus was a *prophet* was fundamental to his teachings and accounted for some of the opposition he encountered.

Reading the Torah

Josephus and Philo refer to public Torah readings as an ancient practice, and the New Testament suggests the tradition had been established by Moses.[12] Probably the practice began with the Jews who returned from exile in Babylonia, becoming more formal and structured over time. The Mishnah indicates that there were regular Torah readings on Mondays, Thursdays, and Sabbaths.[13] For some centuries, what passages were read on each day and how long each reading was differed considerably. In Babylonia, they may have read the entire Pentateuch in one year; in Palestine over three years. Nonetheless, Torah readings were a regular and weekly tradition in both Palestine and the Diaspora. In the course of his lifetime, the average Jew would have heard the Five Books of Moses read in their entirety ten or fifteen times.

The incident in Nazareth set Jesus' ministry in its dynamic context. Jesus spoke his parables aloud. Some Jews accepted them; some Jews were intrigued and came back to listen again; and some Jews were enraged. Despite the personal dangers, he continued to teach.

Following the harrowing incident in his hometown, Jesus journeyed north to Capernaum. From there Jesus traveled from community to community to preach and heal. As in Nazareth, he often encountered resistance and opposition.

Why? What did Jesus teach?

In the next chapter, we explore the secrets in one of Jesus' well-known parables—the Parable of the Sower.

Notes

1. See Matthew 13:54; Mark 6:2; John 18:20; Acts 13:5, 15, 44; 14:1; 17:1–2, 10, 17; 18:4, 26; 19:8.

2. Luke 4:14–16.

3. Isaiah 61:5. Since "aliens" also means beings from space, a better translation of the Hebrew word *zarim* is "strangers."

4. Isaiah 61:5–6.

5. Isaiah 61:9.

6. Isaiah 61:1.

7. Luke 4:22b.

8. Luke 4:30.

9. Paul had a similar experience in Ephesus. After three months of preaching in the synagogue, he was asked to leave and had to rent a hall to continue his teaching. See Acts 19:8–9.

10. Matthew 13:56.

11. Since Jesus expressed some ideas that were similar to the those accepted by the Essenes, several scholars claim he must have been a member of their community at one time. I disagree. In addition to Qumran, the Essenes taught in Jerusalem and Damascus; and former community members lived throughout Palestine. As a result, their beliefs were widely known. Many Jews were aware of their ideas. Besides, Jesus' notions were mostly Pharisaic. See below, pp. 115–18.

12. Josephus: *Apion* 2:175, Philo: *II Som.* 127, New Testament: Acts 15:21.

13. M. Megila 3:4–6.

CHAPTER FOUR

The Parable of the Sower

The Parable of the Sower

Jesus built his parables on the experiences of his listeners. Since most Jews in first-century Palestine were farmers, many parables included allusions to plowing, seeding, and harvesting crops. Among the most graphic was this Parable of the Sower.

> And he [Jesus] told them many things in parables, saying: "A sower went out to sow. And as he sowed, some seeds fell along the path, and the birds came and devoured them. Other seeds fell on rocky ground, where they had not much soil, and immediately they sprang up, since they had no depth of soil, but when the sun rose they were scorched; and since they had no root they withered away. Other seeds fell upon thorns, and the thorns grew up and choked them. Other seeds fell on good soil and brought forth grain, some a hundredfold, some sixty, some thirty." (Matthew 13:3–8)

The same parable was presented in Mark and Luke.

> And [Jesus] he taught them many things in parables, and in his teaching he said to them: "Listen! A sower went out to sow. And as he sowed, some seed fell along the path, and the birds came and devoured it. Other seed fell on rocky ground, where it had not much soil, and immediately it sprang up, since it had no depth of soil; and when the sun rose it was scorched, and since it had no root it withered away. Other seed fell among thorns and the thorns grew up and choked it, and it yielded no grain. And other seeds fell into good soil and brought forth grain, growing up and increasing and yielding thirtyfold and sixtyfold and a hundredfold. (Mark 4:2–8)

And when a great crowd came together and people from town after town came to him, he said in a parable: "A sower went out to sow his seed; and as he sowed, some fell along the path, and was trodden under foot, and the birds of the air devoured it. And some fell on the rock; and as it grew up, it withered away, because it had no moisture. And some fell among thorns; and the thorns grew with it and choked it. And some fell into good soil and grew, and yielded a hundredfold." (Luke 8:4–8a)

Though a good farmer sowed his seeds carefully, some seeds would spill into the rocks and some would be plucked by birds and transported. Most farmers disregarded these sprouts and concentrated on protecting and nourishing the seeds rooted in good soil. From each such seed planted and harvested might come thirty, sixty, or even a hundred more seeds.

Didn't Jesus' listeners already know this? Why did he belabor the obvious?

Even Jesus' disciples were confused. They asked Jesus why he spoke in parables. Why didn't he convey his ideas clearly and directly?

Why Jesus Spoke in Parables

Matthew recorded two answers to the disciples' question. We explore at the second answer first.

This is why I speak to them in parables, because seeing they do not see, and hearing they do not hear, nor do they understand. With them indeed is fulfilled the prophecy of Isaiah that says: "You shall indeed hear but never understand, and you shall indeed see but never perceive. For this people's heart has grown dull, and their ears are heavy of hearing, and their eyes they have closed, lest they should perceive with their eyes, and hear with their ears, and understand with their heart, and turn for me to heal them." (Matthew 13:13–15)

Jesus paraphrased Isaiah 6:9–10, where God told Isaiah, "Go, and tell this people: 'Hear indeed, but do not understand; see indeed, but do not perceive.' Make the heart of this people fat, and their ears heavy, and shut their eyes; lest they see with their eyes, and hear with their ears, and understand with their hearts, and turn and be healed."[1]

Jesus saw many Jews behave as Isaiah predicted. Though alert and successful, they did not understand that God was waiting for them to turn and be healed.

Therefore, he spoke in parables—that by these parables they might understand.

Matthew suggested that Jesus used metaphors to help people comprehend what God intended. Perhaps these stories would provide insights not given through their own experiences or in the instructions of other teachers.

When we turn to Jewish tradition, we learn even more.

In Jeremiah 5:21, we find an image very similar to Isaiah's. Jeremiah described the Jews of Judea as a foolish and senseless people, who "have eyes and do not see, ears and do not hear." Ezekiel 12:2 called the Jews of Judea "rebellious" and used the same image: "They have eyes to see, but see not, ears to hear, but hear not." Apparently, this was a popular expression in the period before the Exile.[2]

The Hebrew verb root *sh-u-v* (to turn) also meant "to repent." In Jewish tradition, repentance involved *turning* away from evil, *turning* toward God for inspiration and guidance, and basing our behavior on God's laws.

Like Isaiah, Jesus was talking about repentance.

To understand Jesus' answer to his disciples, we must first understand the passage Jesus quoted from Isaiah.

Moses, Isaiah, and Jesus

When Moses was instructed to urge Pharaoh to release the Israelite slaves, he was also told that God had "hardened" Pharaoh's heart. No matter how persuasively Moses pleaded, Pharaoh would not hear him.[3]

The same Hebrew word *kabeyd* ("harden") occurred in the Isaiah passage. According to Jewish understandings in the first century, this repetition implied that Isaiah had a comparable experience.

Isaiah would suffer frustration and humiliation when people turned away from him and refused to confront their sins. Nevertheless, Isaiah was commanded to warn the Jews of their impending destruction.[4]

By his answer Jesus suggested that he was a prophet, like Moses and Isaiah, and that his mission was to speak God's word to the people—even though they wouldn't understand.

This was an audacious assertion. In Jewish tradition, no prophet was greater than Moses. Jesus implied he was at least equal to Moses and Isaiah.

Secrets about God's Kingdom

Matthew gave another answer to the disciples' question. After he finished teaching publicly, Jesus and his disciples gathered privately, away from the crowd.

Then the disciples came and said to him, "Why do you speak to them in parables?"
And he answered them, "To you it has been given to know the secrets of the king-

dom of heaven, but to them it has not been given. For to him who has more will be given, and he will have abundance; but from him who has not, even what he has will be taken away." (Matthew 13:10–12)

Jesus told the disciples they possessed information most Jews did not—secret information—and the secrets dealt with the *kingdom of heaven*. The parable form hinted at these secrets but did not express them explicitly.

One of these secrets was presented in verse 12: "To him who has more will be given, and he will have abundance."

The disciples were privileged. Their knowledge gave them an advantage others did not have. When Jesus said "him who has" and "him who has not," he was not referring to wealth or material well-being but to understandings about God's kingdom. The disciples were those who had. Most other Jews had not!

To the disciples "more will be given." They would enjoy "abundance." Not now—their lives were difficult now and filled with sacrifice—but in God's kingdom, in the *kingdom of heaven*.[5]

As for the others—those who heard and saw and didn't comprehend—they would lose everything. Their wealth, their power, their high status, their lives. Everything!

Greater than Amos, Isaiah, and Hosea

A few verses later, Matthew continued these thoughts and provided another secret:[6]

But blessed are your eyes, for they see, and your ears, for they hear. Truly, I say to you, many prophets and righteous men longed to see what you see, and did not see it, and to hear what you hear, and did not hear it. (Matthew 13:16–17).

What an audacious statement! The "prophets and righteous men" of former generations with whom God spoke directly had not been privileged to experience what Jesus' disciples experienced. Though they had longed to understand, they were not given the knowledge. Jesus shared with his disciples secrets about God's kingdom even the former prophets hadn't known.

If by "prophets and righteous men" Jesus meant biblical prophets like Amos, Hosea, Jeremiah, and Isaiah, this was an astounding assertion—and certainly would incur the wrath of most Jews. While he acknowledged their authenticity and respected their teachings, Jesus suggested that the great prophets had not had the insights and understandings that Jesus was conveying to his disciples. Jesus knew things that Isaiah, Jeremiah, and Ezekiel had not.

However, if by "prophets and righteous men" Jesus meant those whom the people considered to be God's spokesmen and were not—false prophets and unfaithful leaders—then Jesus reinforced Jewish tradition.

The secret—to which only his disciples were privileged—was that Jesus was a greater prophet than Amos, Hosea, or Jeremiah. But he left the phrase "prophets and righteous men" deliberately vague to confound his opponents and provide them no clear grounds on which to accuse him.

False Prophets

Biblical prophets mistrusted prophetic guilds and excoriated seers who spoke falsely in God's name.[7] Nonetheless, even in Jesus' day false prophets continued to misguide people.[8] To avoid any misunderstanding, some sages declared that prophecy had ended hundreds of years earlier. According to this tradition, Malachi had been the last authentic prophet.[9]

Jesus denied this assertion and insisted that he was as much a prophet as Elijah, Elisha, and Isaiah.[10] Even more significantly, he suggested that he had access to secrets about God's kingdom some of these biblical prophets had not known.[11]

A Different Answer in Mark

A significantly different answer was recoded in Mark:

> And when he was alone, those who were about him with the twelve asked him concerning the parables. And he said to them, "To you has been given the secret of the kingdom of God, but for those outside everything is in parables; so that they may indeed see but not perceive, and may indeed hear but not understand; lest they should turn again, and be forgiven." (Mark 4:10–12)

According to Mark, the twelve disciples *and others* gathered privately with Jesus, and the *others* (not the disciples) asked why Jesus spoke to the crowds in parables.[12]

Jesus explained that true believers possessed information most Jews did not—secret information—and the parable form hinted at these secrets but did not express them explicitly.

According to Mark, the parable form permitted everyone to hear the secrets but only those "inside" to understand them. For those inside, the mystery of God's kingdom was revealed, while those outside heard only parables, with secrets still to be uncovered.

Mark reversed Matthew. Matthew suggested that the parables were designed to help those who didn't understand to comprehend the secrets, while Mark implied that the parables were designed to hide the secrets, lest those who didn't understand gain insight and repent. How was this significant difference in opinion possible?

Both may be correct. Jesus may have taught one idea on one occasion and the other on a different occasion.

More likely, however, is the notion that each gospel writer presented Jesus' teachings as he (the writer) understood them—and their understandings were significantly different.

Hebrew, Aramaic, and Greek

The difference between Matthew and Mark lies in their understanding of one word—the conjunction that connects Isaiah 6:10a to 10b. In the Hebrew text the word is *pen*, in Aramaic it's *dil'ma*, in Greek *mepote*.

The Hebrew conjugation *pen*—which most English versions translate as "lest"—has several meanings. One is that some precaution has been or should be taken to avert a dreaded consequence; a second is that the event feared has already taken place.[13] The Aramaic equivalent *dil'ma* has the same two meanings,[14] as does the Greek *mepote*.[15]

But *dil'ma* can also take a third meaning, "unless"—that is, the tragedy could be avoided entirely if certain conditions were met. That's how rabbinical exegesis understood it. The sages of the first century regarded the conclusion of Isaiah 6:10 as a promise that God would forgive his people—if they repented.[16]

Isaiah 6:10b—"lest they should . . . understand with their heart and turn to Me to heal them"—cannot mean the prophet was afraid the people would reconcile with God and be healed. Isaiah suffered humiliation and pain to warn the Jews of Judea that they would experience ruin if they didn't change their behavior. His fervent wish was that they would listen and avoid the devastation.

As Jews in the first century understood it, the half-verse was an affirmation of God's mercy. The people could listen and understand, repent and change their ways, and avoid the destruction and exile. That's precisely why Isaiah continued to speak. He desperately wanted them to "turn and be healed."

That must have been Jesus' wish also. He taught in one town after another to bring God's message that if people turned away from their false beliefs and erroneous practices, they might still be healed.

And that's how Matthew understood the tale. For Matthew, *mepote* meant "unless." Jesus taught in parables to help people understand and change—and thereby survive the impending disaster.

Mark may not have known the Palestinian tradition. When he read the Greek word *mepote,* he believed it meant in order to *prevent* the people from being saved. He concluded that Jesus' used parables to *hide* his secrets from the uninitiated.

Luke's Answer

Luke gave an answer comparable to Mark's. Like Mark, he understood the parables as a device for hiding the secrets from the uninitiated.

> And when his disciples asked him what this parable meant, he said, "To you it has been given to know the secrets of the kingdom of God; but for others they are in parables, so that seeing they may not see, and hearing they may not understand." (Luke 8:9–10)

Jesus Explains the Parable

According to Matthew, Jesus explained the parable to his disciples:

> Hear then the parable of the sower. When any one hears the word of the kingdom and does not understand it, the evil one comes and snatches away what is sown in his heart; this is what was sown along the path. As for what was sown on rocky ground, this is he who hears the word and immediately receives it with joy; yet he has no root in himself, but endures for a while, and when tribulation or persecution arises on account of the word, immediately he falls away. As for what was sown among thorns, this is he who hears the word, but the cares of the world and the delight in riches choke the word, and it proves unfruitful. As for what was sown on good soil, this is he who hears the word and understands it; he indeed bears fruit, and yields, in one case a hundredfold, in another sixty, and in another thirty. (Matthew 13:18–23)

As Matthew reported, the "seeds" in the parable referred to Jesus' teachings about God's kingdom—the secrets he and his disciples were conveying to others.[17]

The different places where the seeds landed referred to different kinds of people in Jesus' audiences. The "path" outside the field symbolized the person who was captivated by Jesus' teachings initially, then lost interest the moment something else attracted his attention. The "rocky ground" denoted the person who received Jesus' teachings enthusiastically but fell away when he encountered difficulty or suffering. The "thorns" represented the pleasures and material pursuits that so enticed some listeners they turned aside from Jesus' teachings. The "good soil" represented the people who accepted and followed the teachings of Jesus.[18]

The "yield" they produced was more followers. By their example and by their teaching, these good people brought the message of God's kingdom to others and raised up additional adherents—some thirty, some sixty, some even a hundred new believers.

Though Matthew didn't say it explicitly, the "sower" was Jesus. Each follower who went out and spread the message became a sower also.[19]

Essentially the same explanation was presented in Mark and Luke.

> And he said to them, "Do you not understand this parable? How then will you understand all the parables? The sower sows the word. And these are the ones along the path, where the word is sown; when they hear, Satan immediately comes and takes away the word that is sown in them. And these in like manner are the ones sown upon rocky ground, who, when they hear the word, immediately receive it with joy; and they have no root in themselves, but endure for a while; then, when tribulation or persecution arises on account of the word, immediately they fall away. And others are the ones sown among thorns; they are those who hear the word, but the cares of the world, and the delight in riches, and the desire for other things, enter in and choke the word, and it proves unfruitful. But those that were sown upon the good soil are the ones who hear the word and accept it and bear fruit, thirtyfold and sixtyfold and a hundredfold." (Mark 4:13–20)

> Now the parable is this: The seed is the word of God. The ones along the path are those who have heard; then the devil comes and takes away the word from their hearts, that they may not believe and be saved. And the ones on the rock are those who, when they hear the word, receive it with joy; but these have no root, they believe for a while and in time of temptation fall away. And as for what fell among the thorns, they are those who hear, but as they go on their way they are choked by the cares and riches and pleasures of life, and their fruit does not mature. And as for that in the good soil, they are those who, hearing the word, hold it fast in an honest and good heart, and bring forth fruit with patience. (Luke 8:11–15)

In Matthew, there was an "evil one" who tried constantly to confuse people and undermine their understandings about God's kingdom. In Mark and Luke, this "evil one" was identified as the Devil.

The Devil

The Hebrew word *satan* was rendered in Greek sometimes as *satanas* but mostly as *diabolos*. From *diabolos* we derived devil.

In the Hebrew Bible, *satan* was the accuser who challenged people who may have committed wrongs. He probed a person's motivation and questioned his behavior. As such, Satan worked on God's behalf. In no sense was he a demonic power.[20]

The image changed over time. Satan instigated Job's misfortunes. He incited people to do evil. Repeatedly he attempted to undermine the relationship between God and human beings by leading people to sin. By Jesus' time, Satan was God's adversary.[21]

In addition to "Satan" (now a proper name, not just a description or title), this undermining foe was called Belial (Beliar), Beelzebub (Beelzebul), Mastema, Sama'el, the Evil One, the Tempter, the Accuser, the Prince of Demons, and—some thirty-three times in the New Testament—*ho diabolos* (the Devil).

Rabbi Jose said:

> To what can Michael and Sama'el be compared? To a defending council and a prosecuting attorney standing in court. Satan accused the Jews, and the guardian angel Michael defended them.[22]

Satan accused them every day of the year except on the Day of Atonement.[23] A sage described the angelic princes of the heathen nations appearing before God and accusing the Jews of committing the same sins for which the heathens were condemned.[24]

Sin, suffering, and death were the consequences of Adam and Eve's disobedience in the Garden of Eden. According to the Wisdom of Solomon, the Devil was the tempter.[25]

According to the sages, humans were created with two contrary impulses—the impulse to do good and the impulse to commit evil. Occasionally the evil impulse was personified as Satan. Thus Rabbi Simeon ben Lakish said, "Satan and the evil impulse and the angel of death are the same."[26] An anonymous sage declared, "Satan comes down and misleads a man [evil impulse], then goes up and stirs up God's wrath and obtains permission and takes away his soul [angel of death]."[27] In the Testament of Reuben, Belial's army of "deceiving spirits" were personifications of the very sins they tempted humans to commit—lust, jealousy, envy, covetousness, hatred, and so forth.[28] "Be careful not to refuse charity," one sage warned, "for every one who refuses charity is put in the same category with the followers of Belial."[29]

According to one sage, God hid the "light" of the Messiah under the divine Throne of Glory. Satan asked God for whom He hid the light. God replied the light was for the Messiah. Satan requested to see the Messiah. When he saw him, Satan fell on his face and said, "This is truly the Messiah who will cast me and all the princes of the nations of the world [Satan's angels] into hell."[30]

Most Jews in the first century accepted these images of Satan, and Jesus built on them in his talks. Satan tempted Jesus in the wilderness and Peter and Judas in Jerusalem.[31] When people were sick and had to be healed, often it was because they were possessed by Satan.[32] In this Parable of the Sower, "Satan immediately comes and takes away the word that is sown."[33]

Stay the Course and Have Faith

Jeremias calls this a "contrast-parable."[34] First, Jesus presented the many frustrations a diligent first-century Jewish farmer might experience—some seeds fell outside the field among the rocks or in nearby bushes, the sun scorched them, bushes choked them, and birds ate them. Jesus could have mentioned how the wind sometimes scattered seeds and how locusts, worms, and bugs often devoured them. In contrast, Jesus portrayed the ripened field ready for harvest. Despite the frustrations, the farmer's labor resulted in an extraordinary yield. Each seed yielded thirty, sixty, or a hundred stalks of grain.[35]

The message was designed to quell doubts—doubts on the part of Jesus' audiences and on the part of his followers. Jesus' preaching was not always effective.[36] His teaching engendered controversy and hostility.[37] His own supporters deserted him.[38] Did these not contradict the claims of his mission? Consider the farmer, Jesus taught. In view of the many adverse factors that threaten and destroy his crops, he might well give up and surrender to despair. Nonetheless he persisted, confident that a rich harvest would reward his labors.

The incredible harvest demonstrated God's power and goodness. To human eyes, much of the farmer's labor seemed futile and often resulted in failure, but Jesus presented a more hopeful image. In spite of opposition and failure, God would provide a harvest beyond all conception in His glorious kingdom.

Jesus encouraged his supporters to stay the course and to continue their teaching and healing despite the setbacks and difficulties. "Have you no faith?" he asked his disciples.[39] Not even the faith of a simple farmer?

Jesus Built on Jewish Images

Jesus may have been building on eschatological images in Jewish tradition. Isaiah spoke of the days to come when "Jacob shall take root, Israel shall blossom and put forth shoots and fill the whole world with fruit."[40]

In Genesis 26:12, God blessed Isaac, and Isaac reaped a hundredfold harvest. Commenting on the verse, a sage indicated that the land was infertile and the year poor. Then he asked, "How much more then [would the harvest have yielded] had they had been favorable?"[41]

Queen Cleopatra asked Rabbi Meir if the dead would experience a physical resurrection. He responded, "You may deduce [the answer] from a grain of wheat. If a grain of wheat, which is buried naked, sprouts forth [out of the ground] in many robes, how much the more so [will] the righteous, who are buried in their raiment."[42]

In Jewish tradition, thorns were a common metaphor for evil. Jeremiah encouraged the Israelites to return to God, warning them, "Sow not among the thorns."[43]

In commenting on Exodus 27:8, a sage suggested, "At Sinai they [the Israelites] were like lilies and roses, now [after the incident of the golden calf] they have become like rubble, like thorn-bushes."[44]

In the next parable—the Parable of the Wheat and the Weeds—Jesus amplified his notions of the struggle between his community and the nonbelievers among whom they lived and worked.

Notes

1. Jesus' paraphrase adds *of hearing*—"their ears are heavy *of hearing*" (v 15).

2. It was popular in the first century also. Mark 8:18 used the same image, and Paul quoted Isaiah 6:9 in Acts 28:25–27.

3. Exodus 7:1–5.

4. Isaiah 6:1–10.

5. There is no difference in meaning between *God's kingdom* and *the kingdom of heaven*. In parallel passages Matthew used *kingdom of heaven*, and Mark used *kingdom of God*. For examples, see Matthew 4:17//Mark 1:15; Matthew 13:11//Mark 4:11; Matthew 13:31//Mark 4:30–31; Matthew 19:24//Mark 10:25. Both phrases occurred frequently in postbiblical Jewish literature. O. E. Evans suggests that the phrase *kingdom of heaven* was used to avoid the anthropomorphism that God would appear on earth in person ("Kingdom of God, of Heaven," *The Interpreter's Dictionary of the Bible: An Illustrated Encyclopedia*, ed. George A. Buttrick [New York: Abingdon, 1962], vol. 3, 17).

6. The first explanation (Matthew 13:13–15) seems to be inserted in the middle of the second explanation.

7. 1 Kings 18:20–39; Amos 7:14; Jeremiah 29:24–32. See also M. Sanhedrin 11.5.

8. Josephus, *War*, 1.2.8; 2.8.5; *Antiquities*, 20.5.1; 20.8.6; Luke 1:67; 2:25–27, 36; 7:24–28; Acts 5:36; 21:38.

9. "When the last prophets, Haggai, Zechariah and Malachi, died, the holy spirit ceased out of Israel" (Tosefta Sotah 13.2). See also Psalm 74:9; 1 Maccabees 4:46, 9:27, 14:41; Abot de Rabbi Nathan 1.3; Sanhedrin 11a.

10. Matthew 13:57, Mark 6:4, Luke 4:24. See also Matthew 23:37, Luke 13:33–34, John 4:44.

11. Matthew 13:17.

12. While not among the twelve disciples, these *others* must have been close followers, for Jesus addressed all the people present at that private gathering in the same intimate fashion and included them all in his answer.

13. See Francis Brown, S. R. Driver, and Charles A. Briggs, A Hebrew and English Lexicon of the Old Testament (Oxford: Clarendon, 1907), 814f.

14. See Marcus Jastrow, A Dictionary of the Targumim, the Talmud Babli and Yerushalmi, and the Midrashic Literature (New York: Pardes, 1950), 299.

15. *Mepote* frequently has both meanings in the Septuagint.

16. Strack and Billerbeck cite four examples of the rabbinical exegesis of Isaiah 6.10b. They all agree in understanding Isaiah 6.10b not as a threat but as a promise. See Herman L. Strack and Paul Billerbeck, Kommentar zum Neuen Testament aus Talmud und Midrasch (Munich: C. H. Beck'sche Verlagsbuchhandlung, 1956), vol. 1, 662f.

17. A similar image occurred in 2 Esdras 9:31: "Today I am sowing my law in your heart, which will bring forth fruit in you." See also 2 Esdras 8:6.

18. A similar image occurred in 2 Esdras 8:41: "For just as the farmer sows many seeds upon the ground and plants a multitude of plants, and yet not all that is sown will come up in due season and not all that is planted will take root, so they that have sown [evil] in this world shall not all be saved."

19. Many scholars suggest that the interpretation of the Parable of the Sower was a product of the primitive Church, which regarded the parable as an allegory and interpreted each detail in it allegorically. However, according to Joachim Jeremias (The Parables of Jesus, rev. ed [New York: Charles Scribner's Sons, 1963], 77–79), both the linguistic evidence and the literary analysis show that these interpretations preceded Mark. By the year 65, "the allegorical method of interpretation had already gained considerable ground." To buttress this notion are two comparable images in 2 Esdras. (1) God's word was compared with divine seed. "Today I am sowing my law in your heart" (9:31), and (2) God's planting was compared to human planting. "As the farmer sows many seeds upon the ground and plants a multitude of plants" (8:41).

20. See especially Job 1:6–12, 2:1–7; Zechariah 3:1–2. See also Psalm 109:4, 20, 29—where s-t-n was employed as a verb and applied to human adversaries; and I Kings 11:14, 23, 25—where satan was identified specifically as the foreign kings Rezon and Hadad. The word satan was used as a common noun in the Dead Sea Scrolls (1QH fragments 4:6; 45:3; Formulary of Blessings), and Enoch 40:7 spoke of "satans" in the plural. In 1 Chron 21:1, a satan (indefinite) incited King David to take an illegal census of Israel.

21. Satan incited people to do evil: Jubilees 11:5; 2 Enoch 11:74–80, 22:42; Testament of Dan 1:7; Testament of Joseph 7:4; Wisdom of Solomon 2:24; 1QS 3:20–25. He is God's

adversary: Enoch 67:6; 103:8; Testament of Daniel 5:10–11; Testament of Judah 25:3; Sibylline Oracles 3:71ff; 1QH 3:35; 6:29; 10:34–35; 1 QM 1:10, 13–14. Satan tempted Judas and Peter (Luke 22:3, 31; John 13:27); caused Ananias to withhold his contribution (Acts 5:3); and prevented Paul from visiting the Christians in Thessalonika (1 Thessalonians 2:18). Matthew, Mark, Luke, and John all said something about the Devil.

22. Exodus Rabba, 18.5, as presented in Ephraim E. Urbach, *The Sages: Their Concepts and Beliefs* (Cambridge, Mass.: Harvard University Press, 1987), vol. 1, 143.

23. Pesikta 176a, as presented in George Foot Moore, *Judaism in the First Centuries of the Christian Era* (Cambridge, Mass.: Harvard University Press, 1927), vol. 1, 406f.

24. Pesikta 176a.

25. Wisdom of Solomon, 2:23f, as presented in Moore, *Judaism in the First Centuries of the Christian Era*, vol. 2, 448. It's not clear whether the author imagined that the devil employed the serpent as his agent or that the devil assumed the shape of the serpent.

26. Baba Batra 16a.

27. As presented in Moore, *Judaism in the First Centuries of the Christian Era*, vol. 1, 492.

28. Testament of Reuben, 3:3–6, as presented in Moore, *Judaism in the First Centuries of the Christian Era*, vol. 1, 191.

29. Sifre to Deuteronomy, Re'eh, §177, as presented in Claude G. Montefiore and H. Loewe, *A Rabbinic Anthology* (London: Macmillan, 1938), 423. See also Sanhedrin 111b, as presented in Moore, *Judaism in the First Centuries of the Christian Era*, vol. 1, 166. *B'li ohl* ("without the yoke" [of Torah]) was equated with *beliya'al* ("The Devil").

30. Pesikta Rabbati 161ab, as presented in Montefiore and Loewe, *A Rabbinic Anthology*, 584.

31. Jesus: Mark 1:13. Peter: Matthew 16:23, Mark 8:33, Luke 22:31. Judas: Luke 22:3; John 13:27.

32. Matthew 4:10–11, Mark 3:22.

33. Mark 4:15. Paul warned the Christians in Corinth to beware of false apostles and deceitful helpers, for "Satan disguises himself as an angel of light" (1 Corinthians 11:13–14). Also, Satan hindered Paul's visit to Thessalonika (1 Thessalonians 2:18).

34. Jeremias, *The Parables of Jesus*, 146.

35. Though statistics show that a yield of seven and a half is an average harvest and a tenfold yield is a good harvest (Jeremias, *The Parables of Jesus*, 150, note 84), the Roman historian Pliny noted a shipment of grain to the late Augustus Caesar of four hundred shoots from a single seed and to the emperor Nero a shipment of 360 stalks from one grain. Varro indicated that the normal yield from the fields around Sybaris in Italy is a hundred to one, and a similar yield was reported near Gadera in Syria (northern Galilee) and Byzacium in Africa; Herodotus described corn so abundant in Babylonia that it yielded harvests of two hundred to one or more (Bernard Brandon Scott, *Hear Then the Parable: A Commentary on the Parables of Jesus* [Minneapolis, Minn.: Fortress, 1990], 357). From these examples, it is clear that extraordinary yields did occur on occasion and were not outside the realm of possibility.

36. Mark 6:5.

37. Mark 3:6

38. John 6:66.

39. Mark 4:40.

40. Isaiah 27:6.

41. Midrash Rabba on Genesis 64:6.

42. Sanhedrin 90b.

43. Jeremiah 4:3.

44. Asher Feldman, *The Parables and Similes of the Rabbis* (Cambridge: Cambridge University Press, 1927), 187, quoting Rab. Exod. 42:7.

CHAPTER FIVE

The Parable of the Wheat and the Weeds

The Parable of the Wheat and the Weeds

In this parable, a farmer discovers that an enemy has scattered seeds of weeds on the very soil in which the farmer had sowed his seeds of wheat.

> Another parable he [Jesus] put before them, saying, "The kingdom of heaven may be compared to a man who sowed good seed in his field; but while men were sleeping, his enemy came and sowed weeds among the wheat, and went away. So when the plants came up and bore grain, then the weeds appeared also. And the servants of the householder came and said to him, 'Sir, did you not sow good seed in your field? How then has it weeds?' He said to them, 'An enemy has done this.' The servants said to him, 'Then do you want us to go and gather them?' But he said, 'No; lest in gathering the weeds you root up the wheat along with them. Let both grow together until the harvest; and at harvest time I will tell the reapers, Gather the weeds first and bind them in bundles to be burned, but gather the wheat into my barn.'" (Matthew 13:24–30)

Over time, the stalks of wheat and the weeds grew together. They were separated only at the harvest. The grain was stored away; the weeds were gathered and burned.

How was this comparable to the kingdom of God?

Jesus Explained the Parable

Jesus explained the secrets to his disciples:

> Then he left the crowds and went into the house. And his disciples came to him, saying, "Explain to us the parable of the weeds of the field." He answered, "He who

sows the good seed is the son of man; the field is the world, and the good seed means the sons of the kingdom; the weeds are the sons of the evil one, and the enemy who sowed them is the devil; the harvest is the close of the age, and the reapers are angels. Just as the weeds are gathered and burned with fire, so will it be at the close of the age. The son of man will send his angels, and they will gather out of his kingdom all causes of sin and all evildoers, and throw them into the furnace of fire; there men will weep and gnash their teeth. Then the righteous will shine like the sun in the kingdom of their father. He who has ears, let him hear." (Matthew 13:36–43)

The harvest referred to what would happen soon to bring the current epoch of human experience to a "close."[1]

The "wheat" were the righteous, true believers, those who accepted Jesus' teachings. The "weeds" were the wicked, those who rejected Jesus' teachings.

Like reapers in a field ready for harvest, angels would slice through the peoples of the earth, gathering true believers together under God's love and protection and burning the rest of humanity. Following this conflagration, the "kingdom of heaven" would be established on earth.

Only the "righteous" would survive. All other organizations, communities, and societies would perish—including the priests, sages, merchants, and farmers among the Jewish people who did not accept Jesus' teachings.

Additional Teachings in the Parable
There were additional hints in the parable:

- God allowed evildoers to live among the righteous and tolerated their inequity temporarily, but justice would prevail in the long run. Those who perverted God's law would be punished, and the faithful would be rewarded.
- The punishment of the wicked was burning—searing pain and suffering—and their disappearance from reality. The reward of the righteous was their continued existence in the next age under God's love and protection.
- The angels were God's messengers.
- There was an "evil one" who enticed men and women to transgress against God's laws. The wicked were "sons of the evil one." The righteous were "sons of the kingdom."

Two Alternative Understandings

There is a confusion of metaphors in Matthew's explanation that has resulted in at least two different understandings of the parable.

In verse 38, the righteous were called "the good seed"—giving rise to the image of the sower (Jesus) casting his seed (the righteous) onto the soil (the world). This interpretation emphasized Jesus' missionary efforts. Through his teachings, he raised up disciples who traveled to diverse communities and instructed others who taught others, and so forth. These would be saved from the coming catastrophe.

However, the "seed" was not cut down during the harvest; the wheat and the weeds were. In verse 38, the weeds were the "sons of the evil one." The parallel to the "sons of the kingdom" would be the wheat, not the seeds. Then what were the seeds? The seeds were Jesus' teachings—his parables and speeches. Through his teachings and healings in various communities, Jesus convinced some Jews to give up their erroneous beliefs and follow him. They were the righteous saved from destruction.

Where the first image focused on his missionary concerns and acknowledged the importance of his disciples, the second emphasized Jesus as the unique source of insight and information.

A Third Understanding

There is a third understanding. Like the farmer and his enemy, the wheat and the weeds were engaged in a battle for survival. The weeds hoped to choke off and destroy the wheat.

In Matthew's explanation, God and the evil one were at war. Their opposing armies were the "sons of the kingdom" and the "sons of the evil one." Regardless of how things seemed at present—that is, regardless of how many weeds were sprouting and growing—ultimately God would win. The wicked would suffer pain and death; the righteous would live on in God's glorious kingdom.[2]

Which of these three understandings did Jesus actually speak?

If he spoke to different groups on three different occasions, he may have said them all.

Jesus Built on Jewish Ideas

Many of these ideas were found in Jewish tradition. They were not unique to Jesus.

Harvest was a common biblical metaphor for the Last Judgment. "Let the nations rouse themselves and march up to the Valley of Jehoshaphat; for there I will sit in judgment over the nations roundabout.[3] Swing the sickle, for the crop is ripe. Come and tread, for the winepress is full, the vats are overflowing . . . for the Day of the Lord is at hand in the valley of decision."[4] Also: "For you also, O Judah, a harvest is appointed when I will restore the fortunes of my people."[5]

Angels were God's messengers. At the last minute, an angel prevented Abraham from sacrificing his son Isaac and confirmed God's covenant with him and his descendants.[6] An angel announced the birth of Ishmael and of Samson, protected Jacob, escorted the Israelites through the wilderness, fed Elijah in the desert, and destroyed the Assyrian invaders of Jerusalem.[7] As God stood near, angels "ascended and descended" Jacob's ladder.[8]

Enoch envisioned catastrophe for the wicked. "I turned myself to another part of the earth where I saw a deep valley burning with fire. Into this valley they brought the monarchs and the mighty."[9] The wicked would suffer searing flames and eternal pain. "Into darkness, into the snares and into the flame . . . shall their spirits enter."[10]

The author of 2 Esdras presented a comparable destiny for sinners. "After seven days . . . the earth will give back those who sleep in it [the dead] and the dust those who rest in it. . . . The pit of torment will appear and opposite it the place of repose; the furnace of hell . . . and opposite it the garden of delight."[11]

Jesus did suggest two unique ideas. Jesus defined the "righteous" as those who accepted *his* teachings and not the teachings of the acknowledged sages and leaders of the Jewish people, and he suggested the conflagration was imminent. There was an urgency to Jesus' preaching.

The Impending Conflagration

Isaiah, Jeremiah, and Ezekiel predicted God's ultimate triumph over the heathen nations. Their armies would be defeated ignominiously; their gods would be vanquished. God alone would reign supreme throughout the world.[12]

In the course of this battle, God's justice would prevail. The good would be vindicated and the wicked punished—not just sinners among the foreign nations but also apostates, nonbelievers, and transgressors within the community of Israel.[13]

The peoples of the earth would experience wars, earthquakes, and fires, devastation and destruction. Every facet of human life would be confounded, and human civilization as they knew it would disappear.[14]

Once the heathen nations were vanquished and their kingdoms toppled, and after the wicked among the Jews and non-Jews had suffered their punishment, God's eternal kingdom would be established on earth. "The God of heaven will establish a kingdom that shall never be destroyed, nor will its sovereignty be transferred to another people. It shall crush and wipe out all these kingdoms, but it shall last forever."[15]

In the Apocalypse of Baruch, God explained that the Final Judgment would be divided into twelve periods. "In the first there shall be the beginning of commotions. In the second, slayings of the great ones. In the third, many shall die [by plague and disease]. In the fourth, the sending of the sword [to continue the slaughter by war]. In the fifth, famine and drought [will kill more]."[16] This gruesome description of catastrophe after catastrophe concluded on a note of hope: "When all is accomplished that was to come to pass during these periods, the Messiah shall then begin to be revealed."[17]

Similar predictions were recorded in a *baraita* attributed to Rabbi Nathan:[18] "In the first year the following verse will be fulfilled—'And I will cause it to rain upon one city and cause it not to rain upon another city' [drought].[19] In the second, the arrows of famine will be sent forth. In the third, . . . men, women and children, men of piety, and miracle workers will die, and the Torah will be forgotten. . . . In the seventh, wars."[20] This homily ended with the same promise. "At the end of seven years the son of David [the Messiah] will come."[21]

John the Baptist believed the last judgment was imminent. "Repent, for the kingdom of heaven is at hand."[22] "One who is mightier than I is coming after me. . . . His winnowing fork is in his hand, and he will clear his threshing floor and gather his wheat into the barn, but the chaff he will burn with unquenchable fire."[23] "Even now the ax is laid to the root of the tree."[24]

Jesus shared this understanding that a universal conflagration was imminent and encouraged his listeners to prepare themselves for the collapse of human society.[25] He repeated John's words and taught them to his disciples: "Repent, for the kingdom of heaven is at hand."[26]

This calamity would be like no other in history. "In those days there will be such tribulation as has not been from the beginning of the creation which God created until now, and never will be."[27] Rainstorms would buffet the land; floods and fires would destroy cities; and darkness would cover the earth.[28]

The Kingdom of Heaven Was at Hand

Prepare now! Jesus warned his listeners. Change today! For Jesus, the kingdom of God was not of some distant future; it was now.

The catastrophe would happen within this generation. "This generation will not pass away till all these things take place."[29] "There are some standing here who will not taste death before they see that the kingdom of God has come."[30]

No signs of the impending cataclysm were apparent. No warnings would be heard. "Why does this generation seek a sign? Truly, I say to you, no sign shall be given."[31]

The only way to avoid the devastation and death was to repent. Like the people of Nineveh, who believed Jonah and changed their ways, the Jews could become believers and be saved. This "evil and adulterous generation seeks for a sign; but no sign shall be given to it except the sign of the prophet Jonah."[32] "The men of Nineveh will arise at the judgment with this generation and condemn it; for they repented at the preaching of Jonah."[33]

The Kingdom of Heaven Had Begun

There was nothing to await, Jesus taught. The kingdom of heaven had already begun. For those who understood, the future was already present.

According to Luke, people marveled at Jesus' ability to heal. Jesus saw it as a sign that God's kingdom had begun. "If it is by the finger of God that I cast out demons, then the kingdom of God has come upon you."[34]

Jesus castigated people and called them hypocrites because they refused to believe their own experiences. "When you see a cloud rising in the west, you say at once, 'A shower is coming'; and so it happens. And when you see the south wind blowing, you say, 'There will be scorching heat'; and it happens. You hypocrites! You know how to interpret the appearance of earth and sky; but why do you not know how to interpret the present time?"[35]

Where Jesus Differed from Jewish Tradition

According to most Jewish teachers, the conflagration would come first to punish the wicked and rescue the righteous. Then, after this final judgment, God's eternal kingdom would be established.

Jesus provided a different perspective. He believed the biblical period came to an end with John the Baptist and a new era—the kingdom of God—had already begun. The conflagration would happen next.[36]

In many ways, Jesus' Parable of the Wheat and the Weeds was a response to John's metaphor. The kingdom of heaven would not come into being after the harvest. The kingdom of heaven already existed. Soon God would make his final determination, and the conflagration (harvest) would carry out His judgment.

But for now, according to Jesus, during this intermediary period, sinners and believers lived in same world. "Let both grow together until the harvest."[37] During the conflagration, as a consequence of God's final judgment, they would be separated. "At harvest time [the reapers shall] . . . gather the weeds first and tie them in bundles to be burned, [then] gather the wheat into my barn."[38]

What Were the Seeds?

The field workers reported weeds growing among the shoots of wheat. The owner responded, "An enemy has done this,"[39] relieving the workers of blame. Neither the owner nor his servants were responsible for the weeds. The seeds the owner planted resulted in wheat; the seeds the enemy planted brought forth weeds.

What were the seeds?

The seeds were teachings—about God, about the behavior God demanded, about morality, decency, faith and reward, about life after death and the World to Come, and about the Messiah and God's kingdom. Those who obeyed the teachings of the owner would survive the separation and live on in God's kingdom; those who followed the teachings of the enemy would die during the separation, burn, and disappear.

Who Was the Enemy?

God (or Jesus) was the owner who planted wholesome seeds. Who, then, was the "enemy"?

As discussed in the last chapter, God's enemy was the Devil. On the same earth on which God attempted to raise righteous people, Satan scattered his temptations and broadcast his teachings. Many Jews—often seemingly knowledgeable and respectable Jews—succumbed to his enticements. They were doomed.

According to Jesus, those who opposed him were also God's "enemies," leading people astray by their instruction and causing people to sin. Therefore, some of his listeners concluded that the enemy to whom Jesus referred embraced the Essenes, the Pharisees, and the Sadducees. They were responsible for the weeds.

Angels

Angels were active in the Hebrew Bible. An angel ordered Abraham not to sacrifice his son Isaac and reassured Jacob when his father-in-law Laban tried to cheat him.[40] An angel announced the birth of Ishmael and of Samson.[41]

An angel protected Jacob on his journey, explained to Moses the meaning of the burning bush, escorted the Israelites through the wilderness, set a cloud between them and the pursuing Egyptians, invoked a curse against a village that refused them aid against the Philistines, succored Elijah in the wilderness, and brought defeat to the invaders of Jerusalem.[42] As several psalmists explained, angels protected the faithful.[43]

Abraham hosted three angels in his tent near Beersheba. At Jericho, Joshua saw the angel that commanded God's army. Manoah realized he had spoken to an angel when the being disappeared in flames.[44] In his dream, Jacob saw angels ascending and descending the ladder connecting heaven to earth.[45] Later he wrestled with a spiritual being whom Hosea called an angel.[46]

In the period after the Exile—perhaps as a consequence of the influence of the Babylonian, Persian, and Greek cultures—Jewish ideas about angels became far more complicated. Angels came to be regarded not merely as God's messengers but as beings that controlled various aspects of the natural world.[47] They were organized into a hierarchy, headed by key archangels.[48] They carried human prayers to God and interceded with Him on their behalf.[49] They protected the righteous from harm, punished the wicked, and executed God's calamities. [50]

Angels became identified by name—the archangels Michael, Gabriel, Raphael, and Uriel;[51] the angels of the four seasons Melkiel, Helemmelek, Melejal, and Narel;[52] Raguel, who took vengeance on the world of the luminaries;[53] and Lailah, the angel of conception.[54]

Satan emerged as administrator of his own realm and head of an array of lesser angels and demons. In the Dead Sea Scrolls, the Zadokite Document, the Sibylline Oracles, and the book of Jubilees, he is also called Belial— "worthless."[55] And sometimes he is called Mastema—the "hated" one.[56]

Both the protecting and the destroying angels were organized into armies to carry out the instructions of their leaders.

The Gospels Built on Jewish Ideas
The New Testament reflected many of these traditional Jewish images. Gabriel anticipated the birth of John the Baptist, and an anonymous angel announced the birth of Jesus.[57] An angel warned Joseph to flee with Mary and Jesus into Egypt, encouraged Jesus on the Mount of Olives, rolled aside the stone covering the entrance to Jesus' tomb, and released Peter from prison.[58] Angels surrounded the throne of God in heaven and sang God's praises.[59]

A belief in angels was fundamental to Jesus' teachings. "I tell you, every one who acknowledges me before men, the son of man also will acknowledge before the angels of God; but he who denies me before men will be denied before the angels of God."[60]

New Ideas about Angels

The explanation of the Parable of the Wheat and the Weeds presented ideas not found previously in Jewish tradition: that Jesus was in charge of the angels, and that at Jesus' command the angels will begin their sweep through the nations to gather up all the wicked and incinerate them like noxious weeds.[61]

Those ideas—that Jesus was in charge of the punishing angels and that they would begin their devastation at his command—were incredible assertions and may account for some of the opposition Jesus' teachings aroused.

In the next chapter, we explore six more parables about the kingdom of heaven.

Notes

1. The phrase "the close of the age" was unique to Matthew. See Matthew 13:40, 49; 24:3; 28:20.

2. There may be allusions here to the battles between the "sons of light" and the "sons of darkness" mentioned in the Dead Sea Scrolls.

3. A play on the Hebrew meaning of the name Jehoshaphat—"God judges."

4. Joel 4:12–14 (= Greek 3:12–14).

5. Hosea 6:11. See also Jeremiah 51:33.

6. Genesis 22:11, 15.

7. Genesis 16:11; Judges 13:3–5; Genesis 48:16; Exodus 23:20–23; 1 Kings 19:5; 2 Kings 19:35; Isaiah 37:36.

8. Genesis 28:12.

9. Enoch 53:1–2, a possible allusion to Isaiah 24:21–22.

10. Enoch 103:5.

11. 2 Esdras 7:36–44, as presented in George Foot Moore, *Judaism in the First Centuries of the Christian Era* (Cambridge, Mass.: Harvard University Press, 1927), vol. 2, 339.

12. For example, Isaiah 2:2–4 (compare Micah 4:1–4); 12–17, 18–21; 14:5–7, 13–27, 28–32. Jeremiah 46:1–12, 24–26, 28; 47:1–7. Ezekiel 25:3–5, 8–17; 26:1–18.

13. For example, Isaiah 1:2–4, 10, 11–17, 21–28; 3:8–15. Jeremiah 3:12–18; 18:15–16. Ezekiel 6:4–7, 9, 13; 7:3–4, 8–9, 10–13.

14. For example, Isaiah 24:1–23. Jeremiah 42:16–17, 22; 47:2, 6–7. Ezekiel 7:14–15; 38:1–39:29.

15. Daniel 2:44.

16. The Syriac Apocalypse of Baruch, xvi–xxix, as presented in Ephraim E. Urbach, *The Sages: Their Concepts and Beliefs* (Cambridge, Mass.: Harvard University Press, 1987), 677. Though only a Syriac version survived, the Apocalypse of Baruch was a Jewish work, written shortly after the destruction of Jerusalem in 70.

17. Apocalypse of Baruch.

18. A *baraita* is a quote from rabbinic sources attributed to a sage *(tanna)* of the first two centuries of the Common Era.

19. Amos 4:7.

20. Sanhedrin 97a, as presented in Urbach, *The Sages*, 676.

21. Sanhedrin 97a.

22. Matthew 3:2.

23. Matthew 3:11–12, Luke 3:16–17.

24. Matthew 3:10, John 3:9.

25. Mark 13:3–8, Luke 12:54–56.

26. Matthew 4:17, 10:7.

27. Mark 13:19;

28. Matthew 24:27, 29, 37–39; Mark 13:24–25; Luke 17:24, 26–30.

29. Matthew 24:34. See also Mark 13:30.

30. Mark 9:1.

31. Mark 8:12. See also Luke 17:20.

32. Matthew 12:39. See also Luke 11:29–30.

33. Matthew 12:41.

34. Luke 11:20.

35. Luke 12:54–56.

36. Matthew 11:12.

37. Matthew 13:29.

38. Matthew 13:30.

39. Matthew 13:28.

40. Genesis 22:11, 31:11.

41. Genesis 16:11, Judges 13:3–5.

42. Genesis 48:16; Exodus 3:2, 23:20–23, 33:2, 14:19; Judges 5:23; 1 Kings 19:5; 2 Kings 19:35; Isaiah 37:36.

43. Psalms 35:5–6, 91:11.

44. Genesis 18:1–10, Joshua 5:13–14, Judges 13:20–21.

45. Genesis 28:12.

46. Genesis 32:24–25; Hosea 12:5 (= Greek 12:4).

47. The winds and the stars: Enoch 19:1; 40:4–5; 60:12, 16–21; 61:10; 72:1; 1QH 1.10–11; 47.7–13. The four seasons: Enoch 82:13. Various countries: Daniel 10:19–21. Health: Tobit 3:17; Enoch 10:7, 40:9. Death: 2 Barukh 21:23; possibly Proverbs 16:14.

48. Seven archangels: Tobit 2:15G; Enoch 81:5, 90:21–22; 2 Esdras 5:20. Four archangels: Enoch 40, 87:2–3, 88:1. Three: Enoch 90:31.

49. Daniel 6:2; 10:13, 21. Tobit 12:15. 2 Baruch 6:7, 11G; Enoch 9:10; 15:2; 40:9; 47:2; 99:3, 16. Testament of Levi 3:5, 5:6–7; 1QH 6:13.

50. Daniel 10:13, 20; 11:1, 12:1. 2 Maccabees 11:6. 3 Maccabees 6:18. Susanna 1:45. Enoch 20:5. Jubilees 35:17. 1QH 5:21–22. 1QS 9:15. 1QM 9:16. They were called "angels of punishment" in Enoch 53:3; 56:1; 61:1; 62:11; 63:1. 2 Baruch 21:23; and "angels of destruction" in CDC 4:12 and in the Zadokite Document 2:6, 8:2.

51. Daniel 8:16, 10:13, 12:1. Tobit 3:17, 12:15. Enoch 9:1; 10:4; 19:1; 20:2, 7; 40:9. 1QM 9:26.

52. Enoch 82:13.

53. Enoch 20:4.

54. Niddah 16b, based on Job 3:3.

55. Jubilees 1:20. Sibylline Oracles 3:63, 73. 1QS 1:18, 23–24. Zadokite Document 4:13, 15; 15:18.

56. Jubilees 49:2; Zadokite Document 4:3, 5:18, 6:5, 8:2.

57. Luke 1:11–20, 2:8–14.

58. Matthew 2:13; Luke 22:43; Matthew 28:2–3; Acts 12:7–10.

59. Luke 2:13; Revelations 4:9. See also Isaiah 6:2–3; Enoch 39:12.

60. Luke 12:8–9. See Enoch 99:3. Compare Matthew 10:32–33. This may be a specific allusion to the Sadducees, who denied the existence of angels and other spirits. See Acts 23:6–8.

61. Matthew 13:41–42.

CHAPTER SIX

Other Parables about
the Kingdom of God

After the Parable of the Wheat and the Weeds, Matthew reported six more parables about the kingdom of heaven.

The Parable of the Mustard Seed

Among garden plants the well-cultivated mustard seed grew to become a large, spreading shrub, sometimes as tall as a horse and its rider. Jesus compared the kingdom of heaven to what happened to a mustard seed:[1]

> Another parable he put before them, saying, "The kingdom of heaven is like a grain of mustard seed which a man took and sowed in his field; it is the smallest of all seeds, but when it has grown it is the greatest of shrubs and becomes a tree, so that the birds of the air come and make nests in its branches." (Matthew 13:31–32)

The key to understanding this parable was the image of a tiny mustard seed that grew into a large shrub that protected and nurtured the birds nesting in it.

What Secrets Did the Parable Convey?
What was Jesus' implying?

Like the birds that nested peacefully in the great shrub, true believers who followed Jesus' teachings would be nurtured and protected in the kingdom of heaven.

Just as all of the characteristics of the great mustard shrub were present in the tiny seed, so all of the features of the kingdom of heaven were present in the first century—though visible only to a small number of people.

Three qualities were widely known. First, the mustard plant was particularly hardy. According to Pliny, "Once it has been sown it is scarcely possible to get the place free of it."[2] Second, the mustard shrub had a variety of beneficial uses as a seasoning and a medication. "It is applied with vinegar to the bites of serpents and scorpion stings. It counteracts the poisons of fungi. For phlegm it is kept in the mouth until it melts. . . . For toothache it is chewed."[3] There appeared to be no illness that mustard couldn't cure. Finally, the large mustard bush began as a tiny seed.

All three characteristics provided metaphors in the minds of Jesus' listeners for the kingdom of God: (1) Once established, God's kingdom would spread and grow like the tenacious mustard plant; (2) those invited into God's kingdom would enjoy tasty food and suffer no longer from maladies and afflictions; and (3) though its beginnings were small, ultimately God's kingdom would encompass all humanity and affect the entire world. Most people noted this last quality.

Jesus Encouraged His Followers

Jesus' band of believers was few in number and suffered hardships and the disdain of the community. Often they were frustrated; occasionally they were frightened. Jesus tried to encourage his followers by reminding them they were part of a burgeoning movement. They would be among the survivors protected and nurtured by God.

They ought not to feel discouraged when their hard work convinced just a few people in each community. Like the farmer who planted the tiny mustard seed, the few they converted would spread their message to others who would spread the message to others, ultimately building a large community of true believers in many lands.

Jesus reassured his listeners. Out of the most insignificant beginnings, through processes indiscernible to humans and with compelling certainty, God would create a kingdom that embraced all peoples on earth.

Another Mention of the Mustard Seed

Jesus used the analogy of the mustard seed on another occasion. Apparently the apostles tried to heal a young epileptic and failed. They returned to Jesus feeling discouraged and confused. He said to them, "If you have faith as a grain of mustard seed . . . nothing will be impossible to you."[4]

Jesus used the analogy of the mustard seed to convey many meanings. It was the kingdom of heaven experienced initially by only a handful of true believers. It was the message about God's kingdom the disciples were preaching to others. And it was faith—proper faith—the kind of conviction, knowledge, and understanding that would allow the Jesus' followers to work miracles.

Jesus Built on Jewish Images

The comparison "as small as a mustard seed" was well known in Jesus' day. The rabbis frequently used the mustard seed to indicate the smallest amount—such as the least drop of blood or the least contamination.[5]

A nurturing tree was a familiar Hebrew metaphor for a mighty kingdom that gives shelter to other nations. It was the Assyrian empire. "Assyria was a cedar of Lebanon . . . [that] towered high above all the trees of the forest. . . . All the birds of the air made their nests in its boughs; all the beasts of the field bore their young under its branches."[6] And the Messianic Kingdom: "I will pluck a tender sprig . . . and it will grow into a noble cedar. Birds of every sort will nest in the shade of its branches."[7]

King Nebuchadnezzar shared a disturbing dream. "I saw a tree in the midst of the earth, and its height was great. . . . The beasts of the field found shade under it, and the birds of the air dwelt in its branches. . . . A holy one came down from heaven. He cried aloud and said, 'Hew down the tree and cut off its branches.'"[8] Daniel told Nebuchadnezzar the tree represented his Chaldean empire. Then Daniel informed the king, "You will be driven from among men, and your dwelling shall be among the beasts of the field . . . until you know that the Most High rules the kingdom of men and gives to whom He wishes."[9]

The images presented in the Parable of the Mustard Seed alluded to these prophecies in Ezekiel and Daniel. By the first century, Daniel's prediction had long come to pass. The Greeks had conquered the Chaldeans, and the Romans had vanquished the Greeks. Jews awaited the fulfillment of the rest of Daniel's prophecy.

A similar vision was inscribed in a Dead Sea hymn book. The poet compared the Essene community to a tree: "All the beasts of the forest fed on its leafy boughs . . . and its branches sheltered all the birds." Surrounded by a wicked world, this tree of life was concealed. "All the trees by the water rose above it . . . [and] the seal of its mystery remains unobserved, unrecognized." God Himself guarded its secret. The outsider "sees but does not recognize, and thinks but does not believe."[10]

The Parable in Mark and Luke
Both Mark and Luke recorded essentially the same parable.

> And he said, "With what can we compare the kingdom of God, or what parable shall we use for it? It is like a grain of mustard seed, which, when sown upon the ground, is the smallest of all the seeds on earth; yet when it is sown it grows up and becomes the greatest of all shrubs, and puts forth large branches, so that the birds of the air can make nests in its shade." (Mark 4:30–32)

> He said therefore, "What is the kingdom of God like? And to what shall I compare it? It is like a grain of mustard seed which a man took and sowed in his garden; and it grew and became a tree, and the birds of the air made nests in its branches." (Luke 13:18–19)

The Kingdom of Heaven
Following the conflagration, a new era would dawn for the righteous who survived. God alone would rule, and divine justice would prevail. There would be no sin, no suffering, and no punishment.

These ideas were first articulated by Isaiah and Micah. "In the days to come the mount of the Lord's house shall stand firm above the mountains and tower above the hills; and all nations shall gaze on it with joy. . . . They shall beat their swords into plowshares and their spears into pruning hooks. Nation shall not take up sword against nation, neither shall they learn war any more."[11] To which Micah added: "Every man shall sit under his vine and fig tree, and nothing will alarm him."[12]

In this safe and secure new world, "The wolf shall dwell with the lamb, and the leopard shall lie down with the kid. The calf and the beast of prey shall feed together, and a little child shall lead them."[13]

God's dominion would be universal. All who survived would worship only God and obey His laws. His name would be the only divine name acknowledged. "The Lord will be king over all the earth. At that time, there shall be one Lord with one name."[14]

The new age would begin with a glorious celebration. The Behemoth and the Leviathan[15] would provide meat and fish for everyone at the inauguration banquet.[16]

That banquet would launch an age of endless blessings. "The earth will yield her fruits ten thousand fold. On one vine will be a thousand clusters, each cluster of a thousand grapes, and each grape will yield a *kor* of wine."[17] Every grain of wheat will be as large as the two kidneys of a bullock. One grape will fill an entire cart and provide thirty jugs of wine.[18] Trees would bear fruit every day.[19]

The Parable of the Leaven

To make bread rise, leaven is added to uncooked dough. It only takes a small amount of leaven to affect the entire loaf. Jesus compared the establishment of God's kingdom to what happened when a housewife mixed a bit of leaven into raw bread dough, covered it with a cloth, and let the dough stand overnight. When she returned in the morning, the whole mass had been leavened: "He told them another parable. 'The kingdom of heaven is like leaven which a woman took and hid in three measures of flour, till it was all leavened'" (Matthew 13:33).

What Secrets Did the Parable Convey?

What was Jesus sharing?

No one knew how a small amount of leaven affected the entire loaf, but once started the process was inevitable. The bread rose. With the same inevitability, God's kingdom would be established.

All that was necessary to start the process was to insert a few bits of leaven. Just a few converts in each community could impact the whole.

Women as well as men could be effective in spreading Jesus' message to others.

Leaven

Elsewhere in the gospels, leaven represented the corrupting influences of the accepted leaders on the Jewish people. Matthew warned, "Beware the leaven of the Pharisees and Sadducees."[20] Mark added, "And the leaven of Herod."[21] The editors of The New American Bible suggest that the gospels were pointing to these groups particularly because of their opposition to Jesus.[22] But Matthew 16:12 specifically identified the leaven as their *teachings*. And Luke 12:1 talked about their *hypocrisy*. It was not their opposition but the effect of their teachings and the examples they set that concerned Jesus. Leaven was pervasive. It spread throughout the dough and affected the entire loaf. Like leaven, the examples set by the leaders of the people, their teachings and influences corrupted the entire community.

The sages also spoke of leaven's harmful effects. Interpreting Genesis 6:6, Rabbi Abahu taught that God regretted creating humankind. "What have I made?" God said. "It was I who put the bad leaven in the dough, for 'the inclination of a man's heart is evil from his youth.' "[23] Commenting on the same proof-text, Rabbi Abba Jose said, "Poor is the leaven if its owner [God] testifies that it is bad."[24]

Jesus reversed the image. In the current parable, leaven symbolized the spread of goodness and truth.

Why So Much Leaven?

People knew it took a small amount of leaven to bake a loaf of bread. According to Sellers, the three measures mentioned in this parable would service *twenty-one quarts* of flour—enough flour for twenty-one loaves.[25]

Why this exaggeration?

On the average, bread lasted no more than a week before it molded. To feed a very large family, a woman might have baked ten loaves at a time, but not twenty-one. However, a woman preparing a banquet may have baked twenty-one loaves of bread. The exaggeration suggested how bountiful the kingdom of heaven would be. There would be bread and other food enough for everyone.

The Same Parable in Luke

Luke recorded essentially the same parable: "And again he said, 'To what shall I compare the kingdom of God? It is like leaven which a woman took and hid in three measures of flour, till it was all leavened'" (Luke 13:20–21).

Women

This is the first parable in which the primary actor was a woman.

In the Jewish community, women were both subjugated and emancipated. A woman belonged to her father until her marriage, then she belonged to her husband.[26] She could not serve as a witness in a court of law, she could not divorce her husband (though he could divorce her), and she could not inherit property.[27]

Her primary roles were those of wife and mother, and respect for her in these roles was heavily emphasized.[28]

Nonetheless, prominent women were celebrated in both the Hebrew Bible and the New Testament. Debora was judge and general.[29] Jael, Rahab, and Esther rescued the Israelites from certain death.[30] One of Ruth's descendants was the Messiah, and Mary was Jesus' mother.[31] Some women ran businesses, some were military heroines, and some influenced kings.

Women appeared frequently in the gospel accounts of Jesus' life and ministry.

The Parable of the Hidden Treasure

A man found a treasure in a field and buried it. In his joy, he sold everything he owned and bought the field.

> The kingdom of heaven is like treasure hidden in a field, which a man found and covered up; then in his joy he goes and sells all that he has and buys that field. (Matthew 13:44)

In the unsettled circumstances of the first century, when Romans and brigands confiscated valuable assets, it was not unusual for people to bury treasures in the ground. Jesus' listeners knew this—and knew also that sometimes the owner died before he could recover the treasure or he forgot where he buried it.

What Secrets Did the Parable Convey?

What secrets was Jesus sharing? How was the kingdom of heaven like a buried treasure?

Proverbs 2:3–5 noted that insight and understanding were difficult to achieve but suggested that "if you seek it like silver and search for it as for hidden treasures, then you will understand the fear of the Lord and find the knowledge of God."

The hidden treasure of which Jesus spoke was not any material possession. It was knowledge—knowledge *of* God and knowledge *from* God, knowledge of "righteousness and justice and equity," knowledge that will "deliver you from the way of evil."[32]

More significantly, it was knowledge about the kingdom of heaven. Access to the kingdom of heaven was hidden and unavailable to the uninitiated.

According to Proverbs 3:13–15, "Happy is the man who finds wisdom, and the man who gets understanding, for the gain from it is better than gain from silver and its profit better than gold. It is more precious than jewels, and nothing you desire can compare with it." Jesus agreed. Nothing was more valuable that this special knowledge.

Nothing anyone currently possessed was worth more than participating in God's kingdom. Therefore, having attained this special understanding, a person ought to radically change his life, sell all his possessions, and prepare himself to be accepted by God into His kingdom.

Treasures Found and Jewish Law

Two aspects of this parable are somewhat disturbing:

- The person who discovered the treasure did not inform the owner. Instead, he hid the treasure and bought the field. Was he being dishonest? Was he obligated to inform the owner of the field of the treasure it contained?

- Having found a treasure on someone else's field, the person liquidated everything he owned to purchase the field. Was he imprudent? Was he jeopardizing his and his family's continued sustenance?

Jewish law provided answers to these questions.

Lost and Found

Biblical law required the finder to return a lost item to its owner—even if it meant going out of his way to do so.

> You shall not see your brother's ox or his sheep go astray and withhold your help from them; you shall take them back to your brother. And if he is not near you, or if you do not know him, you shall bring it home to your house, and it shall be with you until your brother seeks it; then you shall restore it to him. So you shall do with his ass; so you shall do with his garment; so you shall do with any lost thing of your brother's which he loses and you find. You may not withhold your help. (Deuteronomy 22:1–3)[33]

By the time of Jesus, there were many laws and customs concerning lost articles. For example, the sages debated how long the finder must announce the goods he found so the owner could come and claim them. Rabbi Meir said, "Until his neighbors know it." Rabbi Judah said, "[For at least] seven days after the last feast, to allow [the owner] three days to travel to his house, three days to return and one day to announce [his loss]."[34]

They tried to define what constituted being "lost,"[35] what kind of property had to be returned if the owner was known or held if the owner was not known,[36] how and for how long the finder must publicize his discovery to make the owner aware of its location,[37] what were the finder's liabilities if the property spoiled or deteriorated under his care,[38] and at what point and under what circumstances the finder could keep the goods as his own property.[39]

The sages even discussed the unlikely circumstance wherein the finder returned the lost property to its owner and then found it lost again. "He restored it [a neighbor's cow or a donkey] again and it escaped yet again, even four times or five. He must restore it, for it [the Torah] says, 'You shall take them back to your brother.'"[40] Even if the finder lost time (wages), he must return the lost article.[41]

Jesus and Jewish Law

Jesus' Parable of the Hidden Treasure contradicted these Jewish images. The finder did not return the treasure to its rightful owner, did not inform the owner of his discovery, did not publicize his discovery so the owner might recover his property, and did not guard the treasure until the owner arrived to claim it. Instead, he kept the treasure secret, sold all of his worldly possessions, and bought the field for himself.

Was Jesus deliberately contradicting Jewish law?

Jesus disagreed with the sages regarding certain Sabbath restrictions and certain dietary rules.[42] It is possible that Jesus also disagreed with the sages regarding lost property—that he believed the person who discovered the buried treasure could keep his discovery secret and acquire it for himself.

I don't think so. I believe we're focusing on the wrong portion of the metaphor. After all, Jesus trained his disciples to bring the message of God's kingdom to the people, and devoted his own energies to that task. They were not keeping the message secret and exploiting it for their own benefit. They were offering the treasure to anyone who would listen. For most Jews, however, who didn't understand, the treasure remained hidden.

The treasure belonged to no one in particular. Anyone could have access to it. Everyone could own it. Like wisdom and righteousness, once a person acquires an understanding of God's kingdom, all other concerns are meaningless. Jesus was saying it was better to sell all property, discard all possessions, disavow all material commitments, and become part of God's kingdom than to suffer devastation and death.

Did Jesus mean this literally? Was he asking believers to sell their homes and abandon their lands to follow him?

Some of his disciples did. Peter, Andrew, James, and John gave up their livelihoods and followed Jesus from town to town, eating with him, sleeping with him, and learning from him. Once successful fishermen,[43] they became entirely dependent for lodging and sustenance on the generosity of others.

Most of Jesus' followers did not sell their fields or abandon their occupations. They provided lodging for Jesus and his disciples.[44] They fed them in their homes.[45] They listened to Jesus preach in their synagogues, stood on the shore of the lake to hear his stories, gathered around him in towns and villages throughout Galilee, welcomed him to Jerusalem, and witnessed his teachings, then returned to their homes and their families.[46] Their contributions of food, shelter, clothing, and money provided Jesus and his disciples the resources to pursue their mission. They too would be saved from destruction and welcomed into the kingdom of heaven.

The Parable of the Valuable Pearl

What would you do if you were a stamp collector who came across the most valuable stamp in the world? Or if you could purchase Buckingham Palace? Would you cash in all your assets and buy it?

Jesus told the parable of a merchant who located the finest pearl he'd ever seen. He sold everything he possessed to purchase the pearl: "Again, the kingdom of heaven is like a merchant in search of fine pearls, who, on finding one pearl of great value, went and sold all that he had and bought it" (Matthew 13:45–46).

What Secrets Did the Parable Convey?

Once again, Jesus suggested that true believers sell everything they own and invest all their resources in the coming kingdom of God.

"The price of wisdom is greater than pearls," declared the Book of Job.[47] Jesus told those in the audience who recalled the biblical reference that the knowledge he was sharing was worth more than any earthly treasure.

Pearls

While the message of this parable was comparable to that of finding a hidden treasure, the use of a pearl as the basis of the metaphor was unusual. Coming from distant seas, pearls were exotic and expensive. Most Jews in the first century didn't own pearls.[48]

Because it was beyond the reach of ordinary people, finding a magnificent pearl was like a finding a hidden treasure.

In later Christian tradition, the pearl became a symbol for Jesus. In Jewish tradition, the pearl became a reference for Torah.

The Parable of the Fishing Net

Jesus described a process of fishing very familiar to Jews who lived along the shores of the Sea of Galilee. Fishermen cast their nets into the sea. When the nets were full, the fishermen dragged the nets behind their boats to the shore, anchored, and sorted among the fish caught. The edible and sellable fish they gathered into their boats; the inedible and unsellable fish they tossed back into the lake.

Jesus compared the kingdom of heaven to this process of fishing.

> Again, the kingdom of heaven is like a net which was thrown into the sea and gathered fish of every kind; when it was full, men drew it ashore and sat down and sorted the good into vessels but threw away the bad. So it will be at the close of the age. The angels will come out and separate the evil from the righteous, and throw them into the furnace of fire; there men will weep and gnash their teeth. (Matthew 13:47–50)

What Secrets Did the Parable Convey?

What was Jesus teaching in this parable? How was the kingdom of heaven like fishing in the Sea of Galilee?

Though Jesus called his disciples "fishers of men," in this parable the fisherman was God. The current age of human experience was coming to a close. When this age ended, angels would sort through all the people on earth and select only true believers to take with them into God's kingdom. All the others would be destroyed. The wicked would be thrown into the fiery furnace and burned to death.

The Parable of the Householder

Every scribe who followed Jesus was like a householder who brought out of his storage both new things and old:

> And he said to them, 'Therefore every scribe who has been trained for the kingdom of heaven is like a householder who brings out of his treasure what is new and what is old.' (Matthew 13:52)

What Secrets Did the Parable Convey?

In the New Testament, a *scribe* was a proponent of Jewish law and tradition and was often mentioned among Jesus' detractors. But there were scribes and Pharisees among Jesus supporters as well.

Within the community of Jesus' followers, scribes performed the same functions as in the Jewish community at large. They preserved and explained Jesus' teachings. Some of Jesus' teachings were based on Jewish tradition; some were new.

Scribes

In the Hebrew Bible, the term *scribe* applied to any individual who composed legal documents and kept records.[49] Shapham the scribe was concerned with the king's finances, and Shebna the scribe administered the king's estates.[50] Barukh wrote Jeremiah's prophecies on a scroll and presented it to King Jehoiakim. The king was displeased and burned the scroll. So Jeremiah dictated a new scroll to Baruch.[51]

A new kind of scribe emerged during the Babylonian Exile. The Jews needed to preserve their heritage in their new and foreign homeland, so scribes began to write down the stories, ceremonies, and traditions they remembered—and to read these scrolls to the exiles on occasions when they assembled in their communities. The scrolls preserved their memories, and the readings reminded them (and eventually their children and grandchildren) what their faith required of them.

Once the texts were widely accepted, their interpretation became more important than their writing. So Jews began to look to scribes who could explain the meanings of the text and instruct them in the proper observance of their traditions. Noted for their ability to apply their understandings of the scrolls to the life needs of the Jewish people, their jobs were "to study the law of the Lord . . . and to teach His statutes and ordinances in Israel."[52]

Initially, many of these scribes were members of priestly families.[53] But there was no requirement of priestly descent. In theory, anyone could be a scribe. As more lay people developed the skills needed to read, explain, and interpret God's law, the group democratized. Eventually they were found in cities and villages throughout the Jewish world, loosely associated with one another, teaching God's word as they understood it.[54]

In Jewish literature and in the New Testament, these scribes were often identified with the Pharisees.[55] But the Sadducees had their scribes,[56] and scribes were members of Jesus' fellowship.[57] According to Jesus, some scribes would be welcomed into the kingdom of heaven.[58]

Leadership Groups within First-Century Jewish Society

In his history of the Jewish people, Josephus noted four significant groups within the Jewish community. He identified three as the Pharisees, Sadducees, and Essenes and called the fourth by a Greek term, *haeresis*, normally translated as "philosophy," "school of thought," or "sect," but what might be viewed less intellectually as a "way of life." None of these groups was an organized school or association. They didn't live in any one location, they didn't follow one teacher, and they often disagreed among themselves.

Nonetheless, Josephus was correct. These groups provided leadership and direction to the Jewish community of Palestine during the two centuries before Jesus and after his death.

Each was a comparatively small association of like-minded people who attempted to persuade the community at large to accept their beliefs and patterns of behavior. Each group had its staunch adherents and also its opponents. Most Jews considered their ideas and were influenced by their opinions but didn't belong to any party.[59]

Let's look at the two largest groups—the Sadducees and the Pharisees.

Sadducees and Pharisees

Certain Sadducees questioned Jesus about his notions of resurrection.[60] According to Jewish law, if a married man died without a son, his brother was required to marry the widow and raise up a child for his deceased brother.[61] The Sadducees based their claim against Jesus on an extreme case involving this law of "levirate" marriage:

> There were seven brothers; the first took a wife, and when he died left no children; and the second took her, and died, leaving no children; and the third likewise; and the seven left no children. Last of all the woman also died. In the resurrection whose wife will she be? For the seven had her as wife. (Mark 12:18–23)[62]

Jesus responded:

> You know neither the scriptures nor the power of God. For when they rise from the dead, they neither marry nor are given in marriage, but are like angels in heaven . . . as for the dead being raised, have you not read in the book of Moses, in the passage about the bush, how God said to him, "I am the God of Abraham, and the God of Isaac, and the God of Jacob"? He is not God of the dead, but of the living. (Mark 12:24–27)[63]

The Sadducees didn't believe in resurrection. Jesus did. So they took him to task for it.

Resurrection was an idea promulgated and promoted by the Pharisees.[64]

The Sadducees based their teachings on their understandings of the Five Books of Moses, with particular emphasis on the priestly sections—the maintenance of the Temple, the sacrifices, the roles of the priests, etc. They viewed Israel as a theocratic community organized under the leadership of the High Priest. Their interpretations of the Torah were different from the sages', and they contested many of the teachings of the Pharisees. In addition to resurrection, the Sadducees also denied all future rewards and punishments, the World to Come, and the advent of a conquering Messiah.[65] They had their own calendar, their own rules about ritual purity, and their own notions about sacrifice. They treated false witnesses more leniently, applied stricter standards for imposing the death penalty, and held owners responsible for the damages caused by both their slaves and beasts.[66]

In each instance above, the Pharisees affirmed the contrary point of view—and Jesus agreed with them. Generally, Jesus accepted the beliefs of the Pharisees and rejected the teachings of the Sadducees.

Jesus had more in common with the Pharisees than with any other major group in the Jewish community. He agreed with their overall philosophy, their fundamental principles, and their interpretations of Jewish law. Most of the ideas Jesus taught were Pharisaic.

He did disagree on some issues and was frequently challenged to explain his position. He didn't believe in divorce, though it was prescribed in the Hebrew Bible.[67] He didn't wash his hands before eating.[68] He dined with sinners.[69] He did not fast when others fasted.[70] He healed on the Sabbath—which the Pharisees saw as forbidden work.[71] On Saturday, his disciples plucked grain from stalks growing in the field—definitely forbidden on the Sabbath.[72]

For the most part, however, Jesus honored the Sabbath. Jesus prayed and preached frequently in synagogues on the Sabbath.[73] He probably wore fringes like other men and wrapped his forehead and left arm in phylacteries.[74] He recited the prayers properly and knew enough Hebrew to read a section of the scroll of Isaiah.[75] After services, he often enjoyed a special Sabbath meal with his disciples or as a guest in another's home.[76] According to John, Jesus said, "I have always taught in synagogues and in the temple, where all Jews come together."[77]

Nicodemus was a Pharisee and one of Jesus' followers.[78] Paul was a Pharisee and the son of a Pharisee.[79] Matthew mentioned scribes who were members of Jesus' community.[80] In the Sermon on the Mount, Jesus said, "I say to you, till heaven and earth pass away, not an iota, not a dot, will pass from the law until all is accomplished. Whoever then relaxes one of the least of these commandments and teaches men so, shall be called least in the kingdom of heaven; but he who does them and teaches them shall be called great in the kingdom of heaven"; further, he called the Pharisees "righteous."[81] Jesus ate in the homes of Pharisees[82] and debated with them openly in Capernaum, Jerusalem, and elsewhere.[83] Later, some Pharisees warned Jesus that Herod Antipas planned to kill him.[84]

It was not their ideas he condemned but their behavior. "Practice and observe whatever they tell you, but not what they do; for they preach, but do not practice."[85] Some Pharisees did not live up to their own high ideals.

Some Pharisees misunderstood their own teachings. "They bind heavy burdens . . . and lay them on men's shoulders; but they themselves will not move them with their finger. They do all their deeds to be seen by men. . . . They make their phylacteries broad and their fringes long, and they love the place of honor at feasts and the best seats in the synagogues and salutations in the market places and being called rabbi by men."[86] "I tell you, unless your righteousness exceeds that of the scribes and Pharisees, you will never enter the kingdom of heaven."[87]

Jesus did not condemn the thoughts and ideas of the Pharisees. He condemned their behavior—not only for the harm they did but, especially, for leading other Jews astray by their example.[88]

When we use only the New Testament as a source for understanding the Pharisees, we get a distorted impression. Pharisees were called "blind guides,"[89] "hypocrites,"[90] "an evil and adulterous generation,"[91] and "a brood of vipers."[92] They picked on Jesus repeatedly, challenging him with their questions and accusations, trying to ensnare him with his own words and deeds.[93] In two gospels, they were listed among those plotting to kill Jesus.[94] These images created a negative impression for subsequent generations of Christians who were not a part of the Jewish community and no longer identified with Jewish tradition.

In Jewish literature, the opposite image prevailed. According to Josephus, "so great is their influence with the masses [of the Jewish people] that even when they speak against a king or a high priest, they immediately gain credence."[95] John Hyrcanus, one of Mattathius' sons and the first Hasmonean ruler, was a disciple of the Pharisees.[96] Queen Alexandra, his daughter-in-law, was strongly influenced by them and established Pharisaic rulings as law.[97] Pharisaic images and interpretations abound in extracanonical books like Judith, Tobit, and First Maccabees.[98] Among the great leaders of the Jewish people during the first two centuries were the Pharisee sages Hillel, Gamaliel, Johanan ben Zakkai, and Akiba. What survived the destruction of the Temple and the disappearance of the sacrificial system was Pharisaic Judaism. Pharisaic beliefs and procedures were the Judaism most Jews practiced in the first century. Jesus was among them. For the most part, Jesus was a Pharisaic Jew.

Jesus and the Sabbath

Let's explore in greater detail Jesus' disagreement with the sages concerning work on the Sabbath.

At that time Jesus went through the grainfields on the Sabbath; his disciples were hungry, and they began to pluck heads of grain and to eat. But when the Pharisees saw it, they said to him, "Look, your disciples are doing what is not lawful to do on the Sabbath." (Matthew 12:1–2)[99]

It was the Sabbath day and Jesus' disciples were hungry, so they plucked from stalks in the field as they walked and ate the grain. Either they were observed by some Pharisees or their plucking was brought to the Pharisees' attention by reliable witnesses. On that basis, these sages accused Jesus of allowing his disciples to break the rules governing work on the Sabbath.

From the discussion that followed, it appears that Jesus and the Pharisees agreed on a set of principles:

- The Sabbath was a sacred day during which certain kinds of work were forbidden.[100]
- Among the work forbidden on the Sabbath was harvesting crops.[101]
- All the Sabbath rules could be set aside to save the life of a human being or an animal.[102]
- These rules—as specified in the Torah, amplified by the prophets and interpreted by the sages—were divinely revealed. To break them was to sin against God.[103]

The Pharisees and Jesus agreed that forbidden work could be performed on the Sabbath to save a human being or an animal in dire straits. They disagreed on what those "dire straits" were.

He said to them, "Have you not read what David did, when he was hungry, and those who were with him: how he entered the house of God and ate the bread of the Presence, which it was not lawful for him to eat nor for those who were with him, but only for the priests?" (Matthew 12:3–4).[104]

Jesus reminded his accusers what happened when David's troops had been hungry during their flight from King Saul.[105] David had lied to the chief priest at Nob about his mission and requested food for his troops. Ahimelech replied that the only bread on hand was the showbread. Both David and Ahimelech knew the showbread was an offering consecrated to God and to be eaten only by priests.[106] David asserted that his soldiers were also "consecrated," and he took the bread.

If it had been appropriate for David and Ahimelech to break the rules to eat to feed the hungry, Jesus was saying, it was appropriate for his hungry disciples to pluck standing grain on the Sabbath. After all, like David's warriors, they were also on a sacred mission.[107]

Jesus provided another biblical example: "Have you not read in the law how on the Sabbath the priests in the temple profane the Sabbath, and are guiltless?" (Matthew 12:5).

As prescribed in the book of Numbers, on the Sabbath the priests burned two unblemished yearling lambs, a meal offering mixed with oil, and a libation in addition to the daily sacrifices.[108] Since lighting a fire and cooking were forbidden on the Sabbath, one might suppose burning sacrifices would also be prohibited. Yet according to the Pharisees themselves, it was not. The duty of Temple service outweighed the requirements of Sabbath rest. So too, Jesus was implying, did the sacred mission of his disciples outweigh the rules forbidding plucking grain on the Sabbath.

Jesus said, "I tell you, something greater than the temple is here."[109] Then he continued, "If you had known what this means, 'I desire mercy, and not sacrifice,' you would not have condemned the guiltless (Matthew 12:7).[110]

Jesus reminded his accusers that the prophets had excoriated people for placing their faith in rituals and sacrifices to the neglect of their fellows. "Hear this, you who trample upon the needy and bring the poor of the land to an end, saying, 'When will the new moon be over, that we may sell grain? And the Sabbath, that we may offer wheat for sale?'"[111] "Your burnt offerings are not acceptable, nor your sacrifices pleasing to me."[112] "I have had enough of burnt offerings of rams and the fat of fed beasts. . . . Seek justice, correct oppression; defend the fatherless, plead for the widow."[113]

Jesus concluded his argument with the following affirmation: "The son of man is lord of the Sabbath."[114]

Most Christians understood the phrase "son of man" as a reference to Jesus himself and concluded that Jesus was declaring that he, Jesus, determined the Sabbath rules and that his message of God's kingdom superceded the Sabbath violations suggested by the sages.[115]

Jews heard the phrase differently. In Hebrew, the phrase *ben adam* ("son of man") meant "a human being"—a descendant of Adam. His first-century Jewish listeners (including the Pharisees to whom he was speaking) understood Jesus to say that the Sabbath was for the benefit of human beings and not the other way around. Shabbat observance should not result in human harm.

That's why Matthew included the following incident immediately after the controversy between these Pharisees and Jesus.

And he went on from there, and entered their synagogue. And behold, there was a man with a withered hand. And they asked him, "Is it lawful to heal on the Sabbath?" so that they might accuse him. He said to them, "What man of you, if he has one sheep and it falls into a pit on the Sabbath, will not lay hold of it and lift it out? Of how much more value is a man than a sheep! So it is lawful to do good on the Sabbath." Then he said to the man, "Stretch out your hand." And the man stretched it out, and it was restored, whole like the other. (Matthew 12:9–13)

According to the sages, one could respond to sudden accidents and danger on the Sabbath. "Any of the [scrolls of the] Holy Scriptures may be saved from burning [on the Sabbath by carrying them to another domain]."[116] "[If a fire broke out on the Sabbath], they may save enough food for three meals—for people, food that is suited for people, and for cattle, food that is suited for cattle."[117] "They may deliver a woman on the Sabbath and summon a midwife for her."[118] "If ravenous hunger seized a man, he may be given even unclean things to eat until his eyes are enlightened [stable].[119] . . . If a man has a pain in his throat [so that he cannot breath or swallow], they may drop medicine into his mouth on the Sabbath."[120] "If a building fell down upon a man and there is doubt whether or not he is there, or whether he is alive or dead, or whether he is a gentile or an Israelite, they may clear away the rubble above him."[121] The rule was clear: "Whenever there is doubt whether life is in danger, this [acting to save a man's life] overrides the Sabbath."[122]

However, chronic conditions could be treated a day later, in which case there was no urgency that justified breaking the Sabbath rules. This was where Jesus differed with the sages. From Jesus' point of view, disease, discomfort, and pain were all urgent concerns and ought to be treated immediately. Making a person suffer another day when relief was available prolonged pain unnecessarily and without cause.

Jesus saw no reason to prolong suffering if it could be cured, and he didn't view healing on the Sabbath as forbidden work. The Sabbath existed to benefit humankind. That's what his listeners understood when Jesus said, "The son of man is the lord of the Sabbath."

In the next chapter, we'll explore eight more parables dealing with the kingdom of God.

Notes

1. Most rabbinic parables begin with the Aramaic words: *mashal l'* (for example, *mashal l'melekh she* . . . "This is a parable. It is like a king who . . ."). The comparison is not

to a specific object or person but to the unfolding of events, circumstances, and relationships. In the current parable, the kingdom of heaven is not like the mustard seed itself but like what grows from a tiny mustard seed.

2. Pliny, *Natural History*, 29.54.170, as presented in Bernard Brandon Scott, *Hear Then the Parable: A Commentary on the Parables of Jesus* (Minneapolis, Minn.: Fortress, 1990), 380.

3. Pliny, *Natural History*, 20.87.236–37, as presented in Scott, *Hear Then the Parable*, 380.

4. Matthew 17:20. See also Luke 17:6.

5. M. Tohoroth 8:8; M. Niddah 5:2.

6. Ezekiel 31:3–6.

7. Ezekiel 17:22–23. The Greek text adds "all kinds of beasts."

8. Daniel 4:10–14.

9. Daniel 4:22.

10. *The Thanksgiving Hymns* (1QH) 8:4–14, 6:15–16, as presented in David Flusser, *Jesus* (Jerusalem: Magnes, 2001), 110f.

11. Isaiah 2:2–4.

12. Micah 4:1–4.

13. Isaiah 11:6, following the Greek text and the Dead Sea manuscript 1QIs4. The Hebrew text is unclear. See also Isaiah 11:7–9.

14. Zechariah 14:6–9. See also Zechariah 8:20–23; Zephaniah 3:9.

15. Created, according to Jewish legend, on the fifth and sixth days of Creation and graphically described in Job 40–41.

16. Louis Ginzberg, *Legends of the Jews* (Philadelphia: Jewish Publication Society of America, 1956), vol. 1, 27–29, with notes in vol. 5, 41–46. See also 4 Esdras 6:51–52; Syrian Baruch 29:1–4.

17. Syriac Baruch 29:5–7, immediately following the description of the Leviathan banquet. A *kor* is about ninety gallons.

18. Sifre on Deuteronomy 32:16–17, as noted in George Foot Moore, *Judaism in the First Centuries of the Christian Era* (Cambridge, Mass.: Harvard University Press, 1927), vol. 2, 365.

19. Shabbat 30b.

20. Matthew 16:11. Read the entire section Matthew 16:5–12. See Mark 8:15; Luke 12:1.

21. Mark 8:15. Other ancient manuscripts read "the Herodians."

22. Page 1076.

23. Tankhuma Noah §4, as presented in Moore, *Judaism in the First Centuries of the Christian Era*, vol. 1, 480. Rabbi Abahu used as his proof-text a quote from Genesis 8:21.

24. Genesis Rabba Noah 34:10, as presented in Claude G. Montefiore and H. Loewe, *A Rabbinic Anthology* (London: Macmillan, 1938), 301. For additional rabbinic uses of this metaphor, see Berakhot 17a; J. Berakhot 7d; Mekhilta Beshallakh 2 (on Ex 14:11).

25. One *se'a* ("measure") equaled one-third *ephah,* and one-tenth *ephah* equaled 2.09

quarts. Therefore, each *se'a* measured slightly less than seven quarts of flour—and "three measures" held almost twenty-one quarts (O. R. Sellers, "Weights and Measures," in *The Interpreter's Dictionary of the Bible: An Illustrated Encyclopedia*, ed. George A. Buttrick [New York: Abingdon, 1962], vol. 4, 834f. See also the articles by Eliezer Bashan (Sternberg) and Haim Hermann Cohn in the *Encyclopedia Judaica*, vol. 16, cols. 375–91).

26. Genesis 3:16. Exodus 21:7. Leviticus 19:29. Judges 19:24. M. Ketuboth 4:4–5; 5:5; 6:1; 8:1–7; 9:1. M. Nedarim 10:1–4; 11:1, 4–5. M. Kiddushin 1:1.

27. M. Ketuboth 13:3; M. Gittin 3:1, 4:7–8, 9:10; M. Baba Bathra 9:1; M. Sanhedrin 3:4–5 (all men); M. Makkot 1:9.

28. Exodus 20:12; Leviticus 20:9; Deuteronomy 5:16, 27:16.

29. Judges 4:4–24.

30. Jael: Judges 4:17–21, 5:24–27. Rahab: Joshua 2:1–21. Esther: Esther 4:1–9:32.

31. The Messiah would be a descendant of King David: Isaiah 9:1–7; Ezekiel 34:23–24, 37:24–25. David was a descendant of Ruth: Ruth 4:18–22. Joseph was a descendant of David: Matthew 1:1–17, 20; Luke 1:27, 2:4. Jesus was the Messiah: Matthew 1:1, 16, 18; Mark 1:1; John 1:17; 17:3; 20:31. Mary was Jesus' mother: Matthew 1:6, 18–25; Mark 6:3; Luke 1:26–38, 2:8–16.

32. See Proverbs 2:5, 6, 8, 12.

33. See also Exodus 23:4.

34. M. Baba Metzia 2:6.

35. M. Baba Kama 10:2. M. Baba Metzia 1:1, 3–8; 2:9–11.

36. M. Baba Metzia 2:1–5, 7–8; M. Makshirin 2:8–10.

37. M. Baba Metzia 2:6; M. Makshirin 2:8–10.

38. M. Gittin 5:3; M. Baba Metzia 3:6.

39. M. Baba Kama 10:2; M. Baba Metzia 1:1, 3–8.

40. Deuteronomy 22:1.

41. M. Baba Metzia 2:9.

42. See below pp. 66–69.

43. Mark 1:16–20; Luke 5:10.

44. Matthew 13:1; 21:17; 26:6; Mark 1:29, 35; 9:33; 10:10; 14:3; Luke 9:12; 19:5–7.

45. Matthew 9:10, 26:17–19; Mark 2:15, 14:12–16; Luke 5:29–30, 7:36, 10:8, 14:1, 22:8–14; John 4:31–34.

46. Matthew 14:14–22, 15:29–39; Mark 6:34–46, 9:12–17.

47. Job 28:18.

48. According to Jeremias, pearls were highly prized throughout the Greco-Roman world. Divers sought them in the Red Sea, the Persian Gulf, and the Indian Ocean. Caesar presented a pearl worth six million sesterces to Brutus' mother, and Cleopatra owned a pearl worth a hundred million sesterces (*The Parables of Jesus*, 199).

49. Jeremiah 32:9–14.

50. 2 Kings 22:3–11; Isaiah 22:15, 36:3.

51. Jeremiah 36:4–32, 45:1.

52. Ezra 7:6, 10–12; Nehemiah 8:1–8, 9, 13.

53. Ezra 7:12; Nehemiah 8:7; 2 Chronicles 34:13.

54. Matthew 7:29; Mark 7:1; Luke 5:17.

55. For example, Matthew 5:20, 12:38, 15:1. Mark 7:1, 5. Luke 5:30, 6:7, 11:53. John 8:3.

56. Luke 20:27–39. Possibly Matthew 20:18, 21:15, 27:41. Mark 10:33; 11:18, 27; 14:1, 43. Luke 9: 22; 19:47; 20:1, 19; 22:2.

57. Matthew 8:19, 23:34; Mark 12:28–34.

58. Matthew 13:52.

59. For an excellent discussion of the meaning of *haeresis*, see Ellis Rivkin, *A Hidden Revolution: The Pharisee's Search for the Kingdom Within* (Nashville Tenn.: Abingdon, 1978), 316–18.

60. This section discusses first the beliefs of the Sadducees, then contrasts them with the ideas of the Pharisees. The Sadducees emerged as a recognized group after the Maccabean Revolution (168–162 BCE). In *Antiquities* (13.10.5–6), Josephus provided the earliest literary reference to the Sadducees, placing them in the era of John Hyrcanus (135–104 BCE).

61. Deuteronomy 25:5–6. See also Genesis 38:8.

62. See also Matthew 22:23–28, Luke 20:27–33.

63. Jesus alluded to Exodus 3:6, which the sages of the first century interpreted to indicate that Abraham, Isaac, and Jacob were alive in heaven. See also Matthew 22:29–32, Luke 20:34–38.

64. See also Matthew 17:9–12; Mark 9:11–13; Acts 4:1–4, 23:6–11.

65. A. C. Sundberg, "Sadducees," in *The Interpreter's Dictionary of the Bible: An Illustrated Encyclopedia*, ed. George A. Buttrick (New York: Abingdon, 1962), 160–63. According to Acts 23:8, they may later have denied the existence of angels and spirits. According to Josephus (*War* 2.8.14, *Antiquities* 13.5.9), they rejected the Greek notion of fate.

66. M. Makkot 1:8, Tosefta Sanhedrin 6:6, M. Yada'im 4:7.

67. Matthew 15:1–2, 19:3–6; Mark 10:2–9. See Leviticus 21:7, 14; 22:13. Numbers 30:10. Deuteronomy 22:19, 29; 24:1–4. Isaiah 50:1. Jeremiah 3:8.

68. Matthew 15:2; Mark 7:1–2, 5; Luke 11:37–38.

69. Matthew 2:16, 9:11; Mark 2:16; Luke 5:30; Luke 15:1–2. See also Luke 7:36–39.

70. Mark 2:18, Luke 5:33.

71. Matthew 12:10; Mark 3:1–6; Luke 6:6–10, 13:14, 14:1–6; John 9:8–33.

72. Matthew 12:1–2, Mark 2:23–24, Luke 6:1–2.

73. Mark 1:21; 3:3; 6:6; Luke 4:6, 31; 6:6; 13:10. According to Luke 4:16, it was "his custom" to attend synagogue on the Sabbath.

74. Matthew 23:5.

75. Luke 4:16–20.

76. Luke 14:1–24. According to Moore (*Judaism in the First Centuries of the Christian Era*, vol. 2, 35), "the Sabbath was a favorite time for entertaining guests at dinner."

77. John 18:20.

78. John 3:1, 7:50–51.
79. Acts 23:6.
80. Matthew 8:19, 13:52.
81. Matthew 5:18–20.
82. Luke 7:36, 11:37, 14:1.
83. Capernaum: Matthew 9:1ff; Mark 2:1ff, 3:1ff; Luke 7:1. Jerusalem: Matthew 21:1ff; Mark 11:1ff; John 8:1. Elsewhere: Mark 10:1ff; Luke 5:1ff, 17:11ff, 19:1ff.
84. Luke 13:31.
85. Matthew 23:3.
86. Matthew 23:4–7. See also Mark 12:38–40, Luke 11:43.
87. Matthew 5:20.
88. However, in Matthew 16:1–11, Jesus warned his listeners three times against the pervasive negative influence of their teachings ("leaven").
89. Matthew 15:14; 23:15, 23. See also Matthew 23:16, 18, 25.
90. Matthew 15:7; 23:13, 14, 22, 24, 26, 28; Mark 7:6.
91. Matthew 12:39, 16:4.
92. Matthew 12:34, 23:32.
93. For example, Matthew 9:11; 12:2, 10, 38; 15:1–2; Mark 2:16, 24; 7:5; 8:11; Luke 5:21, 30, 33; 6:2; John 8:4–5, 13, 25; 9:40.
94. Mark 3:6, Luke 6:7–11.
95. *Antiquities* 13:288.
96. *Antiquities* 13:288.
97. *Antiquities* 13:405–11.
98. Judith 10:5, 12:1–4, 19; Tobit 1:17–19; 2:1–9; 1 Maccabees 7:12–18.
99. See also Matthew 2:23–24 and Luke 6:1–2.
100. Exodus 20:10; 31:14, 15; 35:2; Leviticus 23:3; Deuteronomy 5:14; Jeremiah 17:22, 24; M. Shabbat 7:2.
101. Plucking grain was permitted during the week (Deuteronomy 23:25) but forbidden on the Sabbath (Exodus 34:21). See also Nehemiah 13:15 and the types of work forbidden on the Sabbath in M. Shabbat 7:2.
102. M. Shabbat 18:3; M. Yoma 8:6, 7. See also Mekilta Ki Tissa I, as discussed in Moore, *Judaism in the First Centuries of the Christian Era*, vol. 2, 30f.
103. Numbers 15:32–36, Nehemiah 13:15, Amos 8:5, Isaiah 58:13, Jeremiah 17:19–27, Ezekiel 20, M. Shabbat 1:24, M. Erubim 1:10.
104. See also Mark 2:25–26 (where the priest was Abiathar) and Luke 6:3–4.
105. 1 Samuel 21:2–7 (= Greek 1 Samuel 21:1–6).
106. Leviticus 24:5–9.
107. Jesus also may have been alluding to his own descent from King David.
108. Numbers 28:9–10. See also Rabbi Akiba's ruling in M. Pesakim 6:2.
109. Matthew 12:6.
110. See also Matthew 9:13.
111. Amos 8:4–5. See also Amos 4:4–5, 5:25, 8:10.

112. Jeremiah 6:20. See also Jeremiah 7:21–26.
113. Isaiah 1:11–17.
114. Matthew 12:8. See also Mark 2:28, Luke 6:5.
115. See *The New American Bible*, note to Matthew 12:8, p. 1026, and *The Oxford Annotated Bible*, note to Matthew 12:8, p. 1185. See also Matthew 11:27, John 5:1–18.
116. M. Shabbat 16:1.
117. M. Shabbat 16:2.
118. M. Shabbat 18:3.
119. See I Samuel 14:27.
120. M. Yoma 8:6.
121. M. Yoma 8:7.
122. M. Yoma 8:6. See also Leviticus 18:5; Ezekiel 20:11.

CHAPTER SEVEN

More Parables about the Kingdom of God

The Parable of the Budding Fig Tree

Figs were a staple of Jewish diet in the first century, and Jesus' listeners knew well the cycle of growth exhibited by fig trees. Branches lost their leaves in the winter and remained bare through early spring. Even before the leaves appeared, tiny flowers covered with a soft skin developed on last season's branches. Then the new leaves emerged and covered the branches quickly. By June the tree was in full bloom, and the figs were ripe for picking.

Jesus built on his audience's knowledge in the Parable of the Budding Fig Tree.

> From the fig tree learn its lesson: as soon as its branch becomes tender and puts forth its leaves, you know that summer is near. So also, when you see all these things, you know that he is near, at the very gates. Truly, I say to you, this generation will not pass away till all these things take place. Heaven and earth will pass away, but my words will not pass away. (Matthew 24:32–35)

What Secrets Did the Parable Convey?

In April and May people noticed green buds sprouting along the branches of fig trees and knew from experience that the trees would be covered with leaves and fruit by June. Jesus taught that the kingdom of heaven was like the fig tree. Once the first signs appeared, the rest was inevitable. As certain as a summer harvest of figs was the coming of God's kingdom once the first portents were visible.

Jesus Built on Jewish Images

How do we know Jesus meant the coming kingdom? The prophet Micah predicted it using the same image:

> In days to come, the mount of the Lord's house shall stand firm above the mountains and tower above the hills. Peoples shall gaze on it with joy, and many nations shall go and say: "Come, let us go up to the mountain of the Lord, to the house of the God of Jacob; that he may teach us his ways and that we may walk in his paths." . . . Nation shall not take up sword against nation, neither shall they learn war any more; but every man shall sit under his vine and under his fig tree, and nothing shall cause him to tremble. . . . The Lord will reign over them on Mount Zion now and forever. (Micah 4:1–7)

"The Day of the Lord is coming," Joel warned, a day of destruction and desolation, of "darkness and gloom." Those who repent will be saved. Threshing floors would be full of grain; vats would overflow with wine and oil; and "fig tree and vine will provide their full yield."[1]

Zechariah predicted the scattered Israelites would return from Exile, the Temple would be rebuilt, and the priesthood would be restored. Israel would be saved. "In that day, says the Lord of hosts, every one of you will invite his neighbor under his vine and under his fig tree."[2] In Jewish tradition, vine and fig tree represented safety and security.[3]

The contrary was also true. Vile figs symbolized destruction and death.[4] But Jesus pointed toward a bountiful harvest—the coming of God's kingdom.

God's Kingdom Was Imminent

Some scholars suggest that, by using the phrase "he is near," Jesus was predicting the coming of the Messiah.[5] The translation certainly gives that impression. But the translation is inadequate. In Hebrew and Aramaic, every object is either masculine or feminine. There is no neuter. "God" is masculine, "God's kingdom" is feminine, "the yoke of God's kingdom" is masculine, and "the coming of God's kingdom" is feminine. In each instance, the Aramaic pronoun "he" or "she" would be used to describe these images. Where we would say "it" in English, Aramaic requires "he" or "she."

"He is near" referred to the imminent start of God's kingdom on earth.

It would begin once the first signs appeared. And its advance would be rapid. God's kingdom would be established in "this generation."[6]

With that assertion, Jesus went farther than any previous prediction. He gave a definite time for the establishment of God's kingdom—less than thirty years!

The Same Parable in Luke
Luke presented the same parable, and he stated clearly that Jesus meant the coming of God's kingdom.

> And he told them a parable: "Look at the fig tree, and all the trees; as soon as they come out in leaf, you see for yourselves and know that the summer is already near. So also, when you see these things taking place, you know that the kingdom of God is near. Truly, I say to you, this generation will not pass away till all has taken place. Heaven and earth will pass away, but my words will not pass away." (Luke 21:29–33)

The Same Parable in Mark
Mark's version of the Parable of the Budding Fig Tree was an almost verbatim repetition of Matthew. And, like Matthew, Mark reported the ambiguous pronoun.

> From the fig tree learn its lesson: as soon as its branch becomes tender and puts forth its leaves, you know that summer is near. So also, when you see these things taking place, you know that he is near, at the very gates. Truly, I say to you, this generation will not pass away before all these things take place. Heaven and earth will pass away, but my words will not pass away. (Mark 13:28–32)

What were the signs people would observe? What were "all these things" that were to take place?

The "signs" pointing to salvation and everlasting joy would be as apparent as the small green buds on a fig tree.[7] But Jesus did not describe the signs.

Signs
The terms "sign" and "wonder" occurred frequently in the Hebrew Bible. On eighteen occasions they appeared in the same verse as parallels, indicating that (in those instances) their meanings overlapped. They signified acts of God to be greeted with awe and reverence. While some were natural events (like rainbows, floods, and earthquakes) and some were supernatural events (like the ten plagues in Egypt, Moses parting the Red Sea, and Joshua causing the sun to stand still), all affirmed God's power and majesty in and over the natural world. Both the natural order of the universe and its disruptions depended on God. He was as responsible for the regular alternation of day and night and the fall of rain in spring and fall as He was for the Exodus from Egypt and the Return from Exile. "Signs" of God's activity were as present in ordinary events as in extraordinary events.

For example, according to the story of Creation, the heavenly bodies were to provide direction in travel, support calculations of times and seasons, and indicate weather.[8] The same heavenly bodies displayed portents of the coming cataclysm. "I will give portents in the heavens and on the earth, blood and fire and columns of smoke. The sun shall be turned to darkness, and the moon to blood, before the great and terrible day of the Lord comes."[9]

People also are "signs" of God's activity in the world. The psalmist claimed to have been a portent to his contemporaries.[10] God called Isaiah "a sign and a wonder," and Isaiah designated himself and his children by the same appellation.[11] Sometimes the prophets provided signs; sometimes they were the signs.

When Jesus' contemporaries asked for a sign, they were seeking some external confirmation of Jesus' ideas, some authentication for renouncing the teachings of the accepted leaders of their community and changing their beliefs and behavior to conform to Jesus' instruction. Jesus condemned their requests and declined to provide a sign.[12]

The Parable of the Doorkeeper

A landowner left on a journey and gave a work assignment to each servant. He instructed the doorkeeper to be diligent and watchful. Jesus based the Parable of the Doorkeeper on this real-life experience.

> Take heed, watch; for you do not know when the time will come. It is like a man going on a journey, when he leaves home and puts his servants in charge, each with his work, and commands the doorkeeper to be on the watch. Watch therefore—for you do not know when the master of the house will come, in the evening, or at midnight, or at cockcrow, or in the morning—lest he come suddenly and find you asleep. And what I say to you I say to all: Watch. (Mark 13:33–37)

Jesus built the metaphor on the doorkeeper, not on the man going on a journey, and he instructed his listeners to be alert—like the doorkeeper—and watch for the homeowner's return.

Who was the homeowner?

God was the "master of the house." The "house" was the earth with its people, cultures, and kingdoms. And the owner's coming was the kingdom of heaven.

God's Kingdom Was Imminent

When was the master coming? When would God's kingdom begin?

Though he gave no definite time, Jesus indicated the establishment of

God's kingdom was imminent. Therefore, Jesus encouraged his listeners to get themselves ready—to give up their false beliefs and improper behaviors—lest they be caught by surprise at its sudden presence, be judged sinners, and perish in the devastation to follow.

God's kingdom would appear "sudden" only to those who were "asleep"—not to those who had put their lives in order, had fulfilled their assignment (to obey God's laws), and waited eagerly to participate in the new era.

The Parable of the Return from a Wedding

Once again, Jesus drew on the life experiences of his audience. In the Parable of the Return from a Wedding, he described a landowner traveling to a wedding in another community and returning home. He encouraged his listeners to focus on the servants left behind.

> Let your loins be girded and your lamps burning, and be like men who are waiting for their master to come home from the marriage feast, so that they may open to him at once when he comes and knocks. Blessed are those servants whom the master finds awake when he comes; truly, I say to you, he will gird himself and have them sit at table, and he will come and serve them. If he comes in the second watch, or in the third, and finds them so, blessed are those servants! (Luke 12:35–38)

What Secrets Did the Parable Convey?

The same elements were included here as in the Parable of the Doorkeeper. Their master was away. He could return at any moment. For Jesus, the key issue was the commitment and integrity of the servants. Would they remain diligent in their master's absence—do their work and prepare for his imminent return—or would they rest and neglect their assignments?

The same metaphors also applied. The absent owner was God.[13] His return established God's kingdom on earth. It could happen any time.

Implied were other images common to Jewish thought in the first century. God was never really absent. Eventually, every person would be called to judgment before God for his behavior. There was no fooling God, and there was no escaping His decision. God called on each sinner, until the last day of his life, to repent.[14] Therefore, repent now as if it were the last day of your life.

Once God's kingdom began, there would be no time to repent. Judgment would follow swiftly, and sinners would suffer and die. There was just a short window of time to become true servants of God before the devastation began.

Jesus went farther in this parable than in the previous parable. Not only were they to remain alert and ready—with their "loins girded" and their "lamps burning"—but they were to "open the door" and welcome their master home. Jesus instructed his followers to be proactive and assertive and to greet the new era with joy.

Those who behave in this manner will be blessed. God will prepare a banquet for them, and they will sit at God's table and celebrate in God's presence.[15]

The Parable of the Servant Left Alone

A landowner left and appointed one servant to be in charge of his other servants. Again, Jesus focused on the integrity and commitment of the steward in his master's absence.

> Who then is the faithful and wise servant, whom his master has set over his household, to give them their food at the proper time? Blessed is that servant whom his master when he comes will find so doing. Truly, I say to you, he will set him over all his possessions. But if that wicked servant says to himself, "My master is delayed," and begins to beat his fellow servants, and eats and drinks with the drunken, the master of that servant will come on a day when he does not expect him and at an hour he does not know, and will punish him, and put him with the hypocrites; there men will weep and gnash their teeth. (Matthew 24:45–51)

What Secrets Did the Parable Convey?
Jesus' audience understood the possibilities. The steward could use his significant new power to feed and care for the members of the owner's household, or he could abuse his privileged position and use his new authority for his own self-indulgence. Jesus described the consequences of either choice.

The servant who fulfilled his assignment would be rewarded. His master "will set him over all his possessions." He would be granted additional privileges and would enjoy the benefits of his heightened status.

But if he took advantage of his master's absence—if he "beat his fellow servants," ate and drank to excess from the owner's supplies, and consorted with "drunkards"—he would be severely punished.[16] He would not only lose his job, but his master would "put him with hypocrites" where "men will weep and gnash their teeth."

Hypocrites

The Hebrew verb root *kh-n-f* was often rendered as "hypocrite" or "hypoc-risy" in early translations of the Bible. The King James Version used the word hypocrite eight times in Job and three times in Isaiah.[17]

In the context of Greek drama, *hypocrisy* was the act of playing a part, and a *hypocrite* was the person playacting. Thus, hypocrisy came to mean the act of pretending to be what one was not or affirming a belief one did not hold.

That was not the meaning of *kh-n-f* in the Hebrew Bible. In those passages where a parallel word was given, the synonyms for *kh-n-f* were "evildoer,"[18] "sinners,"[19] and "wicked."[20] Thus, the Hebrew verb root had to do with per-forming sinful acts and the persons who acted sinfully.[21] It did not mean to pretend or to simulate goodness.

Jesus castigated people who acted sinfully, especially community leaders and teachers. He called them to account, asked them to change their behav-ior and amend their teachings, and demanded that they accurately represent God's wishes as reflected in Jewish tradition. He did this in Aramaic, not Greek, and the words he used reflected Hebrew and Aramaic understandings. In the Greek texts where Jesus said "hypocrites" he meant "sinners" and "evildoers."[22]

In this parable, where he warned that the owner would put his wicked servant with hypocrites, Jesus meant that he would be doomed to die like other sinners. He would have no place in God's kingdom.

Weep and Gnash Their Teeth

The phrase "weep and gnash their teeth" occurred six times in Matthew, once in Luke, and nowhere else in the Hebrew Bible or the New Testament. In every instance, the phrase was part of a verse in which someone was being violently punished. The servant in the Parable of the Eight Talents and the Misdressed Wedding Guest were cast into the "outer darkness."[23] In the Para-ble of the Wheat and the Weeds, evildoers would be thrown into the "fur-nace of fire."[24] In this parable, the servant would not only lose his job but would be punished like other sinners and denied access to God's kingdom.

In Matthew, Jesus vividly depicted what he meant.

> So it will be at the close of the age. The angels will come out and separate the evil from the righteous, and throw them into the furnace of fire; there men will weep and gnash their teeth (Matthew 13:49–50)[25]

> Then the king said to the attendants, "Bind him hand and foot, and cast him into the outer darkness; there men will weep and gnash their teeth." (Matthew 22:13)[26]

Both images pointed to the Final Judgment and described the condemnation of the wicked to searing pain, darkness, and death. People wept and gnashed their teeth when they envisioned the suffering that awaited them.

The Same Parable in Luke

Luke provided a version of the Parable of the Servant Left Alone very similar to Matthew's, but in Luke Jesus used the word "unfaithful" rather than "hypocrites."

> And the Lord said, "Who then is the faithful and wise steward, whom his master will set over his household, to give them their portion of food at the proper time? Blessed is that servant whom his master when he comes will find so doing. Truly, I say to you, he will set him over all his possessions. But if that servant says to himself, 'My master is delayed in coming,' and begins to beat the menservants and the maidservants, and to eat and drink and get drunk, the master of that servant will come on a day when he does not expect him and at an hour he does not know, and will punish him, and put him with the unfaithful. (Luke 12:42–46)

To Whom Was Jesus Addressing His Remarks?

According to Luke, Jesus told this Parable of the Servant Left Alone in response to Peter's question about the previous parable—the Parable of the Return from a Wedding. The disciple asked, "Lord, is this parable meant for us or for everyone?"[27] Apparently, Peter wasn't sure.

To whom was Jesus addressing his remarks? Who were the "servants" in this parable?

Peter provided one answer. The servants were Jesus' disciples, and the steward was the person Jesus put in charge of the disciples—possibly Peter himself.[28] When Jesus traveled and was occasionally absent from his disciples, he may have placed one disciple in charge of the community.

The parable may have been directed against the leaders and teachers of the Jewish community.[29] They held their exalted positions at God's behest. But many of them were abusing their authority, using their power for their own self-aggrandizement and leading the people astray. Jesus warned that if they didn't change their behavior quickly, they would suffer the fate of all sinners. During the cataclysm, they would be destroyed.

The parable could have been directed at the people in Jesus' audiences— ordinary people faced with difficult choices. They were responsible for feeding and caring for the members of their families, for orphans and widows, for those less fortunate then they were, and those suffering oppression and disadvantage. Like the steward, they could choose to benefit others or to indulge their own passions. In either case, the consequences were clear. If they chose self-indulgence, they would suffer death and destruction.

I believe the third suggestion is correct. But all three were possible. Nay, all three were probable, if we imagine that Jesus told the same parable to different audiences on separate occasions.

The Parable of the Burglar

Building again on the life experiences of his audience, Jesus compared the coming of God's kingdom to a nighttime burglary.

> But know this, that if the householder had known in what part of the night the thief was coming, he would have watched and would not have let his house be broken into. Therefore you also must be ready; for the son of man is coming at an hour you do not expect. (Matthew 24:43–44)

What Secrets Did the Parable Convey?
A prudent homeowner understood that burglaries often occurred at night when visibility was poor, household members were asleep, and there were few witnesses. Therefore he took pains to be watchful and prepared. He did not "let his house be broken into."

Jesus taught his listeners to be equally expectant of the establishment of God's kingdom. No one knew exactly when it would occur—at what time of the day or season of the year—but it would surely happen. Jesus instructed his audience to realign their beliefs and change their behavior now in order to participate in the kingdom when it occurred.

The Importance of Being Ready
What a strange metaphor. Preparing for the kingdom of heaven was like preparing to thwart a break-in. The element that tied the two images together was the consequence of not being ready. In the case of a burglary, precious items might be stolen and the house ransacked. But they could be repaired or replaced. Life would return to normal. However, in the case of the New Era, sinners would see their property destroyed, their loved ones condemned, and their own lives obliterated permanently. Nothing would ever be the same again.

The Same Parable in Luke
Luke presented a garbled version of the same parable. In his version the homeowner went away and left his house vacant.

> But know this, that if the householder had known at what hour the thief was coming, he would not have left his house to be broken into. You also must be ready; for the son of man is coming at an unexpected hour. (Luke 12:39–40)

In Luke's version, the metaphor doesn't hold. A prudent homeowner could hire guards to prevent a burglar from entering his home, but how could he personally confront the burglar if he were out of town? In the case of the arrival of God's kingdom, how could he welcome the New Era if he were away?

What Secrets Did the Parable Convey?

The difficulties are resolved by referring to other metaphors. As in the Parable of the Unclean Spirit, the house left unattended may be the person's soul, and a vacated soul invited malicious spirits to enter. In this understanding, Jesus reminded his listeners to conjoin their every thought and behavior with God's Spirit.

Or, like Matthew's version, perhaps the word should be "let" not "left." The owner did leave town but let his house be burglarized. That he lost precious goods was a consequence of his own neglect. In this understanding, the lesson in Luke was the same as the lesson in Matthew.

The Son of Man in Jewish Literature

The Hebrew phrase *ben adam* or *ben enosh* was often translated "son of man," but the translation was too literal. *Ben adam* meant "a human being." And every human being—male and female—was a *ben adam*.[30]

The phrase occurred frequently in Ezekiel as God addressed the prophet.

> He [God] said to me, "Son of man, stand upon your feet, and I will speak with you." And when he spoke to me, the Spirit entered into me and set me upon my feet; and I heard him speaking to me. And he said to me, "Son of man, I send you to the people of Israel, to a nation of rebels, who have rebelled against me . . . and you shall say to them, 'Thus says the Lord God.'" (Ezekiel 2:1–4)[31]

The phrase was clearly a form of address—"O human." It was not a title, and it was not unique to Ezekiel. The Aramaic *bar enosh* occurred in Daniel to describe the figure moving out of the clouds toward God. It had a human appearance.[32] Later the phrase was applied to Daniel himself.[33]

Similarly 2 Esdras described the figure who rose from the sea and flew through the clouds as a "son of man."[34] Philo Judaeus of Alexandria suggested that two humans were created at the beginning of the universe—the heavenly man who was the form from which all future humans were created[35] and the first earthly human placed in the Garden of Eden.[36] The heavenly man was *ben adam*, and the earthly man was Adam.

Enoch predicted the coming of a Chosen One in whose presence the righteous would live forever.[37] Sitting on the throne of glory, the Chosen One would select the faithful from among the resurrected and restore them to life.[38]

Elsewhere in Enoch this Chosen One was called "son of man." As in Daniel, he appeared to be a human being with white hair and an angelic face.[39] He would reveal secrets,[40] overthrow the monarchs of those nations that had persecuted the Jews,[41] and establish justice throughout the world.[42]

By the first century there were extant several images of the "son of man" and what functions he would serve. He was a figure in God's company who looked like a human being. Created at the Beginning, he was the form prototype for all future human beings. He was a human being commissioned by God for special purpose. And he was the champion of the oppressed Jews. Under his leadership, evil nations would crumble, sinners would be punished, the righteous would be resurrected and revived, and righteousness would be established forever throughout the world.

The Son of Man in Jesus' Teaching

At the end of the Parable of the Burglar, Jesus reminded his listeners, "Therefore you also must be ready; for the son of man is coming at an hour you do not expect."[43]

When Jesus used the phrase "son of man," which Jewish images did he have in mind?

In at least two instances the phrase *son of man* meant "human being" or "humankind." During the controversy over plucking grain on the Sabbath, Jesus replied to his critics, "The Sabbath was made for man, not man for the Sabbath; so the son of man [that is, humankind] is lord even of the Sabbath."[44] In the argument that accompanied his healing a paralytic, Jesus declared, "The son of man [humankind] has authority on earth to forgive sins."[45]

Jesus referred to himself as *the son of man*. Unlike the animals, Jesus had nowhere to lay his head.[46] His detractors castigated him as "a glutton and a drunkard, a friend of tax collectors and sinners."[47] Words spoken against him could be forgiven.[48] Jesus' followers would be rewarded.[49] He came "to seek and save the lost."[50] By calling himself the *son of man*, Jesus implied that he was a prophet like Ezekiel, Daniel, and Jonah.

In the Parable of the Burglar, the phrase was more than a reference to a mere human being and more than the appellation applied to the prophet Ezekiel. The coming of the son of man was portentous and implied extraordinary changes. Though Jesus did not say it, his listeners probably thought of the champion they awaited and the devastation he would wreak upon foreign nations. Some may have pictured Jesus himself.

Were they justified? Was Jesus describing himself?

Not at this point in his mission. Though he often identified himself as the son of man in the synoptic gospels, he did not say explicitly that he and the "son of man to come" were one. Jesus didn't say that until the end of his career.[51]

The Parable of the Flood

In Israel, especially in the desert, cloudbursts often caused dry riverbeds to flood. Sheep would be swept away, shepherds would drown, and buildings would be demolished by the rushing waters. Jesus used this true-to-life image in the Parable of the Flood.

> As were the days of Noah, so will be the coming of the son of man. For as in those days before the flood they were eating and drinking, marrying and giving in marriage, until the day when Noah entered the ark, and they did not know until the flood came and swept them all away, so will be the coming of the son of man. (Matthew 24:37–39)

What Secrets Did the Parable Convey?

Jesus portrayed the *son of man* coming suddenly—like a flood. Not an ordinary devastation, but a cataclysm as universal as the flood that destroyed every living being on earth, save Noah and those inside the ark. Instead of eating, drinking, and marrying, Jesus warned, his listeners should prepare themselves for an imminent apocalypse.

Noah's neighbors saw him building the ark and observed him herding on board sets of every animal on earth, and still they paid no attention. They didn't change their behavior. They didn't prepare themselves. Even as the clouds formed and the rain began to fall, they continued to eat, drink, and celebrate. Once Noah entered the ark and closed shut the doors, it was too late. They had doomed themselves to death.

Jesus implied there was still time. Though the kingdom of heaven had already begun, the doors to their salvation were not yet sealed. His listeners could still repent and save themselves. Don't wait, he implored. The holocaust could begin at any time.

The image of Noah and the ark reminded his listeners that not everyone was killed. Those in the ark found dry land and started life anew.

So it would be for true believers and faithful followers of God's law. They would survive. They would endure the devastation without suffering, and would begin life again in the New Era.

The Son of Man

Was Jesus the *son of man* in this parable? Did he say he himself would direct (or accompany) the apocalypse?

It might have been what he intended. It might have been what many of his followers believed. But he never said it. What he did say sounded like Enoch. A "son of man" would come, rescue the righteous, destroy the evildoers, and establish a glorious New Era of justice, peace, and prosperity on earth.

The Same Parable in Luke

Luke provided almost the identical image in his version of the Parable of the Flood.

> As it was in the days of Noah, so will it be in the days of the Son of man. They ate, they drank, they married, they were given in marriage, until the day when Noah entered the ark, and the flood came and destroyed them all. (Luke 17:26–27)

The Parable of the Well-Built House

Most Galileans spent time repairing their homes. Gusts of wind ripped thatch from their roofs. Rain soaked their dirt floors. Occasionally storms tore out jagged chunks of their walls. In the Parable of the Well-Built House, Jesus reminded his listeners what it took to build a house that endured the onslaught of ordinary wind and rain.

> Every one then who hears these words of mine and does them will be like a wise man who built his house upon the rock; and the rain fell, and the floods came, and the winds blew and beat upon that house, but it did not fall, because it had been founded on the rock. And every one who hears these words of mine and does not

do them will be like a foolish man who built his house upon the sand; and the rain fell, and the floods came, and the winds blew and beat against that house, and it fell; and great was the fall of it. (Matthew 7:24–27)

What Secrets Did the Parable Convey?

While this parable didn't allude to Noah and the Deluge, it was nonetheless a flood story. Occasionally pounding winds and torrential rains would sweep away buildings. A person's home, cattle, grain, storage, and furnishings could disappear in an instant.

Jesus reminded his audience that a prudent homeowner prepared for these occasional storms. His home was founded on immovable rock. His storage was protected. His grain, oil, and wine were tightly secured. When the storm came, he would survive.

Though he didn't say it in this parable, Jesus taught that devastation would soon befall the Jewish people and destroy every structure and institution they held dear. Only those prepared for the onslaught would survive. All others would perish.

Who was the "wise man"? The person who did whatever was needed to survive the holocaust. As a prudent owner secured his home on bedrock, the wise person put his soul in order. He repented and cemented his relationship with God and carried out God's will in his life. He obeyed the commandments, taught others to obey, and participated fully in the life of his community. In doing so, the wise man built a secure psyche, able to withstand the carnage to come.

Given the same opportunity, the "foolish man" disregarded the warnings, maintained his false beliefs and sinful behaviors, and neglected his relationship with God. Though respected in his community, he remained an unrepentant sinner. His psychic structure would collapse with the coming of God's kingdom, and he would be swept away.

The Same Parable in Luke

Luke provided essentially the same parable. However, instead of a typical Galilean mud house with thatched roof and dirt floors, Luke envisioned a house with a foundation—a clear indication that Luke was not living in Palestine.

Every one who comes to me and hears my words and does them, I will show you what he is like: he is like a man building a house, who dug deep, and laid the foundation upon rock; and when a flood arose, the stream broke against that house, and could not shake it, because it had been well built. But he who hears and does not do them is like a man who built a house on the ground without a foundation; against which the stream broke, and immediately it fell, and the ruin of that house was great. (Luke 6:47–49)

The Parable of Sodom's Destruction

In the Parable of the Flood, Jesus referred to biblical images familiar to his listeners. He did so again in the Parable of Sodom's Destruction. Instead of a deluge, he talked of fire and brimstone.

> As it was in the days of Lot—they ate, they drank, they bought, they sold, they planted, they built, but on the day when Lot went out from Sodom fire and sulphur rained from heaven and destroyed them all—so will it be on the day when the son of man is revealed. On that day, let him who is on the housetop, with his goods in the house, not come down to take them away; and likewise let him who is in the field not turn back. Remember Lot's wife. (Luke 17:28–32)

Jesus Built on Jewish Images

In Jewish tradition, Sodom was perceived as the wickedest city in ancient Canaan. Abraham could not find even ten righteous people living there.[52] After warning Lot, "God rained sulfur and fire upon Sodom and Gemorrah . . . and annihilated those cities and the entire plain."[53] As Lot and his family fled the devastation, "Lot's wife looked back and turned into a pillar of salt."[54] According to one sage, "The men of Sodom hated one another, so God destroyed them both from this world and from the World to Come."[55]

The sulphur that destroyed Sodom and Gemorrah later was used as an instrument of divine punishment against the wicked in Israel, against the king of Assyria, and against Edom and Gog.[56]

Fire also was a means of divine retribution.[57] Wickedness was sometimes compared to fire.[58] Its fitting punishment was burning to death.[59]

Over time, fire became associated with the Final Judgment. The punishing fire of the prophets was transformed in postbiblical literature into what Good called "a theology of fiery judgment."[60] Enoch described an abyss of fire;[61] Daniel, Enoch, Baruch, and others talked about the fire of judgment.[62]

Jesus' included these images in his Parable of the Destruction of Sodom. He warned the Jews in his audience that they were behaving just like the people in Lot's era. They ate, drank, bought and sold, planted and harvested without recognizing that they were doing harm to themselves and their neighbors. Unless they changed, "sulphur and fire" would rain upon them and destroy everything they held dear. They, their children, and all their friends would die.

As in Abraham's time, it would happen suddenly. The people of Sodom and Gomorrah had had no warning. They died still believing they were righteous. But Jesus brought a warning to the people of his day. There was still be time to redeem themselves—before the Final Judgment began.

Don't concern yourselves with household assets, Jesus advised. Don't worry about your crops. They will all be destroyed. Save yourselves. Commit yourselves entirely to reconciling with God. Worry about nothing else. And don't hesitate or falter, Jesus warned. "Remember Lot's wife."[63]

When Jesus said "the son of man," he was not speaking about himself. He was reminding his listeners of images they knew—images presented in Daniel and Enoch—of how human civilization would be destroyed with the inauguration of God's kingdom.

The Parable of the Seed Growing Secretly

Matthew reported the Parable of the Wheat and the Weeds immediately after the Parable of the Sower. Mark placed a different parable in the same position—a parable that occurred only in his gospel—the Parable of the Seed Growing Secretly.

> And he said, "The kingdom of God is as if a man should scatter seed upon the ground, and should sleep and rise night and day, and the seed should sprout and grow, he knows not how. The earth produces of itself, first the blade, then the ear, then the full grain in the ear. But when the grain is ripe, at once he puts in the sickle, because the harvest has come." (Mark 4:26–29)

What Secrets Did the Parable Convey?
While the setting of this parable was similar to the Sower and the Wheat and the Weeds, there has been considerable debate about the identity of the farmer.

If the seeds were the coming kingdom, was it God who sowed and harvested? (In that case, since God knew, why did the text say, "He knows not"?)

If the seeds were Jesus' teachings about God's kingdom, the farmer would be Jesus. (Did Jesus select who would enter the kingdom and who would not? Why then did the text say, "He puts the sickle"?)

If the seeds were the teachings of Jesus, the farmer might be his disciples spreading his teachings in other communities. (Did the disciples select who would enter the kingdom and who would not?)

The seeds could be good deeds. Then the farmer would represent righteous people in the community? (Why did the text say, "He puts the sickle"? Did the righteous select who would enter the kingdom and who would not?)

The confusion about the identity of the farmer resulted from the metaphorical inconsistencies in the parable between the sower and his ignorance, and between the sower and the reaper.

Maybe we expect too much. Parables often contained layers of meaning. The sowing of the seeds may have referred to the preaching and teaching of Jesus' disciples, while the harvesting directly to God's selection of the righteous and His destruction of the wicked.

Whether the seed was planted by God or by any of His agents, the message was the same: The growth of God's kingdom in the world was beyond human comprehension and control.

God's Timetable

Jesus may have hinted at a divine timetable. Just as crops follow an ordained schedule from seed to growth to harvest within a specific period of time, so God already had set in motion the mechanisms for the Final Judgment and the establishment of His kingdom. They would be accomplished inevitably within a given period of time.

A comparable view was expressed in 2 Esdras where a woman's pregnancy symbolized the period of waiting for God's ultimate redemption. "When is this [the Final Judgment] to happen? . . . Go and ask the pregnant [woman] whether her womb will be able to keep her child after her nine months have passed."[64]

Like the birth of a child after nine months of labor (and no more) and the ripening of crops in warm weather (and not earlier or later), the cataclysm, the cleansing, and the celebration of God's kingdom would each take place in its determined time. Humans could not interfere with, hasten, or deter their scheduled occurrence.

This notion may have been directed particularly against zealots and other revolutionaries who hoped by their efforts to overthrow the yoke of Roman oppression and expedite the coming of the Messiah.[65] Jesus was telling them and their supporters that their efforts were futile. God's timetable was already in motion, and their efforts would not influence the divine eschatology in the slightest.

In these revolutionary efforts, Jesus may have detected an unwarranted arrogance. As a result, he asked for more than patience. He called for submission to the will of God and the acceptance of God's plan.

Zealots and Other Rebels

The Aramaic term *kanai* was usually translated as "zealot" (*zelotes* in Greek) and often referred to a Jew who rebelled against Roman rule in Palestine, but the meaning of the term (and the motivation for the rebellion) traced back to earlier biblical images. The Hebrew and Aramaic verb root *k-n-'* signified an intense emotional desire to protect something held dear. That included a husband's *jealousy*,[66] the *rivalry* of Ephraim against Judah,[67] the *envy* of one neighbor for another,[68] and the *ardor* between lovers.[69] As a consequence, no one English word captured its flavor and intensity. *Zeal* came as close as any.[70]

A devastating plague erupted among the Israelites as they journeyed to the Promised Land. When an Israelite brought a Midianite woman into the camp to share with his companions, Phineas executed them both. Phineas' decisive and immediate response stayed the contagion and prevented more people from dying. Phineas was *zealous* to uphold God's law, and God was *zealous* to punish the Israelites for their transgressions.[71]

In the rebellion of the Maccabees against Syrian rule, the author of 1 Maccabees saw a direct parallel to both Phineas' actions and *zeal*. Phineas was the forefather of Mattathias precisely "because he was deeply *zealous*,"[72] and Mattathias "burned with *zeal* for the law, as Phineas did."[73] Mattathias and his sons fled to the mountains and began a campaign against the Seleucid forces that eventually drove them from Palestine.

The prophet Elijah challenged 450 prophets of Baal to a sacrificial duel. He mocked them throughout the day as they hopped around the altar, mutilating themselves and pleading to their deity to accept their offering. Late in the afternoon, he built an altar of twelve stones, placed thereon the wood and the bull and doused them all three times with water. Elijah spoke a simple prayer, and "fire descended from the Lord and consumed the burnt offering." Then Elijah ordered the people to seize the prophets of Baal and execute them.[74]

The Hebrew Bible applauded the prophet's "*zeal* for the Lord."[75] The author of 1 Maccabees wrote: "Because of his great *zeal* for the law, Elijah was taken up into heaven."[76]

These images—what Farmer calls "the theology of zeal"[77]—infused Jewish thought.

In the year 6, Herod's son Archelaus was deposed and exiled to Germany.

The Roman emperor Augustus appointed a Roman prefect over Judea and Samaria and ordered the legate Quirinius to take a census of the Jews in Palestine. Judah the Galilean and Zadok the Pharisee urged their countrymen to resist.[78] According to Josephus, Judah and Zadok established "a fourth philosophy," which grew in numbers until "they filled the nation with unrest."[79]

These rebels found significant support among Jewish farmers and craftsmen in Galilee and Judea, received food and supplies from them, and hid in nearby caves and villages. Occasionally they ventured forth as brigands to prey on local Roman officials, to attack Roman supply trains and harass Roman strongholds and troops.[80]

Josephus mentioned another group of rebels that terrorized Jews who cooperated with the Roman authorities. He called them *sicarii*. "This group murdered people in broad daylight right in the middle of the city. Mixing with the crowds, especially during the festivals, they would conceal small daggers beneath their garments and stealthily stab their opponents. Then . . . [they] simply melted into the outraged crowds."[81]

The first to have his throat cut was Jonathan the High Priest. Others followed.[82] Forming themselves into brigand groups, the sicarii "ranged over the countryside, killing the powerful rich, plundering their houses and setting fire to the villages."[83]

Josephus considered all these rebel groups thieves and blamed them for inciting Roman retaliation against the Jews, but on two occasions he designated some of them as "zealots."[84] They were to be found among all elements of Jewish society, but particularly among the poor and disenfranchised. A few became followers of Jesus.

Simon the Zealot became one of Jesus' trusted disciples.[85] Judas Iscariot may have been another.[86] Before he became a follower of Jesus, Paul was motivated by zeal for the law.[87] He even called himself a "zealot."[88] According to Paul, "thousands of Jews" were zealots.[89] In one sermon to the Jews of Rome, he praised their commitment to tradition.[90]

The theology of zeal drew its inspiration from Judaism's strong commitments to God and His commandments. "I the Lord your God am a jealous God"—or "vengeful God" or "zealous God" (all are possible English translations)—"visiting guilt . . . upon the third and fourth generations of those who reject Me, but showing kindness to the thousandth generation of those who love Me and keep My commandments."[91] God punished transgressors (Jews and non-Jews), and so did some zealots. Carrying their zeal to extremes, some Jews were willing to kill to protect or enforce God's law. After all, just a few generations earlier the Maccabees had rebelled against the Syrians and won.

The next chapter explores parables about servants and workers and what they have to do to be invited into God's kingdom.

Notes

1. Joel 2:1–2, 12–13, 24, 22.

2. Zechariah 3:1–5, 10.

3. See also 1 Kings 5:4–5 (= Greek 1 Kings 4:24–25); 2 Kings 18:31–32; Isaiah 36:16–17.

4. Jeremiah 24:1–10, 29:17. See also Jeremiah 5:17, 8:13; Hosea 2:12; Joel 1:7; Amos 4:9; Habakkuk 3:17.

5. Joachim Jeremias, *The Parables of Jesus*, rev. ed. (New York: Charles Scribner's Sons, 1963), 119.

6. Matthew 24:34.

7. In Joel 2:22, the budding fig leaves were a sign of coming blessing.

8. Genesis 1:14.

9. Joel 2:30–31. Also see Jeremiah 10:2.

10. Psalm 71:7.

11. Isaiah 20:3, 8:18.

12. Matthew 12:39, Mark 8:12, Luke 11:29.

13. The statement in verse 40—"The son of man is coming at an hour you do not expect"—was not part of the parable and reflected Luke's redaction of the text.

14. M. Sanhedrin 6:2; Jerusalem Hagigah 77c on Elisha ben Abuya, as presented in George Foot Moore, *Judaism in the First Centuries of the Christian Era* (Cambridge, Mass.: Harvard University Press, 1927), 522; Midrash Psalms on Psalm 90:12, as presented in Claude G. Montefiore and H. Loewe, *A Rabbinic Anthology* (London: Macmillan, 1938), 321.

15. Jesus used a splendid irony in this parable. Not only would the wealthy landowner enjoy a wedding banquet, but so would his faithful servants.

16. The Greek verb (*dichotomeo*), used only here and in the parallel in Luke, indicates that he might be "cut in two."

17. Job 8:13, 13:16, 15:34, 17:8, 20:5, 27:8, 34:30, 36:13; Isaiah 9:17, 32:5, 33:14. See also Proverbs 11:9.

18. Isaiah 9:16.

19. Isaiah 33:14.

20. Job 20:5.

21. The Greek of the Septuagint captured this meaning precisely in Isaiah 9:17 ("godless, wicked") and Isaiah 33:14 ("godless, impious").

22. For example, in Mark 12:15 their "hypocrisy" becomes their "malice" in Matthew 22:18 and their "craftiness" in Luke 20:23. In fact, the only passage that may retain the original Greek meaning is the verb used in Luke 20:20, where the spies who watched Jesus "pretended to be sincere."

23. Matthew 25:30, 22:13. See also Mathew 8:12.

24. Matthew 13:42. See also Matthew 13:50.

25. See also Matthew 13:40–42.

26. See also Matthew 8:12, 25:30.

27. Luke 12:41.

28. Matthew 16:18.

29. Jeremias, *The Parables of Jesus*, 57–58.

30. *Ben adam*: Numbers 23:19; Job 35:8; Psalms 80:17; Jeremiah 49:18. *Ben enosh*: Job 25:6; Psalms 8:4; Isaiah 51:12, 56:2. See also Psalms 146:3; Daniel 8:17.

31. Almost every subsequent chapter in the book begins with God addressing Ezekiel as "son of man."

32. Daniel 7:13.

33. Daniel 8:17.

34. 2 Esdras 13:3.

35. Genesis 1:27. Philo Judaeus, *On the Account of the World's Creation*, 23:69–71; 46:134.

36. Genesis 2:7. Philo Judaeus, *On the Account of the World's Creation*, 46:134ff.

37. Enoch 39:6.

38. Enoch 45:3, 51:1–3, 61:8.

39. Daniel 7:9, Enoch 46:1.

40. Enoch 46:3.

41. Enoch 46:4–8.

42. Enoch 46:3, 48:4.

43. Matthew 24:44.

44. Mark 2:27–28. See also Matthew 12:8, Luke 6:5.

45. Matthew 9:6. This meaning is clear from the parallel two verses later: "When the crowds saw it, . . . they glorified God, who had given such authority to men" (Matthew 9:8). See also Mark 2:10.

46. Matthew 8:20, Luke 9:58.

47. Matthew 11:19, Luke 7:34.

48. Matthew 12:32, Luke 9:58.

49. Luke 6:22–23.

50. Luke 19:10.

51. See Chapter 19 for a discussion the *son of man* in the Parable of the Last Judgment.

52. Genesis 18:20–32.

53. Genesis 19:24–5. The RSV and most Christian translations read "brimstone and fire," but there is no disagreement. Brimstone is sulfur.

54. Genesis 19:26.

55. Avot d'Rabbi Nathan 12, 26b, as presented in Montefiore and Loewe, *A Rabbinic Anthology*, 468.

56. Wicked: Deuteronomy 29:23; Psalms 11:6. Assyria: Isaiah 30:30, 33. Edom: Isaiah 34:9. Gog: Ezekiel 38:22.

57. Psalms 89:47 (= Greek 89:46); Jeremiah 4:4, 5:14, 21:12; Lamentations 1:13, 2:3; Ezekiel 22:31.

58. Isaiah 65:5, Hosea 7:6.

59. Genesis 19:24, Leviticus 10:2, Joshua 7:15.

60. Edwin M. Good, "Fire," in *The Interpreter's Dictionary of the Bible: An Illustrated Encyclopedia*, ed. George A. Buttrick (New York: Abingdon, 1962), 269.

61. Enoch 18:11, 90:23–26.

62. Daniel 7:11; Enoch 10:6; 21:7; 67:13; 91:9; 100:9; 102:1; 108:3; 3 Baruch 4:16; 2 Baruch 48:39, 43; Judith 16:17; Testament of Judah 25:3.

63. Luke 17:32.

64. 2 Esdras 4:33–40.

65. Jeremias, *The Parables of Jesus*, 152.

66. Proverbs 6:34; 27:4. See also Numbers 5:14, 30.

67. Isaiah 11:13.

68. Ecclesiastes 4:4; 9:6.

69. Song of Songs 8:6.

70. Francis Brown, S. R. Driver, and Charles A. Briggs used the phrase "ardour of zeal" to capture the emotions involved (*A Hebrew and English Lexicon of the Old Testament* [Oxford: Clarendon, 1907], 888).

71. Numbers 25:11.

72. 1 Maccabees 2:54.

73. 1 Maccabees 2:26. See also 1 Maccabees 2:24, 27.

74. 1 Kings 18:20–40.

75. 1 Kings 19:10, 14.

76. 1 Maccabees 2:58. See also Ben Sirakh 8:9–10, where Elijah's ascent into heaven was connected with the establishment of God's kingdom.

77. W. R. Farmer, "Zealot," in *The Interpreter's Dictionary of the Bible: An Illustrated Encyclopedia*, ed. George A. Buttrick (New York: Abingdon, 1962), 938.

78. Josephus, *The Jewish Wars*, 2.118.

79. Josephus, *Antiquities*, 18.8–9. Though Josephus called these zealots a fourth philosophy, in the same chapter he wrote: "They agree with the views of the Pharisees in everything save their unconquerable passion for freedom." What distinguished the Judah and Zadok's revolution was not its "philosophy" but its open rebellion against Rome. Judah and Zadok may have been Pharisees who were more willing than most of their contemporaries to actively resist Roman rule.

80. Josephus, *Jewish Wars*, 2:55–65, 228; *Antiquities*, 17.271–85; 20.113.

81. Josephus, *Jewish Wars*, 2.254–55.

82. Josephus, *Jewish Wars*, 2.256.

83. Josephus, *Jewish Wars*, 2:266. See also 7.254, and *Antiquities*, 20.172.

84. Josephus, *Jewish Wars*, 2:22:1, 4:3:9.

85. Luke 6:15. See also Matthew 10:4 and Mark 3:18 where Simon's Aramaic designation as a zealot is not translated but merely transliterated. The Greek *kananaios* means the same as the Aramaic *kanai* ("a zealot").

86. If the designation Iscariot derived from *sicarius* ("dagger warrior," "assassin").

87. Philippians 3:6, Acts 22:3.

88. Galatians 1:14.

89. Acts 21:20.

90. Romans 10:2.

91. Exodus 20:5–6, Deuteronomy 5:9–10. See also Zechariah 8:2.

CHAPTER EIGHT

Parables about Servants and Workers

The Parable of the Steward and His Master's Debts

A rich man put a steward in charge of his estate. When the landowner discovered that many deliveries had been made without payment, he fired the steward and banished him from his estate.

Before word of his termination spread, the steward approached every merchant who had not paid on his account and offered to change the amount due. As a consequence, he saved each client a considerable amount of money.

> He also said to the disciples, "There was a rich man who had a steward, and charges were brought to him that this man was wasting his goods. And he called him and said to him, 'What is this that I hear about you? Turn in the account of your stewardship, for you can no longer be steward.' And the steward said to himself, 'What shall I do, since my master is taking the stewardship away from me? I am not strong enough to dig, and I am ashamed to beg. I have decided what to do, so that people may receive me into their houses when I am put out of the stewardship.' So, summoning his master's debtors one by one, he said to the first, 'How much do you owe my master?' He said, 'A hundred measures of oil.' And he said to him, 'Take your bill, and sit down quickly and write fifty.' Then he said to another, 'And how much do you owe?' He said, 'A hundred measures of wheat.' He said to him, 'Take your bill, and write eighty.' The master commended the dishonest steward for his shrewdness. (Luke 16:1–8a)

To Whom Was the Parable Addressed?

This parable was not a condemnation of the steward but rather a warning to Jesus' audience. The dishonest steward was prudent in using the things of this life to ensure the future. Listeners should do the same.

Who were these listeners? To whom was the warning addressed?

The answer depends on how we understand the steward's actions.

It was common in Palestine for landed gentry to leave servants in charge of their homes or to hire supervisors to administer their estates. In this instance, the steward was a hired superintendent.[1] He believed his dismissal would disgrace him in the eyes of his peers, and he embarked on his venture "so that people may receive me into their houses when I am put out of the stewardship."

He took the original documents and had them altered. He gave back the receipt to the merchant who had purchased "one hundred measures of olive oil" and had him write a new note in his own hand indicating he had received fifty measures.[2] He returned the original to the purchaser of "one hundred measures of wheat" and had him write a new receipt for only eighty measures.[3] Then he turned in these new documents to his employer.

He cheated the landowner of a considerable portion of what he was due. This was his dishonesty. But he secured his own future. The businessmen of the community would treat him favorably, since he had saved each one of them a considerable sum of money.[4]

The warning was addressed to those Jews in Jesus' audience who were not believers—and not to his disciples. Faced with a crisis that would significantly alter his life, the steward acted swiftly. You should do the same, Jesus taught his listeners. Set your accounts in order, for God is coming to review your behavior and assign your recompense. According to Jesus, they could still save their lives if they accepted his teachings and behaved appropriately.

Jesus was not encouraging his audience to cheat or be dishonest. There was no way to fool God. He was warning his listeners to act swiftly and prudently to right their records with God before they suffered disaster and death.

Sons of Light

At the end of the parable Jesus observed that "the sons of this world are more shrewd in dealing with their own generation than the sons of light."[5]

Light, as a symbol of God's creative power, of God's Law, of God's effect on human life, of God's blessings, and of God's salvation, occurred frequently in the Hebrew Bible and in subsequent Jewish literature.

In the New Testament, the *sons of light* were the disciples and followers of Jesus who would survive the coming Darkness to live eternally bathed in God's Light.[6]

In the Dead Sea Scrolls, the *sons of light* were the members of the Essene fellowship who would defeat the sons of darkness in battle and live on in a world true to the teachings and practices of God.[7]

The similarities between the teachings of Jesus and the Dead Sea Scrolls gave rise to the suggestion that Jesus may have spent some time in Qumran. But the ideas of the Essenes were widely known. In addition to their settlement in Qumran, they established another resident community in Damascus, they met and taught regularly in the Jerusalem Temple, and they preached in communities throughout Palestine. Jesus may have encountered their teachings in a number of different settings.

The Parable of the Tired Servant

Returning from a day's work in the field a servant looked forward to eating and resting, but his master had other plans for him. The master ordered him to prepare a meal and serve him while he ate. After he finished serving his master, the servant could take care of himself.

> Will any one of you, who has a servant plowing or keeping sheep, say to him when he has come in from the field, "Come at once and sit down at table"? Will he not rather say to him, "Prepare supper for me, and gird yourself and serve me, till I eat and drink; and afterward you shall eat and drink"? Does he thank the servant because he did what was commanded? So you also, when you have done all that is commanded you, say, "We are unworthy servants; we have only done what was our duty." (Luke 17:7–10)

What Secrets Did the Parable Convey?

Was it unfair that his master demanded service when the servant was tired? Was the servant's resentment justifiable?

His master had a right to the servant's time and attention. While his employer may thank him or reward him, the servant cannot demand such recompense.

Jesus' message was clear: The apostles, who had given themselves up entirely to their master's service, were expected to do whatever was demanded of them. Doing their best was their duty.

Jesus Built on Jewish Images

There were echoes of rabbinic tradition here. Antigonus of Socho used to say, "Do not be like slaves who serve their master for the sake of receiving a reward, rather be like slaves who serve their master without that expectation."[8] The master was God, and one served God unconditionally, out of reverence and not for some current or future benefit.

Hillel taught, "Do God's will as if it were your own."[9] Rabbi Jose said, "Let all that you do be for the sake of heaven."[10] Rabban Gamaliel repeated the same idea, "Let all who work with the congregation do so for the sake of heaven."[11] Ben Azzai said, "Run [as fast] to carry out the least of the commandments as you would to fulfill the greatest."[12]

In his message to the apostles, Jesus reflected Jewish tradition.

The Disciples Doubt

According to Luke, Jesus' disciples expressed some doubt in their abilities to carry out his teachings. "Increase our faith," the apostles implored.[13]

Jesus told them that faith was reckoned in quality, not in quantity. The strength of their faith would be gauged by their obedience and untiring service—as was emphasized in this Parable of the Tired Servant.

Jesus also demanded humility from his disciples. They were to take no glory in their hard work or even in their forbearance and willingness to forgive. They were merely "unworthy servants" doing their duty.

Wherever they traveled, Jesus and the disciples depended on the goodwill of others for food and lodging and often faced ridicule and harassment. On occasion their lives were placed in danger. Jesus commanded his disciples to be patient, tolerant, and forgiving even in the face of repeated offenses against them. No wonder the apostles said, "Increase our faith!"

The Parable of the Laborers

A landowner went out early in the morning to hire laborers for his vineyard. They agreed to accept one *denarius* a day for their labor and began working. Hours later the owner hired additional laborers for the same wage, and hours later a few more workers for the same wage.

That evening the owner paid all the workers. Those hired last received one denarius. Those hired first also received one denarius. The latter complained, claiming they worked several hours longer and deserved more money.

The vineyard owner insisted they had nothing to complain about. He was paying the wages they had agreed to. What he did with the rest of his assets was none of their business. He could give generously to others if he chose to do so.

> The kingdom of heaven is like a householder who went out early in the morning to hire laborers for his vineyard. After agreeing with the laborers for a denarius a day, he sent them into his vineyard. And going out about the third hour he saw others standing idle in the market place; and to them he said, "You go into the

vineyard too, and whatever is right I will give you." So they went. Going out again about the sixth hour and the ninth hour, he did the same. And about the eleventh hour he went out and found others standing; and he said to them, "Why do you stand here idle all day?" They said to him, "Because no one has hired us." He said to them, "You go into the vineyard too." And when evening came, the owner of the vineyard said to his steward, "Call the laborers and pay them their wages, beginning with the last, up to the first." And when those hired about the eleventh hour came, each of them received a denarius. Now when the first came, they thought they would receive more; but each of them also received a denarius. And on receiving it they grumbled at the householder, saying, "These last worked only one hour, and you have made them equal to us who have borne the burden of the day and the scorching heat." But he replied to one of them, "Friend, I am doing you no wrong; did you not agree with me for a denarius? Take what belongs to you, and go; I choose to give to this last as I give to you. Am I not allowed to do what I choose with what belongs to me? Or do you begrudge my generosity?" (Matthew 20:1–15)

What Secrets Did the Parable Convey?

Jesus seemed to be making a number of points.

- It didn't matter when you accepted Jesus' teachings and joined the fellowship. The reward was the same—eternal life in God's kingdom.
- It didn't matter when you began to travel and preach and teach. The reward was the same—eternal life.
- If God favored a few people along the way out of His generosity, it didn't matter. The reward of eternal life was not diminished.
- If Jesus favored a few people along the way out of his generosity, it didn't matter. The ultimate reward was the same for all—eternal life in God's kingdom.

Unrest within Jesus' Fellowship

Why would Jesus emphasize these ideas? Wasn't the glory of God's kingdom the heart of the message Jesus and his disciples were teaching?

There may have been some dissension or unrest within Jesus' fellowship. Matthew seemed to suggest this. As if in answer to Peter's poignant question, "Lo, we have left everything and followed you. What then shall we have?"[14] he offered the Parable of the Laborers.

Rejoice in the Salvation of Others

The grumbling bothered Jesus. The older workers expected to be treated differently and were disappointed. The vineyard owner did not recognize their greater length of service and their larger accomplishments. He treated older and newer laborers in the same manner and paid them both their wages at the end of the day.

In this parable, Jesus reminded his followers of their mission and cautioned them not to be like the early workers (the complainers)—not to rejoice only in their own redemption but to bring salvation to others. He may even have included a subtle warning that those who expect favored treatment were boasting of their accomplishments and displaying an undesirable haughtiness. By their complaints, they may be putting their salvation in jeopardy. As Antigonos of Socho taught, "Do not be like workers who serve their master for the sake of receiving a reward."[15]

No Greater Reward
Jesus' parable made it abundantly clear. No matter how long they labored, all workers received the same reward. Apostles, first followers, and new converts would all be saved from destruction and welcomed into God's glorious kingdom. There was no greater reward.

Why Five Hirings?
In all, the vineyard owner hired five groups of workers—the first group "early in the morning," the second "about the third hour," the third "about the sixth hour," the fourth three hours later, and the last group "about the eleventh hour." Subsequent Christian tradition interpreted these five hirings as symbolizing the five periods of human redemption from Adam to Jesus or the five stages in human life at which people become Christians.[16] None of these ideas are indigenous to the original parable. The number of hirings and the actual times were not essential. They merely indicated that the owner hired different groups during the day to work in his vineyard and paid them all the same wage—regardless of how long they worked. In fact, the middle three groups disappeared entirely at the end of the parable.

God's Generosity
The vineyard owner kept his promise. He paid each worker exactly what he had agreed to pay in a timely manner at the close of the workday. In what way was he being generous?

Jeremias suggests that Jesus' listeners were surprised when the owner paid the last laborers hired a full day's wage for only one hour of work. To them, this must have seemed extravagant.[17]

For Jesus, it was not the amount of money involved but the principle, since each laborer received a subsistence wage, barely enough to sustain the worker and his family. Pay for just an hour's work—or a few hours work—would not feed a family. The laborer's wife and children would go hungry. The vineyard owner understood this. Out of his compassion for the plight of the poor and the unemployed, he paid a full day's wage. In that sense, he was generous.

According to Jesus, God was generous with humans the same way. Such was the measure of His compassion that He provided a place in His kingdom to the most egregious sinners. Jesus reminded those who saw themselves as better and who criticized Jesus' association with outcasts that, in the process, they were condemning God and disassociating themselves from His endeavors.[18]

The next chapter explores a series of short parables in which Jesus used ordinary experiences with salt and light to explain his ideas.

Notes

1. A slave would have been punished or sold, not dismissed.

2. The Greek text indicated one hundred *baths* of olive oil. A *bath* is a Hebrew liquid measure equal to about nine gallons. Thus, the merchant saved the payment on 450 gallons of oil—a considerable savings.

3. The Greek text indicated one hundred *kors* of wheat. A *kor* is a Hebrew dry measure for grain equal to about ten bushels. The merchant saved the payment on two hundred bushels of wheat—again, a considerable savings.

4. Several scholars have suggested that the "master" who praised the dishonest steward was not Jesus but the landowner. They suggest that the steward did not cheat his employer of money to which the master was entitled but that the steward merely gave up his own commission—50 percent in the case of the oil, 20 percent in the case of the wheat. (See the commentary to Luke 16:1–8a by the editors of The New American Bible; Bernard Brandon Scott, *Hear Then the Parable: A Commentary on the Parables of Jesus* [Minneapolis, Minn.: Fortress, 1990], 255–66; Dan Otto, Via, Jr., *The Parables: Their Literary and Existential Dimension* [Philadelphia: Fortress, 1967], 155–62.)

In my opinion there are two glaring inconsistencies in this suggestion. First, the steward didn't have to create new documents to forgo his commission. He merely had to turn over the money due to his employer. There was no reason for the deception. Second, his employer would praise him only if he collected the money. Reducing the bills brought no benefit to the landowner. But there is no indication in the parable that the steward received payments—even reduced payments—and turned them over to the landowner. Instead, the focus is on his changing the documents to deceive his employer. The landowner certainly would not have praised him for his dishonesty. The "master" in the parable must be Jesus, who praised the steward for securing his future even as he condemned him for his deception.

5. Luke 16:8b. There is considerable discussion about whether this half-verse was part of the original parable.

6. John 12:35–36; 1 Thessalonians 5:4–5.

7. 1Q 1:9–11; 1QS 3:13; 1QM 1:1–15. See also 1Q 3:17–4:26.

8. M. Aboth 1:3.

9. M. Aboth 2:4.

10. M. Aboth 2:12.

11. M. Aboth 2:2.

12. M. Aboth 4:2.

13. Luke 17:5.

14. Matthew 19:27.

15. M. Aboth 1:3. The Hebrew word *avadeem* ("slaves") can be read as *ovdeem* ("workers").

16. See the discussion in Jeremias, *The Parables of Jesus*, 33–34.

17. Jeremias, *The Parables of Jesus*, 37.

18. For a full discussion, see Joachim Jeremias, *The Parables of Jesus*, rev. ed. (New York: Charles Scribner's Sons, 1963), 36–38. Crossan and Reed contend that Roman urbanization and Herodian commercialization in Palestine created profound changes in land ownership. Small farms were incorporated into larger estates, and dispossessed freehold farmers became tenant farmers or day laborers—exactly the kind of situation articulated in this Parable of the Laborers. See John Dominic Crossan and Jonathan Reed, *Excavating Jesus* (San Francisco: HarperSanFrancisco, 2002), 127–28.

CHAPTER NINE

Parables about Lamps, Light, Salt, and Cities

The Parable of the Lamp

Between the Parable of the Wheat and the Weeds and the Parable of the Seed Growing Secretly, Mark inserted a section about how a lamp made concealed items visible.

> And he said to them, "Is a lamp brought in to be put under a bushel, or under a bed, and not on a stand? For there is nothing hid, except to be made manifest; nor is anything secret, except to come to light." (Mark 4:21–22)

What Secrets Did the Parable Convey?

The purpose of light was to illumine. It made no sense to ignite a lamp and cover it with a basket or place it under a bed.

There were understandings of the workings of the universe that most people did not possess. Not only did Jesus' followers possess that secret knowledge, but their mission was to make it manifest throughout the world. Ultimately, everything ought to be revealed.

The Same Idea in Matthew

Matthew presented the same images—without mentioning the lamp.

> So have no fear of them; for nothing is covered that will not be revealed, or hidden that will not be known. What I tell you in the dark, utter in the light; and what you hear whispered, proclaim upon the housetops. (Matthew 10:26–27)

Jesus encouraged his disciples to reveal everything—including the contents of their private conversations. He asked them not to be afraid when they encountered resistance and opposition to what they were teaching.

The Same Idea in Luke
Luke also provided the same image, but his ending was different from Matthew's.

> Nothing is covered up that will not be revealed, or hidden that will not be known. Therefore whatever you have said in the dark shall be heard in the light, and what you have whispered in private rooms shall be proclaimed upon the housetops. (Luke 12:2–3)

Where Matthew reported Jesus' instructions to his disciples in the active tense, Luke recorded Jesus' remarks in the passive voice—"shall be heard" and "shall be proclaimed." In Matthew, Jesus spoke directly to his disciples; in Luke, he addressed a general audience. Jesus may have couched his remarks in the passive to avoid getting others in trouble with the authorities.

There Were Dangers
Jesus warned there were dangers. Some opponents would attack physically, others spiritually and emotionally. The latter were more threatening. The worst detractors could do physically was kill a disciple, but opponents who undermined their faith could remove them from God's kingdom of joy to eternal suffering in Gehenna.[1]

Hell
Gehenna is the Greek and Latin form of the Hebrew phrase *gey kheenom* ("the Valley of Hinnom")—a ravine south of Jerusalem that had been the site of an idolatrous cult whose practices included burning children.[2] So abhorrent were these rites to Jews that the valley's name became synonymous with perversion and wickedness.[3]

By the first century, Gehenna denoted a place where the wicked would suffer fiery torment.[4] Some said they would suffer for a short while immediately after their death, others taught eternally after their Final Judgment.[5]

The Same Parable in Luke and Matthew
In Luke, the story about the lamp occurs after Jesus explained the Parable of the Sower to his disciples. In Matthew, the story about the lamp occurs after

the beatitudes as part of the Sermon on the Mount. Both stories are essentially the same.

> No one after lighting a lamp covers it with a vessel, or puts it under a bed, but puts it on a stand, that those who enter may see the light. For nothing is hid that shall not be made manifest, nor anything secret that shall not be known and come to light. (Luke 8:16–17)

> Nor do men light a lamp and put it under a bushel, but on a stand, and it gives light to all in the house. Let your light so shine before men, that they may see your good works and give glory to your Father who is in heaven. (Matthew 5:15–16)

The Lamp of the Body

The Parable of the Lamp occurred in Luke twice, but the second listing was followed by a completely different text dealing with the human eye as "the lamp of the body."

> No one after lighting a lamp puts it in a cellar or under a bushel, but on a stand, that those who enter may see the light. Your eye is the lamp of your body; when your eye is sound, your whole body is full of light; but when it is not sound, your body is full of darkness. (Luke 11:33–34)

The same metaphor occurred in Matthew, but not in the same place as the Parable of the Lamp: "The eye is the lamp of the body. When your eye is sound,[6] your whole body is light. When your eye is diseased, your whole body is dark" (Matthew 6:22–23a).[7]

In the Hebrew Bible, eyes expressed a person's deepest emotions and mental states. Brightness of the eyes was a sign of physical and emotional well-being,[8] dimness a signal of emotional distress.[9] Arrogance, humility, pity, and mockery were clearly visible in a man's eyes.[10]

Perhaps Jesus had some of these Jewish ideas in mind.

Light

In Matthew, Jesus called his disciples "the light of the world."[11] In Luke, he called them "the sons of light."[12] Paul built on these images in his letters to Christians scattered throughout the Mediterranean world. He instructed the Ephesians to "walk as children of light" and encouraged the Philippians to "shine as lights in the world."[13]

What kind of light were they talking about?

Paul explained his ideas in his letters. "Look to the interests of others," he wrote. "Do nothing from selfishness or conceit. Do all things without grumbling or questioning. Do not be foolish. Do not get drunk with wine. God is at work in you."[14] Paul reminded these early Christians to behave in accordance with the teachings of their faith and to set an example for others. This was what he meant by "light." With the same meaning, Isaiah admonished the Israelites to be "a light to the nations."[15]

This probably was what Jesus meant when he said, "I am the light of the world; he who follows me will not walk in darkness, but will have the light of life."[16] Whoever behaved as Jesus behaved and followed his teachings would evidence his enlightenment. He would be wise and righteous, no longer living in confusion and sin, no longer unrepentant and condemned. His mind and body would be healthy, his soul would be integrated, and his life would be complete.

John seemed to have more in mind. For John, good and evil battled for dominance in the world, light against darkness, chaos against cooperation. Human behavior tipped the balance in one direction or the other. People chose darkness over light, "because their deeds were evil."[17] But those who followed God's dictates and behaved accordingly—whose "deeds have been wrought in God"—experienced the beauty, harmony, and integrity of the world.[18]

Just as Jesus was the Logos in John's metaphysical reality, Jesus was also the Light. He was God's creative force—"the world was made through him"[19]—and he was mankind's ultimate destiny. This was how John understood Jesus' statements. "I am the light of the world; he who follows me will not walk in darkness."[20] Jesus was not just the ideal example to follow. Jesus was the light.

Many of these ideas built on images found in the Hebrew Bible. Light was the first manifestation of God's involvement in the world and had been created prior to and independent of the sun and stars.[21] This spiritual light was essential to and infused all creation. Without God's light, the universe would return to darkness and chaos. Thus, light and darkness were in tension. Both were under the will of God, but light curbed and controlled darkness.[22]

"Seeing the light" was often a synonym for being alive.[23] Light symbolized the pleasures of life, and darkness the turmoil and distress in life.[24] Humans were happy when God's light shone upon them.[25]

Light also designated salvation and rescue from danger.[26] The statement "light is sown for the upright"[27] implied the righteous would enjoy God's salvation—or even more, the righteous would bring about God's salvation.

The faithful (or wise or righteous) person became a light himself. He shone outwardly and inwardly and set an example for others to follow.[28] Thus, Israel was to become "a light to the nations."[29]

Eventually darkness would give way to an eternal day when God would be His people's light.[30]

The Parable of the Salt

Two verses prior to his report of the Parable of the Lamp, Matthew cited a short simile in which Jesus compared his listeners to salt: "You are the salt of the earth; but if salt has lost its taste, how shall its saltness be restored? It is no longer good for anything except to be thrown out and trodden under foot by men" (Matthew 5:13–14).

Mark offered a different ending: "Salt is good; but if the salt has lost its saltness, how will you season it? Have salt in yourselves, and be at peace with one another" (Mark 9:50).

What Secrets Did the Parable Convey?

What was Jesus saying here? How are people like salt?

According to Ben Sirakh, water, fire, iron, salt, wheat, milk, and honey were basic elements necessary for human life.[31] Salt was used as a condiment. A farmer dipped his fresh olives into salt.[32] A baker added water, salt, and spices to dough to make bread.[33] A laborer dipped his bread into salt water, and portions of salt water were added to cooked food.[34]

Salt was used for medical purposes as a disinfectant and skin conditioner. As soon as a baby was born, its umbilical cord was cut and tied, and it was washed. Then the infant was rubbed with salt.[35]

In Ezra, salt appears in a list of provisions for the Temple.[36] Priests sprinkled both the cereal offering and the burnt offering with salt,[37] and twice each day (and more often on holidays) salt was thrown on the head and body of a bird sacrificed as a whole offering.[38] When it was icy after rain or snow in Jerusalem, salt was scattered on the Altar Ramp to prevent priests from slipping.[39] As a consequence, a great deal of salt was used at the Temple; one of the six chambers in the Temple Court was the Salt Chamber.[40]

One incident, known to Jesus' audiences, dramatically acknowledged the life-giving and preservative qualities of salt. The inhabitants of Jericho had complained bitterly to Elisha that their water was tainted. As a result, they could grow no crops. The prophet tossed salt into the spring, made the water wholesome, and prevented further "death and miscarriage."[41]

Jesus taught his listeners that, like salt, their influence would bring healing and hope to the communities in which they lived. By their behavior in their homes and along the streets of their villages, those who followed Jewish teachings could affect life-giving changes in the lives of their contemporaries. Those in his audiences who believed were "the salt of the earth." Like the prophet Elisha, Jesus was tossing them into the world to make it wholesome.

What about Contaminated Salt?

Ben Sirakh noted that salt could be good for the righteous and evil for the sinful.[42] Salt was not intrinsically beneficial. It could harm as well.

In Jewish tradition, the terms "salt," "saltness," and "salty" were often used as images of barrenness or desolation.[43] Moses described a country vanquished by God as a land "devastated by sulfur and salt."[44] The psalmist warned of God's powers to transform "rivers into a desert, springs of water into thirsty ground, a fruitful land into a salty waste."[45] Zephaniah warned their inhabitants that God would turn Moab and Ammon into wastelands, filled with "clumps of weeds and patches of salt."[46] Abimelech razed the city of Shechem and sowed it with salt.[47]

That physical devastation became a metaphor for spiritual anguish. Job's suffering left a vile and loathsome taste in his mouth, and he begged God for release. "Crush me . . . cut me off."[48] Jeremiah echoed Job's assertion: "Cursed is the man . . . whose heart turns away from the Lord. He is like a shrub in the desert, and shall not see any good come. He shall dwell in the parched places of the wilderness, in an uninhabited salt land."[49]

Contaminated salt was destructive to both the soil and the soul. So Matthew concluded his simile with a warning: "You are the salt of the earth; but if salt has lost its taste, how shall its saltness be restored? It is no longer good for anything except to be thrown out and trodden under foot" (Matthew 5:13).

Luke presented the same image. Contaminated salt must be removed and destroyed: "Salt is good; but if salt has lost its taste, how shall its saltness be restored? It is fit neither for the land nor for the dunghill; men throw it away" (Luke 14:34–35).

Taking the opposite approach, Mark emphasized the positive. "Have salt in yourselves," he encouraged, "and be at peace with one another."[50]

The reports in Matthew/Luke and Mark were reverse sides of the same image. Jesus could have articulated the warning on one occasion and the encouragement on a different occasion.

A Covenant of Salt

There was a third way in which salt was understood in Jewish literature. The Hebrew Bible spoke of a "covenant of salt." God established "a covenant of salt" with Aaron to award the holy offerings to him and all his future descendants.[51] Abijah, a descendant of David and king of Judah, justified his invasion of King Jeroboam's territory by claiming that "the Lord God of Israel gave the kingship over Israel for ever to David and his sons by a covenant of salt."[52]

God made promises, and God would fulfill His promises. On that both Jesus' supporters and those resisting him agreed. A great new day was dawning that would see the just vindicated and the wicked punished. In calling his followers "the salt of the earth," Jesus reminded them that they would celebrate in the kingdom of heaven. For God had established an eternal covenant with them—a "covenant of salt."

Who Were the Salt of the Earth?

To whom was the phrase "you are the salt of the earth" addressed?

Matthew set the simile in the Sermon on the Mount and saw it addressed to the crowds assembled on the hillside to hear Jesus' message.[53] Mark placed it in private conversations Jesus had with his disciples in Capernaum.[54] Luke included it in Jesus' comments "to the multitudes," but he mentioned the word "disciple" as well.[55] Both understandings were possible. If Jesus used the simile on several occasions, at one time he may have addressed the multitudes, at another the disciples. Anyone who followed Jesus was "the salt of the earth."

The Parable of the City on a Hill

In the same verse in which Jesus mentioned light, he offered a second simile. Jesus compared his listeners to a city on a hill: "You are the light of the world. A city set on a hill cannot be hid" (Matthew 5:14).

What Secrets Did the Parable Convey?

In Galilee most towns and villages inhabited hilltops. Jesus spent his childhood in the hilltop town of Nazareth. He visited relatives in nearby Cana and heard stories about Sepphoris, Herod Antipas' capital city atop a mountain just four miles away. Even Jerusalem was set on a mountain. Jesus experienced most of his life among people from hilltop communities.

Compared to cities in the plains, a city on a hill needed less fortification, was more easily defended, and was therefore more secure. Jesus' metaphor reminded his followers that their beliefs and practices provided them a strong defense against any catastrophe and assured them that they would survive.

Jesus implied even more. The fortifications, walls, and rooftops of a hilltop city were visible from a distance. To weary travelers they provided direction. To fearful traders they gave encouragement. Soon they would be sheltered and protected within the city's walls.

Like a city on a hill, Jesus reminded his followers, they provided a visible example of the security and certainty that came with living in accordance with God's will. Just by observing them, apprehensive Jews would gain confidence and hope.

The next chapter explores two parables in which Jesus again couched his teachings in locations familiar to his audiences—a vineyard and an orchard.

Notes

1. Matthew 10:26–28, Luke 12:4–5.
2. 2 Kings 23:10; 2 Chronicles 28:3; 33:6; Jeremiah 32:35.
3. Jeremiah 19:1–15.
4. 2 Esdras 2:39; Matthew 5:22, 29–30; 10:28; 18:9; Mark 9:43, 45, 47; Luke 12:4–5; James 3:6; possibly Enoch 27:2–3.
5. M. Eduyoth 2:10; Tos. Sanhedrin 13:3, 4, 5; Philo, *On Execrations* 6; *On Cherubim* 1; Enoch 102:7–8, 103:5ff; 4 Esdras 7:26–44; Ascension of Isaiah 3:13–4:32.
6. From the Aramaic verb-root *sh-l-m* = whole, complete, healthy, fulfilled.
7. As translated in Joachim Jeremias, *The Parables of Jesus*, rev. ed. (New York: Charles Scribner's Sons, 1963), 163.
8. 1 Samuel 14:27.
9. Job 17:7; Psalm 38:10.
10. Proverbs 6:17, 30:17; Psalm 123:2; Ezekiel 16:5.
11. Matthew 5:14a.
12. Luke 16:8.
13. Ephesians 5:8; Philippians 2:15.
14. Philippians 2:3, 4, 13, 14; Ephesians 5:17, 18.
15. Isaiah 42:6. So too Matthew 5:16, Luke 2:32, Philippians 2:15.
16. John 8:12.
17. John 3:19. See also John 12:35.
18. John 3:21.
19. John 1:3. See also John 1:10.
20. John 8:12.
21. Genesis 1:2–4.

22. Psalm 139:11–12, Ecclesiastes 2:13.

23. Psalm 49:19; Job 3:16, 20. See also Job 33:30; Psalm 56:14 (= Greek Psalm 56:13).

24. Isaiah 45:7; Amos 5:18, 20; Psalm 97:11; Job 10:22; 30:26.

25. Psalm 36:9; Isaiah 60:20.

26. 2 Samuel 22:29; Isaiah 9:2, 10:17; Micah 7:8–9; Psalms 18:28, 27:1–2.

27. Psalm 97:11. See also Psalm 112:4; Job 18:5, 38:15.

28. Psalm 34:5; Proverbs 4:18–19, 20:27; Ecclesiastes 2:13–14; 8:1; Daniel 5:11.

29. Isaiah 49:6. See also Isaiah 42:6; 60:3, 5; 62:1.

30. Isaiah 30:26, 60:19–20; Hosea 6:3; Zechariah 14:7.

31. Ben Sirakh 39:26.

32. M. Maaseroth 4:3.

33. M. Betzah 5:4.

34. M. Shabbath 14:2.

35. Ezek 16:4.

36. Ezra 6:9, 7:21–23.

37. Leviticus 2:13, Ezekiel 43:24. According to the last phrase in Leviticus 2:13, every offering was to be sprinkled with salt.

38. M. Zebahim 6:5.

39. M. Erubim 10:14.

40. In the Salt Chamber they stored the salt for the offerings. In the Parwah Chamber they salted the hides of the animal sacrifices (M. Middoth 5:3).

41. 2 Kings 2:19–22.

42. Ben Sirakh 39:27.

43. Deuteronomy 29:23, Jeremiah 17:6, Zephaniah 2:9, Psalm 107:34, Job 39:6.

44. Deuteronomy 29:22 (= Greek Deuteronomy 29:23).

45. Psalms 107:33–34.

46. Zephaniah 2:9.

47. Judges 9:45.

48. Job 6:1–9.

49. Jeremiah 17:5–6.

50. Mark 9:50.

51. Numbers 18:19.

52. 2 Chronicles 13:5.

53. Matthew 5:1.

54. Mark 9:33.

55. Luke 14:25, 26, 33.

CHAPTER TEN

Parables about Vineyards, Orchards, and Fields

The Parable of the Vineyard
Owner and His Tenants

A landowner planted a vineyard, protected it with a hedge, dug a wine press in it, and built a tower, then rented it to tenants. When it was harvest time, he sent his servants to collect his share of fruit. The tenants killed one servant and pelted the others with stones. He sent other servants, and the tenants brutalized them. He sent his son, thinking they would respect him, but the tenants killed the son. So the owner massacred the tenants and leased the vineyard to others.

> Hear another parable. There was a householder who planted a vineyard, and set a hedge around it, and dug a wine press in it, and built a tower, and let it out to tenants, and went into another country. When the season of fruit drew near, he sent his servants to the tenants, to get his fruit; and the tenants took his servants and beat one, killed another, and stoned another. Again he sent other servants, more than the first; and they did the same to them. Afterward he sent his son to them, saying, "They will respect my son." But when the tenants saw the son, they said to themselves, "This is the heir; come, let us kill him and have his inheritance." And they took him and cast him out of the vineyard, and killed him. When therefore the owner of the vineyard comes, what will he do to those tenants? They said to him, "He will put those wretches to a miserable death, and let out the vineyard to other tenants who will give him the fruits in their seasons." (Matthew 21:33–41)

Jesus Built on Jewish Images

Jesus opened this parable with an allusion to the Vineyard Song in which the prophet Isaiah described God's love and care.

> My beloved had a vineyard on a very fertile hill. He broke the ground, cleared it of stones, and planted it with choice vines. He built a watchtower in the midst of it and hewed out a wine press in it. He hoped it would yield grapes, but it yielded wild grapes. (Isaiah 5:1–2)

In the first two verses, Isaiah spoke of God in the third person as his "Beloved." God owned a vineyard, which He cleared and planted. In the succeeding verses, the prophet addressed the crowd in the first person, speaking God's words directly. God was disappointed when the vines He tended yielded "wild" grapes.

> And now, O inhabitants of Jerusalem and men of Judah, judge, I pray you, between me and my vineyard. What more could have been done for my vineyard that I failed to do in it? When I looked for it to yield grapes, why did it yield wild grapes? (Isaiah 5:3–4)

As any vintner would have done, God had no choice but to destroy the vineyard.

> And now I will tell you what I will do to my vineyard. I will remove its hedge, that it may be ravaged; I will break down its wall, that it may be trampled. I will make it a waste; it shall not be pruned or hoed, and briers and thorns shall grow up. I will also command the clouds to drop no rain on it. (Isaiah 5:5–6)

According to Matthew, Jesus told the Parable of the Vineyard Owner and His Tenants in the open portico of the Holy Temple. What images might these allusions to Isaiah's Vineyard Song have created in the minds of his listeners in Jerusalem?

Many understood that the vineyard was Jerusalem. Isaiah's references to "a very fertile hill," "a watchtower," and "choice vines"[1] buttressed that image. Perhaps that's why God called on the "inhabitants of Jerusalem" to judge between Him and His vineyard.

More understood that the vineyard was the Jewish people. Isaiah intimated as much in the next verse: "For the vineyard of the Lord of hosts is the house of Israel, and the seedlings he lovingly tended are the men of Judah."[2]

God looked for justice and righteousness. Instead He saw bloodshed and heard the anguished cry of the oppressed.[3] "Woe to those who join house to house, who add field to field. . . . Woe to those who rise early in the morning, that they may run after strong drink, who tarry late into the evening till wine inflames them . . . Woe to those who . . . acquit the guilty for a bribe and deprive the innocent of his right!"[4]

God sent His servants the prophets to warn the people. Unless they changed their beliefs and behavior, the people of Israel would suffer destruction, devastation, and exile.[5]

The people did not change. They maintained their ways and tormented the prophets.

God fulfilled His promise. Jerusalem was razed, the Temple was ransacked and destroyed, and the Jewish people was driven into exile. Only two tribes and some priests survived. Ten tribes disappeared in Assyria.

Jesus' listeners knew all this. They began to see the Parable of the Vineyard Owner and His Tenants as a parallel to Isaiah's Vineyard Song in which Jesus escalated the violence and the intransigence of the people and brought Isaiah's prophecy up to date.

Jesus used some of Isaiah's words in his opening sentence ("vineyard," "tower," "wine press," "planted," "dug," and "built"), but Jesus meant contemporary Jerusalem and the current Temple, not the capital and shrine destroyed five hundred years earlier by the Babylonians.

Jesus' Views of Jerusalem

Like the prophets of the Hebrew Bible, Jesus took no pleasure in announcing Jerusalem's impending catastrophe. "When he drew near and saw the city he wept over it."[6] He wanted desperately to save it from destruction.

Jesus described the devastation: "The days shall come upon you when your enemies will cast up a bank about you and surround you and hem you in on every side and dash you to the ground, you and your children within you. They will not leave one stone upon another in you."[7] "Your house is forsaken and desolate."[8] For Jesus, "the time of your visitation" had already begun. The disaster would occur within "this generation"—unless the inhabitants of Jerusalem repented.[9]

What Secrets Did the Parable Convey?

The vineyard owner sent one set of servants, and they were beaten and killed. These were the biblical prophets.[10] The owner sent a second set of servants, and they too were slain. These were contemporary prophets, like

Simon and Anna and particularly John the Baptist.[11] Then the vineyard owner sent his son to plead with the tenants. That was Jesus.

The son suffered the same fate as the servants. The tenants murdered him. Jesus predicted he would be brutally slain by the very people he came to save—the people of Jerusalem. He said this aloud, publicly, in the open courtyard of the Temple.[12]

The vineyard owner would punish his tenants. Because they would not change their beliefs and behavior, like their ancestors the Jews of "this gener-ation" would suffer death and devastation. God "will put those wretches to a miserable death and let out the vineyard to other tenants."

Who Might Harm Jesus?

According to Luke, the "scribes and chief priests" suspected Jesus was direct-ing the parable against them.[13] Matthew was more general. "The chief priests and the Pharisees" perceived that all his remarks were pointed against them.[14] Since this included the announcement of his impending death, future generations of Christians ascribed to Jesus the accusation that the chief priests, scribes, and Pharisees would be responsible for his execution.

I'm not convinced that's what Jesus was saying in the parable. The leaders alone were not responsible for the son's death—any more than they were responsible for John's death or the death of the prophets. The people had strayed and become as rebellious and destructive as wild grapes. Therefore, the entire vineyard needed to be destroyed—Jerusalem, the Temple, its priests, the elders of the city, the merchants, bakers, cheese makers, potters, builders, and masons. In short, Jesus condemned everyone who disobeyed God and refused to repent.

The Same Parable in Mark

Mark reported the same story. In Jerusalem, probably in the vicinity of the Holy Temple, Jesus taught the Parable of the Vineyard Owner and His Ten-ants.

A man planted a vineyard, and set a hedge around it, and dug a pit for the wine press, and built a tower, and let it out to tenants, and went into another country. When the time came, he sent a servant to the tenants, to get from them some of the fruit of the vineyard. And they took him and beat him, and sent him away empty-handed. Again he sent to them another servant, and they wounded him in the head, and treated him shamefully. And he sent another, and him they killed; and so with many others, some they beat and some they killed. He had still one other, a beloved son; finally he sent him to them, saying, "They will respect my son." But those tenants said to one another, "This is the heir; come, let us kill him, and the inheritance will be ours." And they took him and killed him, and cast him out of the vineyard. What will the owner of the vineyard do? He will come and destroy the tenants, and give the vineyard to others. (Mark 12:2–12)

While it was the same story as Matthew, Mark added graphic details and intensified the violence.

In Mark, the vineyard owner sent one servant (not a group of servants). The tenants beat him and sent him back empty-handed. He sent another servant, and they wounded him in the head. He sent a third servant, and they killed him. "And so with many others, some they beat and some they killed." The violence escalated with each servant.

In Mark, the sacrifice of the son became even more significant. "He still had one other, a beloved son"—as if to suggest that he was the owner's only son, and the loss would leave him without an heir. Mark might even have been alluding to Abraham's sacrifice of his only son, his beloved son, Isaac.[15] Just as Isaac accompanied his father to Mount Moriah without hesitation or complaint, so Jesus was prepared to obey God—even though it might kill him.

The Same Parable in Luke

Luke reported the same parable.

A man planted a vineyard, and let it out to tenants, and went into another country for a long while. When the time came, he sent a servant to the tenants, that they should give him some of the fruit of the vineyard; but the tenants beat him, and sent him away empty-handed. And he sent another servant; him also they beat and treated shamefully, and sent him away empty-handed. And he sent yet a third; this one they wounded and cast out. Then the owner of the vineyard said, "What shall I do? I will send my beloved son; it may be they will respect him." But when the tenants saw him, they said to themselves, "This is the heir; let us kill him, that the inheritance may be ours." And they cast him out of the vineyard and killed him. What then will the owner of the vineyard do to them? He will come and destroy those tenants, and give the vineyard to others." When they heard this, they said, "God forbid!" (Luke 20:9–16)

Luke's rendition was similar to Mark's version (three visits by individual servants, beloved son, etc.), but less literary and less dramatic. All three servants were merely beaten and dismissed. However, Luke reported an element missing in Matthew and Mark. When the crowd heard Jesus' dire predictions, they cried out, "God forbid!" More than likely, they were appalled at Jesus' prophecy that they would die and that Jerusalem and all its inhabitants would be destroyed. But some may have reacted with grief at Jesus' announcement of his impending murder, and some may have reacted with dismay at his suggestion that they were responsible.

The Vineyard's Destruction

With the vineyard owner's final comments: "He will put those wretches to a miserable death, and let out the vineyard to other tenants who will give him the fruits in their seasons," Jesus came full circle in his recasting of Isaiah's Vineyard prophecy. Words Isaiah had spoken in the eighth century BCE now applied to first-century Israel. "I will tell you what I will do to my vineyard. I will remove its hedge, that it may be ravaged; I will break down its wall, that it may be trampled. I will make it a waste."[16]

Jesus drew on images imprinted in the minds of his audience and applied them to contemporary conditions—the conquest of the northern kingdom by the Assyrians, the conquest of Judah and Jerusalem by the Babylonians, the takeover of Palestine by the Romans less than a hundred years earlier, and the destruction of Sepphoris and the crushing of the Jewish revolutionaries in 6 CE. His listeners had heard the stories for decades and could envision the fate Jesus predicted for them.

The Parable of the Barren Fig Tree

For the third year in a row, a landowner found no fruit on his fig tree. So he decided to cut it down and plant something else. His gardener asked him to wait one more year while he fertilized and tended the barren tree. "If it bears fruit next year, well and good; if not, you can cut it down."

> He told this parable: "A man had a fig tree planted in his vineyard; and he came seeking fruit on it and found none. And he said to the vinedresser, 'Lo, these three years I have come seeking fruit on this fig tree, and I find none. Cut it down; why should it use up the ground?' And he answered him, 'Let it alone, sir, this year also, till I dig about it and put on manure. And if it bears fruit next year, well and good; but if not, you can cut it down.'" (Luke 13:6–9)

What Secrets Did the Parable Convey?

No ending was given to the story, and no moral was suggested. We don't know whether the barren tree bore fruit and, therefore, who was vindicated—the owner or the gardener.

Perhaps clues are contained in the parable itself.

In the Hebrew Bible, the fig tree was a symbol of peace and prosperity. "Judah and Israel dwelt in safety, from Dan even to Beersheba, every man under his vine and under his fig tree, all the days of Solomon."[17] "They shall sit every man under his vine and under his fig tree, and none shall make them afraid; for the mouth of the Lord of hosts has spoken."[18]

The Jews complained to Moses in the wilderness, "Why have you brought the assembly of the Lord into this wilderness, that we should die here, both we and our cattle? Why have you made us come up out of Egypt, to bring us to this evil place? It is no place for grain, or figs, or vines, or pomegranates; and there is no water to drink."[19] Moses comforted and reassured them. "The Lord your God is bringing you into a good land, a land of streams and springs and fountains flowing in valleys and hills, a land of wheat and barley, of vines and fig trees and pomegranates . . . a land where you will eat bread without scarcity, where you will lack nothing."[20]

The prosperity was not automatic. It had to be earned—by obedience to God. "Keep the commandments of the Lord your God; walk in His ways and revere Him."[21]

Through the Parable of the Barren Fig Tree, Jesus reminded his listeners of lessons they already knew: the consequence of disobedience was devastation and death. "I will treat them like loathsome figs which are so bad they cannot be eaten. I will pursue them with sword, famine and pestilence and will make them a horror to all the kingdoms of the earth, to be a curse, a terror, a hissing, and a reproach among all the nations where I have driven them, because they did not heed my words, says the Lord."[22]

The fig tree represented the covenant people; the owner was God; and the gardener was Jesus. For years, the Jewish people had neglected God's laws. As a consequence, they were unproductive and doomed to destruction. There was one more chance. Through Jesus' personal ministry and solicitous care, the Jewish people might yet bear fruit and survive.

However, if the Jewish people did not respond to Jesus' ministrations, it would be destroyed.

Jesus Had the Power to Heal and to Destroy

Another encounter with a barren fig tree reinforced the authenticity of Jesus' dire predictions. In Matthew 21:18–20, Jesus was returning to Jerusalem when he approached a fig tree on the side of the road. Finding no fruit to reduce his hunger, Jesus cursed the tree. At once it withered and died.

The same encounter was reported in Mark 11:12–14, 20–23, with the same results. The tree died.

The message was clear: As Jesus had the power to heal, so he had the power to destroy.

Jews devoted a great deal of time and energy tending their vineyards and orchards. They used the grapes, fruit, nuts, and wine to feed their families, and they sold the surplus to acquire goods and services they couldn't make themselves. Some earned enough money to invest in other enterprises. The parables in the next chapter concern earning and losing money.

Notes

1. The Hebrew word *sorek* ("choice vines") could refer to the Valley of Sorek, just west of Jerusalem.

2. Isaiah 5:7. See also Isaiah 27:2–6.

3. Isaiah 5:7. In Hebrew, "bloodshed" (*mispakh*) and "outcry" (*tza'aka*) are distortions of "justice" (*mishpat*) and "righteousness" (*tzadaka*).

4. Isaiah 5:8, 11, 22–23. Jesus used the same literary device (a litany of woes) in Matthew 23:13–30; Luke 6:24–26, 11:42–52.

5. Isaiah 5:13–14, 24–25.

6. Luke 19:41.

7. Luke 19:42–44.

8. Matthew 23:38. See also Luke 13:35.

9. Matthew 23:36.

10. Elijah was hunted (1 Kings 19:1–14); Jeremiah was flogged (Jeremiah 20:2) and tried for treason (Jeremiah 26:7–16); Uriah, the son of Shemaiah, was captured and killed (Jeremiah 26:20–23); and Zechariah was murdered in Jerusalem (2 Chronicles 24:20–21; Matthew 23:35). See also Matthew 23:34–35, 37; Luke 13:34; Hebrews 11:32–37.

11. John the Baptist was imprisoned and executed by Herod Antipas (Josephus, *Antiquities*, 18:5:2; Matthew 14:3, 10–12; Mark 6:16, 17, 27–29; Luke 3:19–20). For John the Baptist as a prophet, see Matthew 11:13–14, 16:14, 21:26; Mark 8:28, 11:32; Luke 9:19, 16:16, 20:6. For Simon and Anna, see Luke 2:25–31, 36–38.

12. Matthew 21:23. Jeremias denies the notion that Jesus had himself in mind as the son of the vineyard owner who was killed and notes a comparable rabbinic parable in which the slain son was identified as the patriarch Jacob (see Joachim Jeremias, *The Parables of Jesus*, rev. ed. [New York: Charles Scribner's Sons, 1963], 72–74). I disagree. Since Jesus regularly referred to himself as the *son* of man and the *son* of God, his listeners might have inferred that Jesus was the son in this parable also.

13. Luke 20:19.

14. Matthew 21:45.

15. Genesis 22:2.

16. Isaiah 5:5–6.

17. 1 Kings 4:25.
18. Micah 4:4. See also Zechariah 3:10.
19. Numbers 20:4–5.
20. Deuteronomy 8:7–9.
21. Deuteronomy 8:6.
22. Jeremiah 29:17–19. See also Amos 4:9; Hosea 2:12; Jeremiah 5:17, 24:8–10.

CHAPTER ELEVEN

Parables Dealing with Sheep and Money

The Parable of One Lost Sheep

Matthew recorded a parable in which a shepherd tending his flock noticed that one of his sheep had gone astray. He left the flock grazing and searched for the stray.

> What do you think? If a man has a hundred sheep and one of them has gone astray, does he not leave the ninety-nine on the mountains and go in search of the one that went astray? And if he finds it, truly, I say to you, he rejoices over it more than over the ninety-nine that never went astray. So it is not the will of my Father who is in heaven that one of these little ones should perish. (Matthew 18:12–4)

What Secrets Did the Parable Convey?

What was the meaning of this parable? Who was the lost sheep, and who was the caring shepherd?

The shepherd was any person who brought the teachings of Jesus to others. Jesus encouraged his followers to leave the comfort of their own fellowship and journey into the larger community to search for possible converts.

The shepherd was Jesus himself, who often left the fellowship of his followers to bring his message and his healing to those who didn't believe.

The shepherd was Jesus himself, who often assisted persons condemned by society.

The shepherd was God. God not only waited for each person to return ("repent"), He went out to search for each lost soul.

All are possible meanings, and Matthew may have had them all in mind when he recorded this parable. However, the most plausible interpretation of this parable and the one most in keeping with Jewish tradition is the last suggestion. The shepherd was God.

Jesus Built on Jewish Images

The Second Isaiah pictured God as the Shepherd of Israel, tenderly caring and nurturing His people. "He will pasture His flock like a shepherd. He will gather the lambs in His arms and carry them in His bosom."[1]

Ezekiel painted the same image. "Thus says the Lord God: Behold, I Myself will search for my sheep and will seek them out. As a shepherd seeks out his flock when some of his sheep have gotten separated, so will I seek out My sheep. . . . I will pasture them on the mountains of Israel, by the watercourses and in all the settled places of the land."[2]

"They shall have one shepherd," announced Ezekiel as he described Israel's ultimate redemption, "and they shall dwell in the land in which your fathers dwelt. They and their children and their children's children shall dwell there forever."[3]

Jeremiah envisioned the same redemption. "I Myself will gather the remnant of my flock from all the lands to which I banished them, and I will bring them back to their pasture where they shall be fertile and increase. . . . They shall no longer fear or be dismayed, and none of them shall be missing."[4]

"The Lord is my shepherd," stated Psalm 23, "I shall not want."[5]

The Same Parable in Luke

That was Luke's understanding also. God was the Shepherd, and heaven rejoiced at the redemption of the soul who strayed.

> So he told them this parable: "What man of you, having a hundred sheep, if he has lost one of them, does not leave the ninety-nine in the wilderness, and go after the one which is lost, until he finds it? And when he has found it, he lays it on his shoulders, rejoicing. And when he comes home, he calls together his friends and his neighbors, saying to them, 'Rejoice with me, for I have found my sheep which was lost.' Just so, I tell you, there will be more joy in heaven over one sinner who repents than over ninety-nine righteous persons who need no repentance." (Luke 15:3–7)

While the nature of the straying was vague in Matthew, in Luke it was clear. People who sin are like sheep that lost their way and needed to be rescued. God rejoiced in the salvation of every sinner—and, by implication,

He delighted in the benefactor who brought the sinner to repentance. In that sense, any person who convinced another to repent was a shepherd.

Jesus encouraged his disciples to be like caring shepherds willing to search far and wide for even one stray sheep, and he reminded them that God and all the creatures of heaven rejoiced when they were successful.

Though not part of the parable itself, Luke wrote for his collection of four parables an introduction that implied that the Parable of One Lost Sheep applied to Jesus as well. "Now the tax collectors and sinners were all drawing near to hear him. And the Pharisees and the scribes murmured, saying, 'This man receives sinners and eats with them.'"[6] For Luke, Jesus was also the shepherd.

Publicans and Sinners

Some Pharisees criticized Jesus for his ministry to people on the margin of society—the mentally ill, the physically abused, prostitutes, and tax collectors. Expressing more than disapproval, they suggested that Jesus was an irreligious man and warned his followers not to associate with him. Jesus countered by asserting that if "publicans and sinners" were as immoral as these Jewish leaders suggested, it was precisely toward them a helping hand should be extended.

Jesus did not defend the behavior of these transgressors. Like a physician, he responded to those who were spiritually ill and needed healing. Like a shepherd, he searched for lost sheep to bring them back to the fold. He did precisely what he believed the Pharisees and scribes themselves should be doing.

In Matthew, Jesus told the Parable of One Lost Sheep to his disciples as they conversed about the kingdom of heaven.[7] The emphasis was on the importance of their mission. Jesus challenged his disciples to be like the shepherd in the parable, to search diligently and persistently for lost sheep. In doing so, they would be fulfilling God's wishes. "It is not the will of my Father who is in heaven that one of these little ones should perish."

In Luke, the Parable of One Lost Sheep was Jesus' response to critics who decried his fraternizing with "tax collectors and sinners."[8] Jesus reminded his detractors that God revealed laws and sent prophets to encourage people to repent. In order to bring sinners to repentance, one has to associate and communicate with them. Nothing was more important, and no group was more significant. As Luke reminded his readers, "There will be more joy in heaven over one sinner who repents than over ninety-nine righteous persons who need no repentance."

The Parable of One Lost Coin

A woman noticed one of ten coins was missing. Carefully she put the nine coins away and began to search for the missing coin.

> Or what woman, having ten silver coins,[9] if she loses one coin, does not light a lamp and sweep the house and seek diligently until she finds it? And when she has found it, she calls together her friends and neighbors, saying, 'Rejoice with me, for I have found the coin which I had lost.' Just so, I tell you, there is joy before the angels of God over one sinner who repents. (Luke 15:8–10)

A woman was the main character in this parable. She owned, handled, and lost money. Jesus knew wealthy women.[10]

What Secrets Did the Parable Convey?

Both the Parable of One Lost Sheep and this parable shared the same messages: (1) God was so concerned about people who lacked the ability to find Him that He sought them; (2) the followers of Jesus should follow God's example and search for each lost soul; and (3) each new convert was a cause for celebration in heaven—and within the community of Jesus' followers.

The Parable of the Ten Coins

Zacchaeus was a very rich man and the chief tax collector in Jericho. When Jesus heard that Zacchaeus gave away half his fortune to the poor, he shared the story of a nobleman preparing to journey to a distant country where he was to become its new king. Before he departed, he gave each one of ten servants one silver coin to invest for him while he was gone. When he returned, he asked each servant for an accounting.

The first servant reported that the original coin left with him had earned ten more coins. The second stated that the coin left with him had earned five coins. The third servant apologized and returned the original silver. He had stored the coin in a napkin and never invested it. The nobleman generously rewarded the first two servants and punished the third.

> He proceeded to tell a parable. . . . "A nobleman went into a far country to receive a kingdom and then return. Calling ten of his servants, he gave them ten *minas*[11]

and said to them, 'Trade with these till I come.' But his citizens hated him and sent an embassy after him, saying, 'We do not want this man to reign over us.' When he returned, having received the kingdom, he commanded these servants to whom he had given the money to be called to him that he might know what they had gained by trading. The first came before him, saying, 'Lord, your mina has made ten minas more.' And he said to him, 'Well done, good servant! Because you have been faithful in a very little, you shall have authority over ten cities.' And the second came, saying, 'Lord, your mina has made five minas.' And he said to him, 'And you are to be over five cities.' Then another came, saying, 'Lord, here is your mina, which I kept laid away in a napkin; for I was afraid of you, because you are a severe man. You take up what you did not lay down and reap what you did not sow.' He said to him, 'I will condemn you out of your own mouth, you wicked servant! You knew that I was a severe man, taking up what I did not lay down and reaping what I did not sow? Why then did you not put my money into the bank, and at my coming I should have collected it with interest?' And he said to those who stood by, 'Take the mina from him, and give it to him who has the ten minas.' (And they said to him, 'Lord, he [already] has ten minas!') 'I tell you, that to every one who has will more be given; but from him who has not, even what he has will be taken away.'" (Luke 19:11–26)

What Secrets Did the Parable Convey?

Two themes intermingled in this parable:

- A wealthy nobleman gave his servants money to invest for him. The parable related the rewards for those who invested successfully and the punishment for those who did not.
- A wealthy nobleman sought to become king. His subjects opposed his appointment. The nobleman overcame their resistance, became king, and punished those who spoke against him.

Let's explore each theme independently.

First Theme: Invest Coins

Each time Jesus spoke he gave away insights. Any listener who applied these teachings diligently and successfully to his life would receive a reward far more valuable than silver and gold. He would earn eternal life.

Jesus suggested that ordinary Jews should reassess their current priorities and allegiances and change their ways of behaving—a message that could have been interpreted by both Roman and Jewish authorities as opposition to their requirements and rulings. Maybe this was why the sages and their disciples often challenged Jesus. They asked him why he ate with sinners,[12] why he allowed his disciples to pluck grain on the Sabbath,[13] why he didn't wash his hands before eating,[14] and how he advised his followers about paying tribute to Caesar.[15] In their public confrontations with Jesus, they challenged him to justify why he led people astray by blatantly disregarding their rulings.

Second Theme: Become King

According to Luke, Jesus told the Parable of the Ten Coins just before or during his entry into Jerusalem the week before Passover. That would make the parable one of the last Jesus shared. Expectation ran high among both his followers and detractors about what Jesus would do within the capital. Some people hoped that he would proclaim his royal authority and announce the inception of the kingdom of God.

Maybe that was why the leading authorities asked Jesus, "Are you the Messiah?"[16] They understood the Parable of the Ten Coins as a reference to Jesus himself. He was the nobleman who would become king and require an accounting from his trusted servants. Those who denied and opposed him he would punish.

Jesus didn't say he was the nobleman. He left the man's identity deliberately vague. But Jesus had already told his disciples he was the Messiah,[17] and both he and the authorities knew some people were calling him the Messiah.[18] It was no wonder that Pontius Pilate asked him directly, "Are you the king of the Jews?"[19]

While I believe Jesus' emphasized these two notions in this Parable of the Ten Coins, other interpretations are possible.

First Theme: Invest Coins

The nobleman was God. God had provided the Jews with material and spiritual resources. Their task was to use those resources in ways acceptable and pleasing to God, so that, when their accounting came, they would be rewarded. Preserving and protecting what they had, like the third servant, was not what God wanted them to do.

The nobleman was Jesus. Jesus was giving the Jews secrets worth more than silver and gold. Yet some people denied and disregarded them. Those who joined Jesus' fellowship and followed Jesus' teachings would be rewarded. All others, like the third servant, would be punished.

The nobleman was Jesus, the coins were his supporters, and the goal of the movement was to raise up more followers. Whether their master was present or not, worthy supporters labored continually to convince others of the authenticity of their message and to enlarge the community of believers.

Second Theme: Become King

The nobleman was the Messiah. Foreigners now ruled King David's territory, but their reign was temporary. The rightful king—a descendant of David—would return and reassert his dominion over Israel. Rome would be vanquished. Sinners would be punished. God's kingdom would be established on earth. Those who recognized the inevitability of the Messiah's reign (like the first two servants) would let go of their current material pursuits and devote their energies, talents, and resources to obeying God's laws.

Jesus' listeners could have drawn any or all of these assertions from the Parable of the Ten Coins.

The Emperor in Rome

Within the Roman Empire, the emperor appointed kings. When Jesus' listeners heard this parable, they imagined that the nobleman had sailed to Rome to plead his case before the emperor and that some time would pass before he returned. In his absence, he gave his servants money to invest.

That was precisely what had happened when Herod the Great died in 4 BCE. His sons expected to inherit his property and his title, but the Jews protested. They contested Herod's will and sent a delegation to Augustus to recount the son Archelaus' cruelties. In Rome, Archelaus had to defend himself against their accusations. Archelaus won—though he was appointed tetrarch and not king over Judea.

Upon his return from Rome, the new tetrarch inflicted brutal revenge upon the Jews who had opposed his succession, embarrassed him, and forced him to endure a costly trial. A decade later he was summoned again to Rome, dethroned, and banished to Germany. A Roman prefect (procurator) was appointed to govern Judea.

Twenty-five years later, people still talked about Herod the Great, Archelaus his son, and his two brothers, who still ruled over the Jews. Jesus and his listeners knew the stories. Many of them had experienced their cruelty and violence firsthand.

To Whom Was This Parable Addressed?

Some scholars assert Jesus addressed his detractors—the Pharisees and scribes who questioned and criticized him.[20] Some suggest he instructed his disciples.[21] But Luke presented the parable as part of Jesus' discourse to the crowds who gathered about him somewhere on his journey from Jericho to Jerusalem, and I find no reason to question that image. Jesus addressed the Jews who stood before him—for the most part ordinary Jews, though there may have been some priests or scribes among them.

Life in First-Century Palestine

The parable presented some interesting aspects of life in first-century Palestine: There were recognizable socioeconomic classes—rich and poor, free and slave, noblemen and workers. Servants were entrusted with money, entitled to invest the money in any business they chose, and expected to return significant profits. Some ventures earned 500 to 1,000 percent of the original investment.

A comparable parable was reported in Matthew, but a great deal more money was entrusted to the servants and only the first theme was emphasized. It's called the Parable of the Eight Talents.

The Parable of the Eight Talents

A wealthy man left on a journey and gave his servants money to invest—five talents of silver to one, two talents to another, and one talent to the third. Some time later, when the man asked for an accounting, the first servant handed him ten talents (double the money he had received), and the second servant offered four talents (also doubling his money). The third servant returned only the original silver. He had buried the talent in the ground for safekeeping and had not invested it. The first two servants received generous rewards; the third servant was dismissed and banished.

> For it will be as when a man going on a journey called his servants and entrusted to them his property; to one he gave five talents, to another two, to another one, to each according to his ability. Then he went away. He who had received the five talents went at once and traded with them; and he made five talents more. So also, he who had the two talents made two talents more. But he who had received the one talent went and dug in the ground and hid his master's money. Now after a long time the master of those servants came and settled accounts with them. And he who had received the five talents came forward, bringing five talents more, saying, "Master, you delivered to me five talents; here I have made five talents more." His master said to him, "Well done, good and faithful servant; you have been faith-

ful over a little, I will set you over much; enter into the joy of your master." And he also who had the two talents came forward, saying, "Master, you delivered to me two talents; here I have made two talents more." His master said to him, "Well done, good and faithful servant; you have been faithful over a little, I will set you over much; enter into the joy of your master." He also who had received the one talent came forward, saying, "Master, I knew you to be a hard man, reaping where you did not sow, and gathering where you did not winnow; so I was afraid, and I went and hid your talent in the ground. Here you have what is yours." But his master answered him, "You wicked and slothful servant! You knew that I reap where I have not sowed, and gather where I have not winnowed? Then you ought to have invested my money with the bankers, and at my coming I should have received what was my own with interest. So take the talent from him, and give it to him who has the ten talents. For to every one who has will more be given, and he will have abundance; but from him who has not, even what he has will be taken away. And cast the worthless servant into the outer darkness; there men will weep and gnash their teeth." (Matthew 25:14–30)

What Secrets Did the Parable Convey?

While similar, there are some significant differences between the previous parable in Luke and this parable in Matthew:

- Ten servants were mentioned in the previous parable, but the investment results of only three servants were reported. How the other servants fared was never reported. In this parable, only three servants and their results were noted.
- In this parable *talents* were given instead of minas. Each talent was worth sixty minas.[22]
- Eight talents were given—not ten minas as in the previous parable—but much more money was involved.[23]
- In this version, each servant received a different amount. In the prior parable, each servant received one mina.
- In this version, each of the first two servants doubled his master's investment—a pretty good return, but far less than ten times and five times the investment in the first parable.
- No punishment for the unproductive servant was indicated in the first parable. In this version, he was dismissed and forced to live outdoors in the dark.

While the message was the same in both parables, Matthew dramatically escalated both the value of the teachings Jesus was giving away and the punishment his listeners would receive for not applying them diligently in their lives.

Napkin versus Burial

In both parables, the unproductive servant preserved the original coin and returned it to his master. In Luke, he hid the mina in a napkin; in Matthew he buried the talent in the ground. There was a significant difference in the meaning of those acts.

The sages regarded burial as an appropriate security against loss or theft; binding property in a napkin was not. "If a man left money in his fellow's keeping and his fellow bound it up [in a cloth or sack] . . . [and it was lost], he is liable [to replace the money], since he did not guard it properly. But if he guarded it properly [that is, if he buried it] [and it was lost], he is not liable."[24]

By burying the talent, the third servant in Matthew acted prudently in accordance with Jewish law. If he had invested the money and lost, he believed, Jewish law would have made him responsible to pay it back from his own resources. By burying the money, he preserved his master's assets and reduced his own liability at the same time.

The servant in Luke who wrapped the mina in a cloth and did not bury it—so that the cloth remained visible and accessible to others—acted imprudently. His inadequate protection of the money entrusted to him jeopardized his master's assets and made him personally liable to replace any loss.

Both servants determined to preserve the assets they received—and therein lay a deeper meaning. If the money entrusted to their care was a metaphor for the Torah and Jewish teaching in general, then they were fulfilling the demands of Jewish law. One of the objectives of the sages was to preserve and protect Jewish tradition for future generations.

A rabbinic homily emphasized this idea: "I shall tell you a parable. To what may this be compared? To a man with whom the king deposited some object. . . . [Then Rabbi Eliezer turned to Rabbi Johanan ben Zakkai, who was mourning the death of his son.] Master, you had a son. He studied Torah, the Prophets, and the Holy Writings. He studied Mishnah, Halakha and Agada. And he departed. . . . Shouldn't you be comforted [knowing] you've returned your trust unimpaired?"[25]

Torah was to be protected. "Make a fence around the Law," the sages taught.[26] It was God's revelation, the source of Jewish legend, law, and lore, to be studied diligently and guarded continuously. As the Jews protected the Torah, so the Torah protected the Jews.

Another rabbinic parable reinforced this notion: A king, gone for many years, returned to find his bride-to-be still awaiting their marriage. "If it had not been for the magnificent marriage contract you wrote for me, my companions would long ago have made me give you up." Then the metaphor was applied to the people of Israel. "The Israelites go into their synagogues and houses of study and take up the book of the Law, and they read therein, 'And I will turn unto you and make you fruitful and multiply you, and I will establish my covenant with you,'[27] and they are comforted. When the end shall have come, God will say to the Israelites, 'My children, I marvel that you have waited for me all these years.' And Israel will say, 'Lord, if it had not been for the Torah which You wrote for us, the nations would have caused us to abandon You long ago.'"[28]

Some in Jesus' audience would have applauded the third servant. He acted diligently to preserve and protect Jewish tradition.

Why then was the master so upset? Why did he punish the third servant?

From this point of view, the parable was a criticism of Pharisaic teaching. Jesus deliberately suggested that the regulations and restrictions of the sages were no longer appropriate. This was no time to hang on to exactly what they had been entrusted. New investments were required. With the coming of God's kingdom, those who held tight to the old ways would lose everything. They would be swept up by the whirlwind and destroyed like the rest of the sinners on earth. In order to survive the holocaust, people needed to commit themselves to Jesus, change their thinking, and revise their behavior. Their reward would exceed any asset they now possessed.

Each Servant Was Responsible
Each servant was free to choose. No one determined what his choice would be. Therefore, each was responsible—for his reward and for his punishment.

To Whom Was the Parable Addressed?
Who was the audience for this parable? Was it still the ordinary people of Jerusalem?

In chapter 24, Matthew reported Jesus speaking privately to his disciples; in chapter 26, Matthew described Jesus sharing with them his premonitions about being crucified.[29] Though no location was given in chapter 25, Matthew presented it as a continuation of the same discourse and envisioned this parable as an address to the disciples.

However, our analysis of the parables indicated they were not instructions to the disciples alone. On the contrary, the Parables of the Budding Fig Tree, the Flood, the Burglar, the Servant Left Alone, and the Ten Maidens—though grouped together in these chapters by Matthew—were addressed to the Jews assembled in Jesus' audiences. In order to warn and encourage them, he recounted one parable after another, again and again, wherever and whenever the crowds gathered to listen. His disciples were present and may have gleaned more from his metaphors, but Jesus addressed the people—ordinary Jews he was desperate to save.

The Parable of the King Who Settles Accounts

Jesus compared the kingdom of heaven to a king who wanted to settle accounts with his servants. One slave owed him ten thousand talents and could not pay. The king ordered him, his wife, his children, and all his possessions sold in partial payment. The slave begged for more time and promised to pay the entire debt. Out of pity, the king released him and forgave the debt.

Shortly thereafter, the slave encountered another slave who owed him a hundred denarii and could not pay. The second slave begged the first for more time and promised to pay back the entire debt. But the first slave refused and sent the second slave to jail.

The king castigated the first slave. "Should you not have mercy on your fellow servant, as I had mercy on you?" he asked, and he sent the first slave to jail.

> Therefore the kingdom of heaven may be compared to a king who wished to settle accounts with his servants. When he began the reckoning, one was brought to him who owed him ten thousand talents; and as he could not pay, his lord ordered him to be sold, with his wife and children and all that he had, and payment to be made. So the servant fell on his knees, imploring him, 'Lord, have patience with me, and I will pay you everything.' And out of pity for him the lord of that servant released him and forgave him the debt. But that same servant, as he went out, came upon one of his fellow servants who owed him a hundred denarii; and seizing him by the throat he said, 'Pay what you owe.' So his fellow servant fell down and besought him, 'Have patience with me, and I will pay you.' He refused and went and put him in prison till he should pay the debt. When his fellow servants saw what had taken place, they were greatly distressed, and they went and reported to their lord all that had taken place. Then his lord summoned him and said to him, 'You wicked servant! I forgave you all that debt because you besought me; and should not you have had mercy on your fellow servant, as I had mercy on you?' And in anger his lord delivered him to the jailers, till he should pay all his debt." (Matthew 18:23–34)

True Repentance

The sum of ten thousand talents was so vast as to put the debtor beyond all reasonable possibility of repaying it.[30] Yet out of his compassion and without hesitation, the king forgave the entire debt.

Once again, Jesus emphasized the importance of true repentance. Our most horrendous sin would be forgiven if we truly repented. However, a sign of true repentance was our willingness to forgive others who sinned against us. The unforgiving person was doomed to eternal darkness.

Using this parable as his medium, Jesus reinforced Jewish understandings about repentance:

- God would hear your pleas and react with compassion.
- No matter how enormous were your sins, all could be forgiven.
- The measure of your repentance was your behavior. If you treated others decently, responded with compassion to their travails, and forgave their trespasses, your repentance was sincere. Otherwise, you were still a sinner and would experience the dungeon and death.

There were people in positions of responsibility and power who appeared to be among God's fortunate. They were not. God judged their sincerity and behavior by the same standards and found many of them wanting. They were sinners and would suffer divine retribution. Their wealth and status would not protect them.

While they mouthed the prayers correctly, offered the proper sacrifices, and recited penitential poems, many Pharisees and priests were insincere. Their behavior belied their words. Instead of extending mercy and forgiveness, they judged others harshly, condemned them, and abused them.

According to Matthew, Jesus concluded with the warning: "So also my heavenly father will do to every one of you, if you do not forgive your brother from your heart."[31] While most scholars agree this verse was not part of the original parable, it agreed with his teachings: "For if you forgive men their trespasses, your heavenly Father also will forgive you; but if you do not forgive men their trespasses, neither will your Father forgive your trespasses."[32]

Those who truly repented and became reconciled with God reached out with compassion to help others and forgave them their trespasses. Those who did not behave in this fashion—regardless of how often or how loudly they confessed—were still sinners and would suffer devastation and death.

Isaiah had said it centuries earlier: "Because this people drew near with their mouth and honored Me with their lips, but kept its heart are far from me, and its worship of Me has been a commandment of men learned by rote, therefore, behold, I shall further baffle this people. . . . The wisdom of their wise men shall fail, and the prudence of their discerning men shall vanish."[33]

Jesus reinforced it in the first century: "This people honors me with their lips, but their heart is far from me; in vain do they worship me, teaching as doctrines the precepts of men."[34]

The Parable of the Two Debtors

Two men owed a wealthy creditor and could not pay. One owed him five hundred denarii; the other fifty denarii. The creditor forgave them both.

> A certain creditor had two debtors; one owed five hundred denarii, and the other fifty. When they could not pay, he forgave them both. Now which of them will be more grateful?[35] Simon answered, "The one, I suppose, to whom he forgave more." And he [Jesus] said to him, "You have judged rightly." (Luke 7:41–43)

What Secrets Did the Parable Convey?

What was Jesus teaching?

Simon provided the answer: The man who was forgiven more would feel more intense appreciation. That is, the greater the accumulation of a person's sins, the deeper his or her feelings of gratitude, relief, and fulfillment when those sins are removed.

Jesus and Simon the Pharisee

According to Luke, Jesus shared this parable at a banquet in the home of a prominent Pharisee.

> One of the Pharisees asked him [Jesus] to eat with him, and he went into the Pharisee's house and took his place at table. And behold, a woman of the city, who was a sinner, when she learned that he was at table in the Pharisee's house, brought an alabaster flask of ointment, and standing behind him at his feet, weeping, she began to wet his feet with her tears, and wiped them with the hair of her head, and kissed his feet, and anointed them with the ointment. Now when the Pharisee who had invited him saw it, he said to himself, "If this man were a prophet, he would have known who and what sort of woman this is who is touching him, for she is a sinner." (Luke 7:36–39)

Concluding that Jesus was a prophet—either because of what he saw him do or heard him say[36]—Simon the Pharisee invited Jesus to a banquet at his home. Overwhelmed with gratitude that her sins have been forgiven, a woman of ill repute barged in during the banquet and "began to wet his feet with her tears, and wiped them with the hair of her head, and kissed his feet, and anointed them with the ointment." The host was surprised that Jesus would allow a sinner to approach him and touch him. Doubts assailed the Pharisee. Perhaps Jesus was not a prophet after all.

Sensing his disapproval, Jesus turned to his host: "And Jesus answering said to him, 'Simon, I have something to say to you.' And he answered, 'What is it, Teacher?'" (Luke 7:40).

Jesus told him the Parable of the Two Debtors. Clearly one debtor was the sinful woman, now cleansed of her sins. But who was the second debtor?

> Then turning toward the woman he said to Simon, "Do you see this woman? I entered your house, you gave me no water for my feet, but she has wet my feet with her tears and wiped them with her hair. You gave me no kiss, but from the time I came in she has not ceased to kiss my feet. You did not anoint my head with oil, but she has anointed my feet with ointment. Therefore I tell you, her sins, which are many, are forgiven, for [which] she displayed much gratitude; but he who is forgiven little, shows little gratitude." (Luke 7:44–47)

Jesus contrasted the woman's behavior with that of his host. She expressed love and gratitude, while he stood in judgment—reproving her and doubting Jesus. Instead of responding with joy at her release, Simon criticized her nearness and the many rules she was breaking. His behavior was ungracious and inhospitable. He evidenced no compassion or concern. The host was the second debtor.

Jesus Disagreed with the Sages
This was another instance in which Jesus took exception to the rules and traditions of the sages.

As it was in other passages, the Greek word *hamartolos* was translated "sinner." The woman was a sinner. Most scholars presume she was a prostitute. But her sin was not defined.[37] She could have been a child molester, a thief, or a drunkard. Wherever it occurred, the Greek word was never defined and covered a multitude of sins.

Jesus was condemned by some Pharisees of dining with tax collectors and *sinners*.[38] Some saw him eating and drinking and called him "a glutton and a drunkard, a friend of tax collectors and *sinners*."[39] In the course of their examination of the blind man Jesus healed, they called Jesus "a *sinner*."[40]

It was a term of approbation, but it was not a Pharisaic term. Jesus used the same term when he described his opponents as "an adulterous and *sinful* generation."[41] At Gethsemane, Jesus was betrayed into the hands of *sinners*.[42] Peter called himself "a *sinner*."[43]

No one assumes they were all prostitutes or that their sin had anything to do with sex. In like manner, there is no justification for accusing the woman in this parable of being a harlot.

What was clear from Simon's reaction was his opinion that she was still sinning. She loosened her head covering, unbound her hair to wipe Jesus' feet, touched him, and kissed his feet in public—acts considered immodest and forbidden by Jewish law.[44] Jesus viewed her behavior as an outpouring of the joy and gratitude she felt on being cleansed of her sins. Simon had no sense of her relief and exuberance, seeing rather her behavior as a vindication of her reputation. She was indeed a sinning woman.

In a larger context, then, Jesus accused the Pharisees of condemning behavior without examining the cause, of branding people without knowing who they were or what they were experiencing, and of focusing merely on outward appearance without emphasizing redemption within. As a consequence, they thoroughly misunderstood the true meaning of repentance.

Jesus could tell by the gratitude and exuberance she expressed that the woman had been redeemed. So he said to her matter-of-factly, to indicate that he understood her condition, "Your sins are forgiven."[45]

The other guests at the banquet misunderstood Jesus' words: "Then those who were at table with him began to say among themselves, 'Who is this, who even forgives sins?' And he said to the woman, 'Your faith has saved you; go in peace'" (Luke 7:49–50).

They accused Jesus of announcing that he had the power to abrogate sins and that he forgave her transgressions. From their point of view, Jesus claimed God's power. At that moment, the tension in Simon's house must have been intense. Luke didn't report whether they attacked Jesus or just left in a huff. Jesus' last words were to reassure the woman. "Your faith has saved you; go in peace."

The Perfect Wife

The qualities of a perfect wife were listed at the end of the book of Proverbs. Written from a male's point of view, it described how industrious she was. Up before dawn and working long after sunset, she planted a vineyard with her own hands; produced her own cotton, wool, and linen fabric; sewed clothing for herself and her children; and made and sold linen garments (and gave the profit to her husband). "Her husband trusts in her and lacks no good thing." She was wise, kind, charitable, industrious, self-contained, and optimistic. Her children blessed her, and her husband praised her.[46]

Such a wife was hard to find and more precious than rubies.[47] Most Jewish women didn't express all these qualities, but it was the ideal. The woman in the parable fell far short of this standard.

According to the sages, a woman should not appear in public bareheaded. This woman did. A woman should not let her hair fall loose or speak in public to other men. These were grounds for divorce.[48] This woman did.

Jesus also was at fault. According to the Hebrew Bible, anyone and anything that came into contact with a menstruant woman was defiled—and defiled anything he or it touched afterwards.[49] Since only a husband might know whether or not a woman was sufficiently beyond her menstrual cycle to be clean, the rule adopted by first-century Jewish men was not to touch any woman. By allowing the woman to touch him, Jesus broke this rule and put himself and everyone else at the banquet in jeopardy.

Jesus didn't know whether or not the woman was clean.[50] It didn't matter to him. He felt it was more important to acknowledge her gratitude and joy. Once again he defied convention and expressed his opposition to the teachings of the sages.

The Amount of Sin and Forgiveness
God's forgiveness was not automatic and was not determined by the size of the sins. Forgiveness flowed from God's grace. Without hesitation, and by virtue of His own decision, God forgave.

The size of the loan was irrelevant. In the parable, neither debtor could repay. Though Simon may have sinned less than the woman, he was still a sinner and required forgiveness.

One act of forgiveness was no different from the other. Not bigger than or small than, each was a sublime gift. It was not the debts that were forgiven but the debtors. The sinners were cleansed and made whole.

Jesus was telling his host he shouldn't judge either the woman or Jesus. The host himself was a sinner who needed to repent. I'm sure Simon didn't like being called a sinner in front of his guests.

Simon looked with disdain upon the woman who intruded on his banquet. He saw her as a person who committed egregious sins. In the parable, she was the debtor with the large loan. Yet she was forgiven.

Jesus taught that every sinner could obtain God's forgiveness, regardless of the amount or intensity of his transgressions. No one was undeserving, and no one was beyond God's reach. Those Jews who thought so (and taught so) misunderstood the process of repentance.

Taxes and Tax Collectors

Four kinds of taxes were collected by the Romans from the people of Palestine: a tax on land, a poll tax, a tax on personal property, and custom duties on items exported or imported. The residents of Jerusalem paid a house tax. In addition, Jews throughout the empire provided a half-shekel payment to support the Temple in Jerusalem.[51] The land and poll taxes were collected by Roman officials. Tolls on personal property and custom charges were farmed out to private contractors, who paid a stipulated sum in advance for the right to collect these charges in a given locality and to try to make a profit on the transaction.[52] Both the Romans and the contractors hired Jews to do the actual collecting. The half-shekel tax was collected by Temple priests.

Most Jews (including many of their leaders) resented these taxes and viewed them as a form of Roman persecution. Roman wars led to demands for more money, goods, and services. Roman suppression of civil unrest and rebellion often devastated whole regions. Droughts, especially years of multiple droughts, diminished considerably the abilities of farmers to produce surplus crops to sell. Many farmers fell deep into debt. Many lost their land and became tenant-farmers or, worse, unemployed workers searching for temporary employment anywhere they could find it. Taxes often amounted to 40 percent of their earnings.[53]

In the New Testament, tax collectors had an unsavory reputation. So often were they denounced that "tax collectors and sinners" became a popular cliché.[54]

That negative image echoed in Jewish literature. Tax collectors were grouped with murderers and robbers. To avoid loss, one could deceive a tax collector.[55] The word of a tax gatherer could not be trusted, nor could his oath be believed.[56] As a consequence, he could not testify in a court of law or hold a communal office. Money in the pocket of a tax collector was considered stolen property.[57]

Jesus associated with tax collectors not because he condoned their behavior but because he hoped to rescue and redeem them. Tax collectors came to be baptized and asked what to do. Jesus said to them, "Collect no more than is appointed you."[58]

Like anyone else who sinned, tax collectors could be saved. Zacchaeus, the chief tax collector in Jericho, repented and now gave half his earnings to the poor. When he discovered someone he previously defrauded, he repaid him fourfold.[59] Another tax collector, Levi, left his position to follow Jesus about the country.[60] A third (or possibly the same man) was listed among Jesus' disciples, called "Matthew the tax collector."[61] A repentant whore or bureaucrat had a far better chance to survive the coming catastrophe than an unrepentant Pharisee. "I say to you, the tax collectors and the harlots go into the kingdom of God before you."[62]

The Parable of the Tower Builder

Farmers built stone towers in their fields to store equipment and produce, for lodging, and as lookout posts to guard their crops from animals and thieves.[63] Jesus told a parable about a farmer who never finished his tower.

> For which of you, desiring to build a tower, does not first sit down and count the cost, whether he has enough to complete it? Otherwise, when he has laid a foundation, and is not able to finish, all who see it begin to mock him, saying, "This man began to build, and was not able to finish." (Luke 14:28–30)

Not every farmer built a tower on his property. It was a daunting and expensive task. In small agricultural communities, everyone in town must have noticed the tower under construction. After some time, they noted no further work on the structure. Only the foundation stood, rooted in the soil. The townspeople began to talk among themselves and mock the builder for wasting his time and money to build a foundation and no tower.

What Secrets Did the Parable Convey?
What was Jesus teaching?

Luke set this parable in a series of addresses to Jesus' disciples. If the disciples were his audience, Jesus informed them, they had begun an arduous task—like building a tower. They ought to be sure from the outset that they had calculated the costs and understood the resources necessary to complete their mission. If not, they would suffer scorn and mockery.

According to Jeremias, Jesus was telling potentially new supporters not to commit at all rather than to fall short and fail.[64]

Hultgren suggests a different message. The parable was intended not to drive away potential disciples but to get those already involved to remember that their task was far from finished. The tower was only partially built. They needed to "continue and complete" that which they had already begun.[65]

Echoes of the Book of Proverbs

Those among his followers who knew the Hebrew Bible may have heard echoes of the book of Proverbs:

> A house is built by wisdom, and is established by understanding; by knowledge are its rooms filled with all precious and beautiful things. A wise man [understands] strength, and a knowledgeable man exerts power; for by stratagems you wage war, and victory comes with much planning. (Proverbs 24:3–6)

The question at the beginning of the parable was rhetorical. There was a plan, though most people couldn't perceive it, because only the foundations had been established. But the rest of the tower would be completed soon. God would finish what He started. God's kingdom would be established on earth. The construction had already commenced, and those who mocked would perish. "A house is built by wisdom and is established by understanding." Jesus' followers possessed that understanding. They would enjoy "precious and beautiful things" as residents of God's house. In due time, after much work and planning, they would celebrate their "victory."

The Parable of a King Preparing for War

According to Luke, Jesus immediately succeeded the previous parable with a parable about a king waging war on another king.

> What king, going to encounter another king in war, will not sit down first and take counsel whether he is able with ten thousand to meet him who comes against him with twenty thousand? And if not, while the other is yet a great way off, he sends an embassy and asks terms of peace. (Luke 14:31–32)

What Secrets Did the Parable Convey?

This parable dealt with the same circumstances and raised the same critical questions as its predecessor, but enhanced the consequences. Though he suffered shame, the tower builder lived. The king risked losing his life. More, his mistake might cause the death of thousands of his soldiers. The king had better be certain of his decision. The encounter has become deadly, and the consequences were life threatening.

Most scholars suggest this second parable was a parallel to the first and taught the same lesson to Jesus' disciples. Be prudent, Jesus advised. Think through carefully what it means to be a disciple before committing to become one. Your life will be altogether altered.[66]

According to this suggestion, the parable referred to the disciple's inner struggle and the phrase "sends an embassy and asks for terms of peace" advised the disciple to seek accommodations with the community at large if he could not commit his entire being to the mission that lay before him.

Many of his supporters did that. Though they believed in Jesus and his teachings, they lived and worked with their families at home.

For some, the parable had a different meaning. Those who saw God as the tower builder imagined that He was also the king in this parable.

God could not lose the war. Victory for His forces was inevitable—even if they were outnumbered. The followers of Jesus were few in number and lacked the wealth, power, status, and resources of their opponents, but they possessed insight and understanding. They knew.

The war had already begun. It didn't matter that they were outnumbered. God was on their side, and size was irrelevant. Look at the successes of David against the Philistines and the Maccabees against the armies of Syria. Didn't the book of Proverbs say that "a house is built by wisdom, and is established by understanding"? Well, they had the knowledge. Their "victory" was assured. Eventually, they would enjoy all the "precious and beautiful things."

As long as they maintained their faith and behaved as God wished them to do, they would be saved. Their goal was to save others as well.

In the next chapter, we discover what happened to a man who completed everything and decided to enjoy his success.

Notes

1. Isaiah 40:11.

2. Ezekiel 34:11–13. See also verses 15–16.

3. Ezekiel 37:24–25.

4. Jeremiah 23:3–4.

5. Psalm 23:1.

6. Luke 15:1–2.

7. Matthew 18:1. Mark 9:33–50 contains a similar discussion between Jesus and his disciples, but the Parable of One Lost Sheep is not mentioned.

8. Luke 15:1–2.

9. Literally, *ten drachmas*. In the first century, a *drachma* was the daily wage of a hired laborer.

10. Joachim Jeremias (*The Parables of Jesus*, rev. ed. [New York: Charles Scribner's Sons, 1963], 132–35) suggests the woman was poor, but she possessed the equivalent of

ten days' wages—and possibly more, since the parable didn't indicate that these coins were her total assets.

11. A *mina* was worth one hundred drachmas—about a hundred times the daily wage of a hired laborer. Since the Revised Standard Version was published in Great Britain, the text has translated *mina* into the familiar British currency—"pounds." In the United States we would say "dollars." At eight dollars an hour, the average hired laborer in the United States would make sixty-four dollars a day. One mina in today's currency would be worth $6,400.

12. Matthew 9:11; Mark 2:16; Luke 5:30, 15:2. See also Luke 7:36–39.

13. Matthew 12:1–2, Mark 2:23–24, Luke 6:1–2.

14. Matthew 15:1–2; Mark 7:1–2, 5; Luke 11:37–38.

15. Matthew 22:15–22, Mark 12:13–17.

16. Mark 14:61. See also Matthew 26:63; Luke 22:67.

17. Matthew 16:16, 20; Mark 8:29–30; Luke 9:20–21.

18. Matthew 9:27; 12:23; 15:22; 20:30–31; 21:9, 15; 24:5, 23; Mark 10:47–48; 11:10; Luke 18:38–39; John 4:29; 7:26, 31, 41–42; 11:27.

19. Luke 23:3. See also Matthew 27:17, 22.

20. Jeremias, *The Parables of Jesus*, 62; Dan Otto Via, Jr., *The Parables: Their Literary and Existential Dimension* (Philadelphia: Fortress, 1967), 115.

21. James E. Talmage, *Jesus the Christ* (Salt Lake City, Utah: Church of Jesus Christ of Latter-Day Saints, 1962), 535.

22. In today's money, each talent was worth $384,000.

23. Ten minas would equal $640,000 in today's currency. Eight talents would equal $3.172 million.

24. M. Baba Metzia 3.10. Later rabbinic authorities understood the phrase "guarded it properly" to mean burial in the ground (Baba Metzia 42a).

25. Aboth D'Rabbi Nathan 14, as presented in Bernard Brandon Scott, *Hear Then the Parable: A Commentary on the Parables of Jesus* (Minneapolis, Minn.: Fortress, 1990), 230.

26. M. Avot 1.1.

27. Leviticus 26:9.

28. Pesikhta Rab Kahana 19, 139b, as presented in Scott, *Hear then the Parable*, 233–34.

29. Matthew 24:3, 26:1–2.

30. The contrast between ten thousand talents and a hundred denarii would be comparable today to the difference between $38 million and a single dollar. According to Josephus (*Antiquities*, 17.318), the entire annual tribute of Galilee and Perea in 4 BCE amounted to two hundred talents—a fiftieth of that sum. The enormous amount was intentional and contrasted sharply with the second servant's debt of a hundred denarii. (See Jeremias, *The Parables of Jesus*, 30.)

31. Matthew 18:35.

32. Matthew 6:14–15.

33. Isaiah 29:13–14.

34. Matthew 15:8–9.

35. As Jeremias suggests, the Greek word *agapan* should be translated as "gratitude" rather than "love."

36. Jeremias presumes Jesus must have preached a sermon in the synagogue that greatly impressed Simon. (See Jeremias, *The Parables of Jesus*, 126.)

37. Some scholars suggest that the phrase "woman of the city" indicated she was a prostitute (see Jeremias, *The Parables of Jesus*, 127), but the phrase could mean simply that the lady lived in the town and therefore was known to Simon and his guests.

38. Matthew 9:10–13; Mark 2:15–17; Luke 5:30–32, 15:1–2. See also Luke 18:13–14.

39. Matthew 11:19, Luke 7:34.

40. John 9:24.

41. Mark 8:38.

42. Matthew 26:45, Mark 14:41.

43. Luke 5:8.

44. Tosefta Sota 5:9.

45. Luke 7:48.

46. Proverbs 31:11–29.

47. Proverbs 31:10.

48. M. Ketubot 7.6.

49. Leviticus 12:1–8, 15:19–33, 18:19–20, 20:18. Contact with a menstruant woman was as grave as contact with a corpse (M. Zabakhim 5.11). The uncleanliness that resulted from menstruation was compared to that from idol worship (M. Avoda Zara 3.6).

50. He would have had to know that her bleeding had ceased seven days earlier and that she had performed the rituals of immersion and purification. See Leviticus 15:19–33; M. Berakhot 3.6.

51. Madeleine S. Miller and J. Lane Miller, *Harper's Encyclopedia of Biblical Life*, rev. ed. (New York: Harper and Row, 1978), 268.

52. Bernard J. Bamberger, "Tax Collector," in *The Interpreter's Dictionary of the Bible: An Illustrated Encyclopedia*, ed. George A. Buttrick (New York: Abingdon, 1962), 522.

53. Richard A. Horsley, *Bandits, Prophets and Messiahs: Popular Movements at the Time of Jesus* (San Francisco: HarperSanFrancisco, 1988), 58, 60.

54. Matthew 9:10–11, 11:19; Mark 2:15–16; Luke 5:30, 7:34, 15:1. In Matthew 21:31–32, it was "tax collectors and harlots."

55. M. Nedarim 3.4.

56. M. Baba Kama 10.2; M. Tohorot 7.6. See also M. Hagiga 3.6.

57. M. Baba Kama 10.1.

58. Luke 3:12–13.

59. Luke 19:2, 8.

60. Luke 5:27–28.

61. Matthew 10:3.

62. Matthew 21:31. See below, pp. 346ff, for the Parable of the Pharisee and the Publican.

Both Matthew and Mark told of an incident in Bethany toward the end of Jesus' life in which a woman—another woman—entered the home of Simon the leper and anointed Jesus' head (Matthew 26:6–13, Mark 14:3–9). These reports represented an entirely different tradition and will not be discussed here.

63. Arland J. Hultgren, *The Parables of Jesus: A Commentary* (Grand Rapids, Mich.: William B. Eerdmans, 2002), 139.

64. Jeremias, *The Parables of Jesus*, 196.

65. Hultgren, *The Parables of Jesus*, 140.

66. Hultgren, *The Parables of Jesus*, 142–44; Jeremias, *The Parables of Jesus*, 196.

CHAPTER TWELVE

The Parable of a Rich Man Who Decided to Enjoy Himself

The Parable of a Rich Man Who Decided to Enjoy Himself

A prudent person plans for the future. During the summer he repairs the thatch on his roof to withstand the fall winds and winter rains to come. At the end of one harvest he lays aside seed to plant next season's crop. He builds larger storage facilities to protect possessions he expects to accumulate. But when does he cease? When can he stop saving and start to enjoy his accumulations?

Jesus told the tale of a wealthy man who decided to enjoy himself.

> And he told them a parable, saying, "The land of a rich man brought forth plentifully; and he thought to himself, 'What shall I do, for I have nowhere to store my crops?' And he said, 'I will do this: I will pull down my barns, and build larger ones; and there I will store all my grain and my goods. And I will say to my soul, Soul, you have ample goods laid up for many years; take your ease, eat, drink, be merry.' But God said to him, 'Fool! This night your soul is required of you; and the things you have prepared, whose will they be?' So is he who lays up treasure for himself, and is not rich toward God." (Luke 12:16–21)

The man owned barns full of produce and possessions, yet he was both a *sinner* and a *fool*.

He committed three grievous sins:

- He intended to use his assets to satisfy only himself—with no regard for the needs of others.

- He failed to acknowledge that God was the source of his success.
- He presumed that he and not God was in charge of his own destiny—even of the length of his life.

As Jewish sources indicate, these sins were well known to Jesus' Jewish audience.

The Earth Is the Lord's

When Samuel's mother Hannah gave her infant son into the care of Eli the priest at Shiloh, she recited a prayer of joy and thanksgiving in which she acknowledged, "All the earth is the Lord's."[1] David used the same phrase in Psalm 24: "The earth is the Lord's and the fullness thereof, the world and those who dwell therein."[2] In the New Testament, Paul repeated the same phrase.[3]

By the first century, both the phrase and the theology it represented had become an oft-quoted principle in Jewish thought. Not only did God create the universe, He owned it. He determined how its resources would be allocated and to whom.

In the same prayer, Hannah spoke these words: "The Lord makes poor and makes rich; He casts down, He also exalts."[4] No matter how ambitious a person was or how hard he worked, his wealth was a gift from God.[5] And God could rescind the money, the land, and the status instantaneously if He decided to do so. For God has set the world in order.[6]

To the person who has wealth but withholds contributions to the needy, God says: Remember that I made him poor and you rich, and I can send reverses against you and make you poor.[7]

In commenting on the conjunction in Deuteronomy 15:10, another sage compares economic successes and reverses to the turning of a wheel. God says: I made him poor and you rich. Don't cause me to turn the wheel and make you poor.[8]

The rich man in our parable sinned because he took pride in his wealth and did not acknowledge that God was the source of his success.

Do Justice

In discussing Psalm 82:3, a sage noted: It does not say "Have pity on" but "Do justice to."[9] It is a requirement, a moral obligation. And the sage closed by quoting "The earth is the Lord's and all the fullness thereof."[10]

Not only was success a gift from God, but it entailed obligations. Wealth was to be used to help the poor and the needy.

Sages told this story about the mother of Rabbi Tanhum bar Hiya. Though she only needed one pound of meat, when she went shopping she bought two pounds—one for her son and one for the poor. Why did God create both rich and poor? That one might be sustained by the other.[11]

One sage told this parable to illustrate the commandment "If your brother becomes poor and his hand fails you, you shall strengthen him" in Leviticus 25:35: "He is like a load resting on a wall. One man can hold it and prevent it from falling, but once it has fallen to the ground five men cannot raise it up again." He continued, "Even if you have strengthened him [helped him] four or five times, [if he needs it] you must strengthen him yet again."[12]

No commandment was more important than helping the poor. Rabbi Hiya said, "Whoever turns his eyes away from almsgiving is as if he worshipped idols [an abominable sin]."[13]

What we call charity today comes from the Latin word *caritas* and refers to free-will offerings of the heart. But the sages talked about *tzedaka*—righteousness—not voluntary contributions but acts of kindness required of all Jews. *Tzedaka* was a divine imperative. To turn aside from doing an act of charity was to break God's law.

The command in Deuteronomy 16:20 echoed through the centuries in the sayings of the prophets and the teachings of the sages: "You shall surely perform righteous acts."[14] The rich man in our parable sinned because he planned to use his wealth only for his own enjoyment.

Choose Life

Like property and possessions, life itself was a gift from God. According to Jewish tradition, humans had no power over its creation, its qualities and characteristics, or its conclusion. All were under God's control.[15]

As with wealth, the gift of life was to be used to fulfill God's will. "You shall therefore keep My laws and My ordinances, by doing which a man shall live."[16]

An early or sudden death was believed to be the penalty for sins. "For You, O God, will bring them down into the nethermost pit. Those murderous, treacherous people shall not live out half their days."[17] Rabbi Akiba taught that the years of a man's life were predetermined. If he was worthy, he lived the entire period. If he was not worthy, his years were reduced.[18]

The rich man in our parable sinned when he presumed that he controlled his destiny and the length of his life.

As well as being a sinner, the rich man was a *fool*. He should have known better.

- Jewish tradition warned him time and again not to concentrate on accumulating wealth but on attaining spiritual growth and well-being.
- On death, God will judge a person not on how much wealth he attained but on the spiritual and moral qualities of his life.
- Had he been other than a fool, he would have realized the vanity of hoarding wealth.

In reality, he had no control—not over his assets and not over his life. He died, and his wealth went to others. Despite his decision "to eat, drink, and be merry," he never enjoyed his riches himself.

What Secrets Did the Parable Convey?

According to Jesus, what happened to the rich man in the parable could happen to any person who gathered wealth only for his own enjoyment.

It was all right to accumulate wealth, but the wise man thought about becoming "rich" in God's sight—not in the eyes of his neighbors. His afterlife depended on it! "Do not lay up for yourselves treasures on earth, where moth and rust consume and where thieves break in and steal, but lay up for yourselves treasures in heaven."[19] Later Jesus said, "If you would be perfect, go, sell what you possess and give to the poor, and you will have treasure in heaven."[20]

In these regards, Jesus was teaching Jewish tradition.

The Epicureans

Epicurus taught that the gods lived a life of endless bliss and didn't care what happened to human beings. People should follow their example and achieve lives of undisturbed tranquility (*ataraxia*). The worst pains could be endured without losing happiness, and there was nothing to fear in death.

Later generations of Epicureans carried some of his ideas to excess—drinking, carousing, and sexual indulgences—in order to achieve a continuous state of bliss.

Jews abroad encountered Epicureans in Athens, Rome, and Alexandria, while Jews in Palestine could visit Epicurean centers in Gadera, Gaza, and Caesarea. Individual Epicureans may have journeyed to other holy-land communities as well. Under Antiochus Epiphanes, Epicureanism received particular support.[21]

While these ideas intrigued some Jews, the leaders of the Jewish community generally opposed them. Rabbi Eleazar taught, "Be alert to study the Law and know how to answer an Epicurean."[22] An unnamed sage said,

"These have no share in the World to Come: who says there is no resurrection of the dead, . . . [who says] the Law is not from Heaven, and an Epicurean."[23]

Eventually, the Aramaic word for Epicurean—*apikoros*—became a term of opprobrium, a frequent epithet applied to both Jews and non-Jews who opposed the teachings of the sages and led lives filled with indulgence and licentiousness.

Ecclesiastes

Five decades after the death of Epicurus, the author of Ecclesiastes noted that no human ever achieved absolute righteousness. "Surely there is not a righteous man on earth who does good and never sins."[24] So "don't be overly righteous, and don't make yourself overly wise. . . . Don't be overly wicked, and don't be a fool."[25] He admonished people to avoid the impossible and strive for moderation.

Again and again he wrote, "There is nothing better for a man than that he should eat and drink and find enjoyment in his toil."[26] Wealth is God's gift.[27] A person should enjoy the fruit of his hard work.

But the constant pursuit of riches—like the pursuit of power and status—ultimately was empty and without merit, worthless. "Vanity of vanities! All is vanity. What real value is there for a man in all the gains he makes."[28]

Rich and poor, slave and master, the wise man and the fool all suffered the same end. "The wise man dies just like the fool."[29] "What befalls the fool will befall me also."[30] It did no good to rail against one's fate or to try to overcome the inner workings of the universe. "What has been is what will be, and what has been done is what will be done. There is nothing new under the sun."[31]

Then why strive to acquire wisdom? Why try to act morally—"if all is futile and the pursuit of wind"?[32]

God "has no pleasure in fools."[33] Wisdom brought a man good fortune, protection, and joy. It helped him to both earn a livelihood and spend it advantageously. And it motivated him to live a virtuous life.[34] Better to choose wisdom than folly, advised the author of Ecclesiastes.

In the Parable of the Rich Man Who Decided to Enjoy Himself, Jesus alluded to and extended these images in the book of Ecclesiastes. It was not enough merely to use your resources wisely and enjoy the benefits God had given you. God expected more of you. Change your ways today, Jesus advised, lest you die tonight as both a *sinner* and a *fool*.

Jesus' Teaching about Worldly Goods

An introduction provided the context of the parable. A younger brother appealed to Jesus to convince the older to give him his portion of the inheritance.[35] Jesus declined to resolve the dispute. Instead, he told the Parable of the Rich Man Who Decided to Enjoy Himself.

It is unclear whether the younger brother addressed Jesus from the crowd or whether he waited until after the crowd dispersed and approached him privately.[36] A few verses later, Jesus addressed his disciples,[37] yet his advice applied to the larger audience and represented his teaching about worldly goods.

"Take heed, and beware of all covetousness; for a man's life does not consist in the abundance of his possessions."[38] "Do not be anxious about your life, what you shall eat, nor about your body, what you shall put on, for life is more than food, and the body more than clothing."[39] In short, the possession of property was irrelevant to survival in the World to Come. "Do not seek what you are to eat and what you are to drink, nor be of anxious mind, for all the nations of the world seek these things. . . . Instead, seek His kingdom, and these things shall be yours as well."[40]

Jesus' intent was not merely to emphasize the notions that no person knows the day of his death and that sometimes death comes suddenly. His focus was on God's kingdom, on the approaching holocaust, and on the certain knowledge that all the people in his audience would die painfully if he couldn't change their beliefs and behavior.

They were just as foolish as the rich man who died suddenly if they concerned themselves with property and possessions when the cataclysm had already begun.

Notes

1. LVB (*The Living Bible*) 1 Samuel 2:8. Other translations have "the pillars of the earth are the Lord's."

2. Psalm 24:1. The translation is according to the old JPS (The Jewish Publications Society edition of *The Holy Scriptures*), the KJV, and the RSV. The new JPS renders "The earth is the Lord's and all that it holds; the world and its inhabitants." See also David's prayer in 1 Chronicles 29:11.

3. 1 Corinthians 10:26. See also Acts 4:24, 17:24.

4. 1 Samuel 2:7.

5. Ecclesiastes 5:18.

6. 1 Samuel 2:8. See also Psalm 24:2, Deuteronomy 8:17–18, Ecclesiastes 6:2, Hosea 12:8–9, Job 42:10.

7. Tanhuma Mishpatim §8, as noted in George Foot Moore, *Judaism in the First Centuries of the Christian Era* (Cambridge, Mass.: Harvard University Press, 1927), vol. 2, 169.

8. The Hebrew conjunction *biglal* ("because") is derived from the same verb root as *galgal* ("wheel"). Both are things that "go around." See Moore, *Judaism in the First Centuries of the Christian Era*, vol. 2, 169.

9. Midrash on Psalm 82, as presented in Claude G. Montefiore and H. Loewe, *A Rabbinic Anthology* (London: Macmillan, 1938), 385–86.

10. Psalm 24:1.

11. Pesikta Rabbati 191b, as presented in Montefiore and Loewe, *A Rabbinic Anthology*, 439.

12. Sifra 109b, as presented in Montefiore and Loewe, *A Rabbinic Anthology*, 412.

13. Ketubot 68a, as presented in Montefiore and Loewe, *A Rabbinic Anthology*, 413.

14. The Hebrew word *tzedek* also means "justice," but this translation emphasizes the notion that charity is also a divine obligation.

15. 1 Samuel 2:6; Psalm 49:7–9, 104:29–30; Job 4:9, 34:14–15.

16. Leviticus 18:5. See also Deuteronomy 32:46–47.

17. Psalm 55:24 (= Greek Psalm 55:23a). See also Psalm 37:35–36; Proverbs 10:27; Job 15:32, 22:16.

18. Yevamot 50a, as presented in Ephraim E. Urbach, *The Sages: Their Concepts and Beliefs* (Cambridge, Mass.: Harvard University Press, 1987), 265.

19. Matthew 6:19.

20. Matthew 19:21.

21. From 175 to 164 BCE, Antiochus IV Epiphanes was the ruler of the Syrian empire, which included Palestine. See H. A. Fischel, "Epicureanism," in *Encyclopedia Judaica*, ed. Cecil Roth (Jerusalem: Macmillan, 1971–1972), vol. 6, 818.

22. M. Avot 2:14.

23. M. Sanhedrin 10:1.

24. Ecclesiastes 7:20.

25. Ecclesiastes 7:16–17. My translation.

26. Ecclesiastes 2:24. See also 3:12, 22; 5:19; 8:15; 9:9.

27. Ecclesiastes 2:24. See also 3:13, 5:18, 6:2, 8:15.

28. Ecclesiastes 1:2–3. My translation.

29. Ecclesiastes 2:16. See also 2:14b, 6:8.

30. Ecclesiastes 2:15.

31. Ecclesiastes 1:9.

32. Ecclesiastes 2:17.

33. Ecclesiastes 5:3 (= Greek Ecclesiastes 5:4).

34. Ecclesiastes 2:26; 7:11–12, 16–17, 19.

35. The elder brother would rather keep the inheritance undivided. Jeremias suggests that such a jointly held inheritance was praised in Psalm 133:1 ("Behold how good and pleasant it is for brethren to dwell together in unity") and undergirded Matt. 6.24; Luke

16:13 ("No servant can serve two masters"). See Jeremias, *The Parables of Jesus*, rev. ed. (New York: Charles Scribner's Sons, 1963), 164 and 194, note 1.

36. Luke 12:13.

37. Luke 12:22.

38. Luke 12:15.

39. Luke 12:22–23.

40. Luke 12:29–31.

CHAPTER THIRTEEN

Parables about Dinners and Banquets

The Parable of the Royal Wedding Feast

Excited about the coming marriage of his son, a king planned an elaborate wedding feast and invited many people to attend. As the date drew near, he reminded those invited of the celebration. Quite a few indicated they could not attend. He sent out his servants again the day before the wedding, and they repeated his words to each invited guest: "Everything is ready. Come to the marriage feast." But the guests rejected the reminder and murdered the messengers. Enraged, the king sent his troops to kill the murderers and raze their city.

Then the king instructed his servants to go into the streets and invite everyone they saw to the wedding feast. Eventually, the banquet hall was filled with guests.

> Again Jesus spoke to them in parables, saying, "The kingdom of heaven may be compared to a king who gave a marriage feast for his son, and sent his servants to call those who were invited to the marriage feast; but they would not come. Again he sent other servants, saying, 'Tell those who are invited, Behold, I have made ready my dinner, my oxen and my fat calves are killed, and everything is ready; come to the marriage feast.' But they made light of it and went off, one to his farm, another to his business, while the rest seized his servants, treated them shamefully, and killed them. The king was angry, and he sent his troops and destroyed those murderers and burned their city. Then he said to his servants, 'The wedding is ready, but those invited were not worthy. Go therefore to the thoroughfares, and invite to the marriage feast as many as you find.' And those servants went out into the streets and gathered all whom they found, both bad and good; so the wedding hall was filled with guests." (Matthew 22:1–10)

To Whom Did Jesus' Parable Apply?

The invitation of the king was a command to attend; yet even when the servants came to get them, those invited refused to come. Some fled to their fields, some to their businesses. The few still left in the city killed the king's servants.

Why would ministers of the court, wealthy merchants, businessmen, and priests insult the king? Why would they kill his servants and put their status, property, and families at risk?

Jesus' listeners knew the invited guests acted foolishly and would suffer the king's wrath. Who were these foolish respondents? To whom did Jesus' metaphor apply?

As usual, Jesus here presented a parable with many meanings. His listeners could apprehend some or all of its meanings. Three interpretations were possible.

In the first interpretation, God was the king and the prophets were His servants. Jesus declared that Jews were rejecting God's laws and abusing His prophets. Especially wicked were the leaders of the people. Like their ancestors, they would suffer devastation and destruction.[1]

In this interpretation, Jesus affirmed his status as a *prophet*. Like the biblical prophets, Jesus also faced humiliation and rejection from the very people he sought to warn.[2] Jesus may even have been hinting that, like some prophets, he too would be killed.[3]

In the second interpretation, Jesus was the king and the disciples were his messengers. Jesus asserted that by rejecting his teachings and abusing his disciples, Jews denied God's law. Especially rebellious were the leaders of the people. They would suffer devastation and death.[4] In this interpretation, Jesus not only affirmed his status as a *prophet* but subtly implanted in his listeners' minds the image that he was a *king*.

The wedding banquet reminded his listeners of the great feast by which the Messianic reign would be established.[5] According to some sages, only Israelites would partake. Others suggested that righteous gentiles would also participate.[6] Jesus asserted that anyone who truly repented and based his behavior on Jesus' teaching would enjoy life in God's kingdom—Jew and gentile.[7]

In the third interpretation, God was the king and Jesus was the son getting married. The refusal to attend the king's feast was a deliberate affront to both the king and his son. Jesus reminded his listeners that as God's *son* he possessed some of His authority and ruling power.

Later Christian tradition emphasized this last interpretation: God was the king, Jesus was the son, and the apostles (and later the Church) were the servants.[8] The invited guests who refused to come were the Jews who rejected Jesus and his teachings. The guests brought in from the streets were the Jews and gentiles who accepted Jesus and his teachings. Only believers in Jesus would survive to enjoy the celebration of the establishment of God's kingdom. The rest of the Jewish people—including their the leaders and teachers—would be annihilated.

While some of Jesus' followers may have understood the parable in that way, most of his listeners did not. Jesus' divinity was not widely accepted in the Jewish community. The phrase "son of God" meant something entirely different to first-century Jews than it did to Christians in subsequent centuries.[9]

Jewish Weddings

According to the Hebrew Bible, marriage was the natural state for men and women and the fulfillment of God's plan. "The Lord God said, 'It is not good for man to be alone. . . . Therefore a man leaves his father and his mother and clings to his wife, so that they become one flesh.'"[10] Although polygamy had been practiced by the patriarchs and by the upper classes during the early years of the monarchy,[11] the biblical conception of marriage was essentially monogamous[12] and the many references to marriage in later biblical literature took it for granted that a man had only one wife.[13]

The sages extolled marriage. Pointing to various biblical passages, Rabbi Jacob said, "One who has no wife remains without good, without a helper, without joy, without blessing and without atonement." Others added, "Without peace and without life." Another said, "He is not a whole person." Others said that the unmarried man "diminishes the likeness [of God]."[14]

As a consequence, celibacy was not common in the first century and was disapproved by the rabbis. According to Rabbi Ishmael, a man should be married at eighteen. Since God commanded humans to "be fruitful and multiply,"[15] if a man passed twenty without taking a wife, he transgressed against God's law and deserved to be punished.[16]

The Essenes disagreed. In rejecting worldly pleasures, they also rejected marriage and practiced continence.[17] While some members of the Qumran community were married and had children, most were single and celibate.[18] As a consequence of its prohibition against procreation, the Qumran community constantly had to attract new members to replace those who departed or died, or decline in numbers.[19]

Jesus also taught that abstinence was superior to sexual intercourse, though not everyone was capable of such control. "There are eunuchs who have been so from birth, and there are eunuchs who have been made eunuchs by men, and there are eunuchs who have made themselves eunuchs for the sake of the kingdom of heaven. He who is able to receive this, let him receive it."[20] The ideal was to remain a celibate "for the sake of the kingdom of heaven."

In his letter to the Christian community in Corinth, Paul promoted celibacy. "It is well for a man not to touch a woman."[21] Marriage was a concession to human weakness. "To the unmarried and the widows I say that it is well for them to remain single as I do. But if they cannot exercise self-control, they should marry. For it is better to marry than to be aflame with passion."[22]

While there had been marriage celebrations in biblical times, the details were vague. When Jacob and Leah married, "Laban gathered all the people of the place and made a feast."[23] As groom, Samson posed a riddle for his guests and gave them a week to solve it.[24] Processions and music were part of the celebrations, and the bride and groom wore special attire.[25]

By the first century, the details were widely known. The Jewish wedding consisted of two ceremonies—*kiddushin* and *nisu'in*. Usually they occurred one after another on the same occasion, but theoretically they could be separated by as much as a year. In a technical sense, both were marriage ceremonies. A bride who completed only the *kiddushin* portion was her husband's wife and required a divorce before she was free to marry again—even if she never finished the *nisu'in* section.[26]

During the *kiddushin* ceremony, in the presence of at least two male witnesses, the groom gave his bride a gift of value (usually a ring) and recited the wedding formula: "With this ring, you are consecrated unto me as my wife according to the law of Moses and Israel."[27] The bride and groom praised God in the blessing over wine and drank from a common cup. They recited a second blessing, which read: "Blessed are You, O Lord our God, King of the Universe, . . . who disallowed unto us those who are betrothed to us, but sanctified unto us those who are married to us. . . . Blessed are You, O Lord, who hallows Your people Israel by prescribing marriage under a bridal canopy and by a sacred ceremony."[28] Since cohabitation was forbidden until after *nisu'in*, this benediction was a warning to the bride and groom not to sleep together until the second ceremony was completed.

During the *nisu'in* ceremony, seven blessings were recited over the bride and groom, and the bride took up her residence in the groom's household.[29] At that point, the wedding was complete.

Processions were part of the celebration. Often accompanied by music, the two wedding parties left their places of assembly separately and merged at an arranged location—usually at the bridegroom's home—where the wedding feast took place.[30]

A joyous celebration followed the wedding ceremonies, with food, drink, singing, and dancing. There was a dispute between the schools of Hillel and Shammai as to how one should dance before the bride;[31] Rav Aha even danced with the bride on his shoulders.[32]

By attending a wedding ceremony and celebration, a person fulfilled one of God's commandments; whoever entertained the bride and groom was comparable to a person who offered a thanksgiving sacrifice at the Temple.[33] Sages interrupted their lessons and, with their students, joined the wedding procession.

A gentile lady once asked Jose ben Halafta how God had occupied Himself since creating the universe. "He's engaged in matching couples for marriage," the sage replied. The lady declared she could do as well herself and mated a thousand male and female slaves. The next morning they came to her—one with a cracked head, another with an eye gouged out, and a third with a broken leg. One man said, "I don't want her"; another said, "I don't want him." Whereupon the lady admitted that the task of creating successful marriages was worthy of both God's attention and intelligence.[34]

Jesus, his family, and his disciples attended a wedding in the village of Cana, a few miles north of Nazareth. According to John, when the groom's family ran out of wine at the wedding feast, Jesus instructed servants to fill six thirty-gallon jars to the brim with water. When the steward tasted the water, it had turned to fine wine.[35] In the Parable of the Ten Maidens, Jesus alluded to young ladies waiting for the groom to come to the bride's house for the wedding celebration.[36] In addition, Jesus talked about the wedding feast in his response regarding the rules of fasting, in his instructions to his followers, and in the Parable on the Place of Honor.[37] The Parable of the Royal Wedding Feast was Jesus' most elaborate exploration of a Jewish wedding celebration.

Son of God

In the Hebrew Bible, Israel was God's son. "Israel is my first-born son."[38] "When Israel was a child, I loved him, and out of Egypt I called my son."[39] "And you shall say to Pharaoh, . . . 'Let my son go that he may serve me.'"[40]

The people of Israel shared a special relationship with God, a relationship that entailed special responsibilities. "You are the children of the Lord your

God. You shall not gash yourselves or shave the front of your heads because the dead."[41]

Isaiah promised that one day Israel would be redeemed and reunited. "I will say to the north, 'Give back!' and to the south, 'Do not withhold! Bring my sons from afar and my daughters from the end of the earth.'"[42] Then "the number of the people of Israel shall be like the sands of the sea, which cannot be measured or counted. Instead of being told, 'You are not My people,' they shall be called, 'children of the living God.'"[43]

These same images occurred in postbiblical literature. Israel was the son of God.[44] Jacob was His first-born son, and Jacob's descendants were God's children.[45] God punished them like a father and considered the righteous to be His children.[46] Sometime in the future, God would be reunited with His children.[47]

David was also called God's son,[48] and the psalmists applied the term to his successors.[49] Occasionally, God addressed the Messiah as "My son."[50] And some Jews may have interpreted Psalm 2 to refer to Israel's future Redeemer, a descendent of King David.[51]

The New Testament sometimes referred to Israel as God's son.[52] In general, however, the "sons of God" were Jesus' followers and supporters. In this regard, we see a shift in understanding. No longer were the people of Israel or even the righteous "children of God." According to Jesus, those Jews who rejected his teachings and continued their erroneous behavior were sinners. They would not be saved. Only those who accepted Jesus' insights and synchronized their behavior to his ideas obeyed God's will. They were the true children of God. In the coming apocalypse, they would be saved.

While everyone in his fellowship was a child of God, Jesus himself was unique. He was the perfect exemplar, the son of God par excellence. No other person could match his understandings, his talents, and his behavior. By following Jesus, they would overcome the vicissitudes of their current lives. The Romans would no longer oppress them; taxes would no longer plague them. There would be plenty to eat and God's Presence to enjoy. No wonder they began to identify Jesus with the Messiah. In their minds, he was leading them toward the same long-awaited redemption.

The term "son of God" conveyed to believers all the extraordinary qualities, power, and status they saw in Jesus. Eventually, it was capitalized and became "Son of God."

Jesus never used the phrase about himself. "Son of God" was a designation others gave him. When speaking of himself, Jesus used the term "son of man."[53]

The Parable of the Misdressed Wedding Guest

The story of the royal wedding feast was supplemented by the following parable.[54] At a wedding feast, the king noticed that one of his guests was not wearing proper attire. The king asked him how he got in without wearing a "wedding garment." Receiving no response, the king had the guest bound and tossed outside into the darkness.

> But when the king came in to look at the guests, he saw there a man who had no wedding garment; and he said to him, 'Friend, how did you get in here without a wedding garment?' And he was speechless. Then the king said to the attendants, 'Bind him hand and foot, and cast him into the outer darkness; there men will weep and gnash their teeth.' For many are called, but few are chosen. (Matthew 22:11–14)

What Secrets Did the Parable Convey?

How is it that all the other guests secured proper attire for the wedding feast but this guest did not?

Scholars propose a number of scenarios to answer this question.

"Proper attire" may have meant something ordinary, like modest dress that covered the arms and legs or clean clothes, which this guest deliberately rejected—thereby showing intentional disrespect for or rebellion against the king.

It is possible that the guests who came to the wedding were given clothes to wear by the king's servants and that this guest deliberately disregarded the garment provided—thereby again indicating his disrespect for or rebellion against the king. In 2 Kings 10:22, King Jehu directed the wardrobe master to provide garments for all the worshippers of Baal—an indication that special clothes were kept by the king to clothe invited guests—but there is no example of such a custom in the time of Jesus.

Perhaps this guest did not enter the wedding feast properly. As a result, he did not receive the clothes. He was an intruder who had sneaked in and had not been attended to by the king's servants. In another context, Jesus said, "He who does not enter the sheepfold by the door but climbs in by another way, that man is a thief and a robber."[55]

Perhaps a physical garment was not intended. The Greek word *enduma* referred to something a person put on *like* a garment—an attitude or a demeanor. This guest did not display the proper attitude or behavior.

I believe this last suggestion was what Jesus had in mind. What the guest lacked was not a physical garment but an attitude. He had not repented. His behavior reflected no change of heart, no new understanding. As a consequence, he was ineligible for God's kingdom.[56]

That's why the guest had no answer to the king's question. There was no acceptable answer.

Jeremias cites a rabbinic parallel that supports this contention. Attributed to Rabban Johanan ben Zakkai, who lived a generation after Jesus, the parable told of a king who invited guests to a banquet but did not specify the hour. The wise attired themselves, while the foolish continued to work. The summons came suddenly. Those who were properly attired were admitted to enjoy the banquet; those who were not dressed in clean clothes were not admitted.

The parable occurred in a discussion about repentance. Rabbi Eliezer said, "Repent one day before your death." The scholars asked him, "How can a person know the day of his death?" He answered, "Since he may die tomorrow, it's imperative that he repents today. In this manner, he will be in a state of penitence throughout his life."[57]

In this instance, the proper attire for the banquet was repentance. And so it was in Jesus' Parable of the Misdressed Wedding Guest.

Garments of Salvation

There was another garment Jesus may have had in mind—a wedding garment God Himself would provide. The prophet Isaiah promised:

> He [God] has clothed me with garments of triumph,
> Wrapped me in a robe of victory,
> Like a bridegroom adorned with a turban,
> Like a bride bedecked with her jewels. (Isaiah 61:10)[58]

On Judgment Day, God would clothe the redeemed in wedding clothes— "garments of salvation" and "a robe of righteousness."

Ethiopian Enoch described the robe as follows: "And this shall be your clothing: a garment of life from the Lord of Spirits. Your clothing shall not grow old, and your dominion shall not pass away from before the Lord of Spirits."[59]

Jesus himself spoke of God's Kingdom as an occasion for a new garment and new wine.[60] In the Parable of the Father and His Two Sons, following his son's contrite repentance the father clothed his returning son in the finest robe and prepared a banquet for him.[61]

As Isaiah predicted and as Jesus taught, those who repented and obeyed God's laws would survive the coming apocalypse. Clothed in "garments of salvation," they would feast at the banquet God prepared for them.

Jesus Built on Jewish Images

A widely held rabbinic view of God was affirmed in this parable. God (the king) not only viewed his guests in a general way but examined each and every guest individually. Even in the midst of a crowd, no one—not a single guest—would escape His scrutiny. "Their ways are continually before Him; they cannot be hidden from His eyes."[62]

The sages taught that God waited to receive a sinner's confession and removed every obstacle that might hinder a sinner's penitence from reaching Him. The gates of prayer sometimes closed, but the gates of repentance never closed.[63] According to one Midrash, God held open the door to encourage Adam's repentance, but Adam declined the opportunity.[64] When the angels closed the openings in the firmament through which confessions ascended to God's ears, God drilled a hole beneath His throne where the angels dared not venture.[65]

In Jewish tradition, the World to Come was compared to a feast. "On this mountain the Lord of hosts will make for all peoples a banquet of rich viands, a feast of choice wines. . . . He will destroy death forever."[66]

The same image was emphasized in the New Testament. "Many will come from east and west and sit at table with Abraham, Isaac, and Jacob in the kingdom of heaven."[67]

The Parable of the Great Banquet

A man once gave a great banquet and invited many to attend. On the day of the banquet, he sent his servant to tell those who had been invited that everything was ready. The guests offered excuses and declined to attend. In anger the host told his servant to go into the streets and "bring in the poor and maimed and blind and lame." He concluded, "None of those men who were invited shall taste my banquet."

> He said to him, "A man once gave a great banquet, and invited many; and at the time for the banquet he sent his servant to say to those who had been invited, 'Come; for all is now ready.' But they all alike began to make excuses. The first said to him, 'I have bought a field, and I must go out and see it; I pray you, have

me excused.' And another said, 'I have bought five yoke of oxen, and I go to examine them; I pray you, have me excused.' And another said, 'I have married a wife,
and therefore I cannot come.' So the servant came and reported this to his master.
Then the householder in anger said to his servant, 'Go out quickly to the streets
and lanes of the city, and bring in the poor and maimed and blind and lame.' And
the servant said, 'Sir, what you commanded has been done, and still there is room.'
And the master said to the servant, 'Go out to the highways and hedges, and compel people to come in, that my house may be filled. For I tell you, none of those
men who were invited shall taste my banquet.'" (Luke 14:16–24)

What Secrets Did the Parable Convey?
Scholars have noted the points of resemblance between this parable and the
Parable of the Royal Wedding Feast. Few have considered the many differ-
ences.

- This parable in Luke was told in the home of one of the chief Pharisees,
  probably in some town in Perea. The parable in Matthew was told
  within the Temple precinct in Jerusalem, as Pharisaic opposition to
  Jesus reached a climax.
- The invited guests in the parable in Luke offered excuses and apologies.
  The refusal of the guests to come to the wedding feast in Matthew was
  markedly more offensive and coupled with escalated violence and
  murder.
- In this parable, the host was a wealthy private citizen. In Matthew, the
  host was a king.
- In Luke retribution was limited to exclusion from the banquet. In Matthew, the punishment was the slaughter of the murderers and the
  destruction of their city.
- In the Parable of the Royal Wedding Feast, much of the story focused
  on the many occasions the servants reminded the invited guests about
  the banquet and their reactions to these announcements. In this parable, much of the story described the attempts of the servant to bring
  strangers far and wide to the banquet and the kind of people they were.
- In the first, the king involved several groups of servants. In this parable,
  the host used only one servant.

Why these significant differences?
Here are some possible explanations:

- Both parables teach the same lessons. Jesus was just being more dramatic in Matthew than in Luke.

- Jesus shared the Parable of the Great Banquet on more than one occasion. On one occasion, he emphasized one aspect of the story; on another, he concentrated on a different element. In telling the story, Matthew and Luke reproduced these differences Jesus himself had articulated.
- The differences reflected the viewpoint of each gospel writer more than they represented actual differences in Jesus' message.

While most scholars accept the third suggestion, I believe the second explanation is correct. The stories were a reflection of different areas of emphasis in Jesus' own teachings.

In both parables, the banquet depicted the glorious experiences of the redeemed in God's kingdom after the impending catastrophe. And both stories emphasized that those people who refused the invitation would not survive the holocaust to share God's bounties in the New Era.

Who Were the People Invited to the Banquet?

Who was originally invited?

While Matthew didn't specify, Jesus' audience understood that a king would invite noblemen, aristocrats, and members of the social elite to celebrate his son's marriage. In Palestinian-Jewish society, the elite included the High Priest, his chief priests, their relatives and family members; surviving members of the Hasmonean royal family; leaders of the Sadducees and Pharisees and their families; and wealthy landowners, merchants, businessmen, and tax collectors, and the members of their families. All refused the invitation. Some continued their agricultural and business pursuits; others belittled, brutalized, or murdered the king's servants.

The same kinds of people were invited in Luke's tale. They bought and sold land and purchased blocks of oxen at a time. They were the wealthy, powerful, and influential aristocratic elite, who did business with the Romans, taxed the Jews, and ran the cities.

In Matthew, they were replaced by people from the streets—ordinary people—cheese makers, butchers, donkey drivers, carpenters, masons, wheelwrights, smiths, their family members and helpers, porters, servants, travelers, and beggars. These were the kind of people in Jesus' audiences—the people neglected, ignored, and often despised by the social elite.

Luke widened the gap between the aristocracy and the people who actually attended the banquet. The host instructed the servant to bring in not just ordinary people but those on the margins of society, "the poor and maimed and blind and lame."

First the servant went nearby "to the streets and lanes of the city." Then he went out into the countryside "to the highways and hedges" to find guests to fill his master's hall. He brought in "the poor and maimed and blind and lame," not just from the cities but also from farms and villages throughout the land, areas experiencing economic hardships, oppressive debt, and burdensome taxation, people frequently neglected by the very aristocracy that demanded their fidelity and respect.

Who Was the Servant?

Who was this servant? And why was only one servant mentioned in Luke, whereas groups of servants were noted in Matthew?

In Matthew, the servants represented the prophets—both ancient and contemporary—who conveyed God's message that (1) God was displeased with the rampant lawlessness and hypocrisy of the Jews (especially of the leaders of the people); (2) unless they changed their behavior, these sinners would experience devastation, disaster, and death (their high status would not protect or save them); and (3) the righteous would be rescued and rewarded: "I will turn their mourning to joy, I will comfort them and cheer them in their grief. . . . My people shall enjoy My full bounty, declares the Lord."[68]

In Luke, the servant was Jesus. As far as Jesus was concerned, the time for judgment had arrived. The banquet was ready, as were the weapons of God's retribution. The apocalypse would begin at any moment, and the acknowledged leaders and teachers of the people would suffer and die in the catastrophe. They would not participate in the great banquet God had prepared for the righteous. Only the poor, the blind and the lame, the humble and the meek, the self-sacrificing and the sympathetic would survive.

This was Jesus' message—especially to the Pharisees, Sadducees, and sages in his audiences. There was no more time; the banquet had begun. Either they repented and righted their relationships with God or they would be left out *forever*.

Jews and Non-Jews in Heaven

After the servant brought in the poor, the maimed, the blind, and the lame from the city streets, he reported there still was room in the banquet hall. He was told to gather more guests from the "highways and hedges"—that is, from the roads and farms outside of town. As a consequence, additional invitations were extended.

Jeremias has suggested that the infirm and the disadvantaged already in the city referred to Jews who accepted Jesus' teachings and that the guests who lived beyond the city were non-Jews who converted.[69] The two invitations indicated more than the host's desire to fill every place at the banquet. They voiced Jesus' teaching that both Jews and gentiles would be welcome in God's kingdom.

In his response to the Roman centurion who pleaded with Jesus to heal his servant, Jesus clearly indicated that gentiles have a place in God's kingdom. "Truly, I say to you, not even in Israel have I found such faith. I tell you, many will come from east and west and sit at table with Abraham, Isaac, and Jacob in the kingdom of heaven, while the sons of the kingdom will be thrown into the outer darkness; there men will weep and gnash their teeth."[70]

The Parable of the Ten Maidens

Jesus compared the kingdom of heaven to ten maidens who took their lamps and went to greet the bridegroom. Five brought no oil to replace the fuel that burned while they waited, but the other five took extra jugs of oil with their lamps. At midnight they were awakened by the announcement that the bridegroom approached. The five prepared maidens lit their lamps and went to meet the bridegroom. The other five ran to find more olive oil, and the bridegroom arrived while they were away. Only those maidens who were prepared accompanied him into the marriage feast. The other maidens arrived after the door was shut, and the host would not let them in.

> The kingdom of heaven shall be compared to ten maidens who took their lamps and went to meet the bridegroom. Five of them were foolish, and five were wise. For when the foolish took their lamps, they took no oil with them; but the wise took flasks of oil with their lamps. As the bridegroom was delayed, they all slumbered and slept. But at midnight there was a cry, "Behold, the bridegroom! Come out to meet him." Then all those maidens rose and trimmed their lamps. And the foolish said to the wise, "Give us some of your oil, for our lamps are going out." But the wise replied, "Perhaps there will not be enough for us and for you; go rather to the dealers and buy for yourselves." And while they went to buy, the bridegroom came, and those who were ready went in with him to the marriage feast; and the

door was shut. Afterward the other maidens came also, saying, "Lord, lord, open to us." But he replied, "Truly, I say to you, I do not know you." (Matthew 25:1–12)

What Secrets Did the Parable Convey?

Most Jews in Jesus' audiences would understand two images suggested by this parable. In the first, the bridegroom was a metaphor for the coming kingdom.

Once again, Jesus likened God's kingdom to a wedding celebration. Only those prepared would attend and enjoy the festivities. All others, though they expected to participate and pleaded to be allowed into the reception, would be excluded.

No one knew exactly when the kingdom of God would begin. Therefore, every person ought to set his life in order continuously so as to properly welcome the New Age the moment it started.

In the second image, the bridegroom was God. Jesus reminded his listeners that on Judgment Day God would examine each person's life and determine who would enter His kingdom and who would remain outside in the darkness. Pleading and praying would be ineffective then. God's decisions would be irrevocable. That Day of Judgment could begin at any moment.[71]

In each of these assertions, Jesus was reinforcing Jewish ideas.

Some of his supporters may have derived a third image from in the story, one that reinforced their perception of Jesus' unique role in human history. They might have imagined the bridegroom was Jesus. Jesus' presence and preaching indicated that the kingdom of God had arrived. The feast could begin at any moment.

This was a perception peculiar to Jesus' followers and not understood or shared by most Jews in the first century.

The Fate of the Five Unprepared Maidens

The five maidens who prepared themselves joined the wedding procession, accompanied the groom into the celebration, and enjoyed the feast. They were "locked in" and safe. But what about the five young ladies who were locked out and refused entry? What happened to them?

They were destined to die. The darkness would be permanent. The cataclysm about which the biblical prophets spoke, the sages taught, and Jesus and his disciples preached had already begun. All nations on earth would be purged, and everyone not invited into the banquet would be killed.

Though he couched this parable in the future, it was an immediate future. The bridegroom was on his way and would arrive at any minute. Be prepared,

Jesus was saying. Get yourselves ready. Even if he tarried until midnight, that was just a few hours away.

Be Prepared

The sudden arrival of the bridegroom had parallels in Jesus' teachings about a flood that found people unprepared, about the unexpected entry of a thief, and about the unanticipated return of the estate owner from a feast or journey.[72] The common elements in these stories were the sudden and unexpected arrival of a person or event and the devastation that followed.

The Parable of the Ten Maidens was a warning. God's joyous kingdom awaited those properly prepared, but would bring death and darkness to those unprepared. "Be ready," Jesus said, "for the son of man is coming at an hour you do not expect."[73]

Message to the Members of His Fellowship

While the maidens represented the Jewish community at large, Jesus also may have included a special message to the members of his fellowship: There was no automatic entry into the kingdom of heaven. Everything depended on maintaining proper behavior. The foolish maidens who came unprepared and were rejected could include Jesus' followers.

Jesus said, "Not every one who says to me, 'Lord, Lord,' shall enter the kingdom of heaven."[74] Jesus continued, directing his remarks specifically to the disciples. "On that day many will say to me, 'Lord, Lord, did we not prophesy in your name, and cast out demons in your name, and do many mighty works in your name?' And then will I declare to them, 'I never knew you; depart from me, you evildoers.'"[75]

They must have been shocked. Some had left their families and given up their livelihoods, followed him from town to town, gone on distant journeys for him to preach and heal, and suffered humiliation on his behalf. They were his closest supporters, and still he called them "evildoers." What did he mean?

At least two understandings are possible.

Jesus was reminding even his disciples that they could do more. Their faith was not as strong as it could be. Their worries about their ultimate status and well-being indicated misplaced priorities. Their squabbles among themselves pointed to an unbecoming haughtiness. In that sense, the disciples were still "evildoers."

Jesus was reminding even his disciples that they—like all humans—were potentially "evildoers." They could backslide and sin—and be excluded from

God's kingdom. Their good work to date did not guarantee them entry. Only if they remained repentant and continued to succor and care for others would they be welcomed into the celebration of God's vindication.

The Narrow Gate

In that sense, entry into heaven was through a narrow door. "And someone said to him, 'Lord, will those who are saved be few?' And he said to them, 'Strive to enter by the narrow door; for many, I tell you, will seek to enter and will not be able.' "[76]

On another occasion, Jesus contrasted the gate to sin and devastation with the gate to morality and everlasting life. "The gate is wide and the way is easy that leads to destruction, and those who enter by it are many. . . . The gate is narrow and the way is hard that leads to life, and those who find it are few."[77] Jesus called on his listeners to choose the moral path and "enter by the narrow gate."[78]

The Master Will Reject Those Outside

In the Parable of the Ten Maidens, the door could not be opened from the outside. Someone inside had to open the door to let in the five foolish maidens. So the maidens stood outside in the dark and pounded on the door, pleading with the master of the house, "Lord, lord, open to us." But he replied, "Truly, I say to you, I do not know you."[79]

Jesus' audience recognized the double entendre. The Hebrew word *adon* ("master, lord") usually referred to the master of a house or the owner of an estate, but it also meant God. Jesus warned his listeners to prepare themselves for the coming of God's kingdom, lest they wind up in the darkness pleading for their lives and God responded, "I do not know you."

Jesus presented the same idea on another occasion using a slightly different metaphor. Having finished his work, the homeowner locked the door. "Once the householder has risen up and shut the door, you will begin to stand outside and to knock at the door, saying, 'Lord, open to us.' He will answer you, 'I do not know where you come from.' Then you will begin to say, 'We ate and drank in your presence, and you taught in our streets.' But he will say, 'I tell you, I do not know where you come from; depart from me, all you workers of iniquity!' "[80]

At the Final Judgment, God would reject the "workers of iniquity" among the Jewish people. They would be left out of the kingdom of heaven and be condemned to suffer darkness, devastation, and death.

The bridegroom was on his way. He could arrive at any moment. With his arrival, the cataclysm would begin. Human civilization would crumble. Even the stars in heaven would change. And it would happen within this generation. So Jesus warned his listeners, "When you see all these things, you know that he is near, at the very gates."[81]

The Meaning of the Oil in the Parable

The disciples healed by anointing others with oil,[82] and the Samaritan treated the wounds of the traveler with oil.[83] On one occasion, Jesus dined with Peter and others in the home of a Pharisee when a woman entered and washed Jesus' feet. From an alabaster flask she poured oil and rubbed it on his feet.[84]

Perhaps this was the meaning of the oil in the Parable of the Ten Maidens. The oil represented the healing and care the first five maidens provided. The other maidens hadn't performed similar good deeds before the bridegroom arrived.

In the Parable of the House Built on Rock, Jesus defined who was wise and who was foolish. "Every one then who hears these words of mine and does them will be like a wise man. . . . And every one who hears these words of mine and does not do them will be like a foolish man."[85]

These definitions applied to the ten maidens in this parable. The five prepared maidens accepted Jesus' teachings and behaved accordingly. They would enter the kingdom of heaven and enjoy the banquet. The five maidens who did not would be locked out and perish.

Verse 13

According to Matthew, Jesus concluded with the warning: "Watch therefore, for you know neither the day nor the hour,"[86] but this verse was not part of the original parable. Sleeping was not the issue. All the maidens slept, and all were awakened by the announcement that the bridegroom had arrived. But the maidens who had not provided extra oil for their lamps could not find their way in the dark to the bridegroom until they obtained additional oil. By the time they arrived, the procession was over and the door had been shut. What was condemned was not that the young ladies fell asleep but that the five maidens had failed to secure oil in advance for their lamps. They were unprepared. As a consequence, they missed the banquet entirely.

The exhortation to watchfulness in verse 13 was a later addition to the parable.

The Bridegroom as the Messiah
Some readers presume the bridegroom was the Messiah, but "the allegorical representation of the Messiah as a bridegroom is completely foreign to the whole of the Old Testament and to the literature of late Judaism." According to Jeremias, this image appeared for the first time in the writings of Paul.[87] The Jews in Jesus' audience would not have pictured the Messiah as a bridegroom.

Maidens, Not Virgins
Because the women were described by the Greek word *parthenois* ("virgins"), the story was often called the Parable of the Ten Virgins. But *parthenos* could also designate a young woman. More recent translations render *parthenois* as "maidens" or "bridesmaids," without any reference to their sexual history.[88]

The Parable of the Place of Honor

According to Luke, Jesus was invited to share a Sabbath dinner at the home of a wealthy Pharisee. During the dinner, he shared several parables and teachings about banquets. The Parable of the Great Banquet was one of them. Another was the Parable of the Place of Honor.

Noting how guests at a dinner party frequently scrambled to sit closest to the person with the highest status, Jesus shared his view of proper etiquette.

> Now he told a parable to those who were invited, when he marked how they chose the places of honor, saying to them, "When you are invited by any one to a marriage feast, do not sit down in a place of honor, lest a more eminent man than you be invited by him; and he who invited you both will come and say to you, 'Give place to this man,' and then you will begin with shame to take the lowest place. But when you are invited, go and sit in the lowest place, so that when your host comes he may say to you, 'Friend, go up higher'; then you will be honored in the presence of all who sit at table with you." (Luke 14:7–10)

What Secrets Did the Parable Convey?
Unlike other parables, no comparison was given. What was Jesus saying?

Jesus was instructing his followers how to behave properly in his presence.

Jesus was instructing his followers how to behave properly at any dinner they attended.

Jesus was reminding his followers how people who were invited to the banquet celebrating the establishment of God's kingdom would behave.

But Jesus was saying more.

Jesus Built on Jewish Images

Jesus reminded his listeners of the demands of Jewish etiquette. The book of Proverbs admonished, "Do not put yourself forward in the king's presence or stand in the place of the great, for it is better to be told, 'Come up here,' than to be put lower in the presence of the prince."[89] In meetings of the Sanhedrin, each member sat in the place that was proper for him and each judge declared his opinion in a prescribed order.[90] In noncapital cases, the eldest judge declared his opinion first; in capital trials, the youngest spoke first.[91] In a letter written in the early sixties (CE), James chided Christians for seating the well-dressed men in the best places in their synagogues and telling the poor to sit on the floor.[92]

Jesus Chided the Pharisees

The parable may have pointed to the Pharisees. Twice on other occasions Jesus chastised Pharisees for accepting seats of honor in synagogues and at public feasts. "Woe to you Pharisees, for you love the best seat in the synagogues and salutations in the market places."[93] "Beware of the scribes, who like to go about in long robes and love salutations in the market places and the best seats in the synagogues and the places of honor at feasts."[94] Jesus went even farther. Not only did they lack humility and a sense of social propriety, but these Pharisees were immoral hypocrites as well. They "devour widows' houses and for a pretense make long prayers." They deserved and would receive "the greater condemnation."[95]

These remarks against the Pharisees undermined their status and authority and angered the sages who heard them. Did Jesus understand that?

Of course he did. In all three synoptic gospels (that is, Matthew, Mark, and Luke), conversations about Jesus, confrontations with Jesus, and investigations of Jesus among and by the authorities increased as his ministry progressed.

Did Jesus Deliberately Anger the Authorities?

Did he do it deliberately? Did Jesus intend to anger the authorities?

Jesus was a man on a mission. He yearned to save as many people as possible before the impending catastrophe began. So he preached passionately, charismatically, and honestly. Most of his ideas were Pharisaic, but occasionally he disagreed, and he did not shirk from expressing his opinions. He con-demned anyone who exhibited haughtiness, hypocrisy, or immorality—and that included Roman authorities, wealthy Jewish landowners, priests, sages, and synagogue leaders. He hadn't set out to foment resistance and anger, but both were consequences of his honesty and intensity. Jesus "called them as he saw them," and those who disagreed with his depictions and predictions fought back.

As we saw in the discussion of his preaching after reading from the scroll of Isaiah in his hometown synagogue, ordinary Jews who knew him well could get so upset with his ideas that they would retaliate physically.

The Exalted Will Lose, the Humble Will Survive

Jesus concluded with this last observation: "Every one who exalts himself will be humbled, and he who humbles himself will be exalted."[96]

Normal expectations would be completely overturned with the coming of God's kingdom, and persons of exalted status—sages, priests, and aristo-crats—would be humiliated. People who acted humbly and considered others would be honored.

The same observation was recorded in Matthew 23:12 and Luke 18:14.

As if to reinforce this image, after the Parable of the Place of Honor Luke inserted another teaching about reaching out to the disadvantaged. "When you give a feast, invite the poor, the maimed, the lame, [and] the blind, and you will be blessed." Jesus concluded with the following statement: "They cannot repay you. You will be repaid at the resurrection of the just."[97]

Resurrection

While they didn't say so explicitly, many biblical passages suggested physical resurrection. In Deuteronomy, God said, "I slay and I revive; I wounded and I will heal."[98] And Hannah affirmed the same image in her prayer, "God slays and revives; He casts down into Sheol and raises up."[99] The witch of Endor called up the prophet Samuel from the netherworld to speak to King Saul.[100]

According to Isaiah, when God would redeem the people of Israel, the dead would live again. "Your dead will revive; your corpses will arise. Awake, and shout for joy."[101]

In Ezekiel, the blanched bones of Israel's slain came to life again. "The hand of the Lord . . . set me down in a valley. It was full of bones. . . . Sud-denly there was a sound of rattling, and the bones came together . . . there were sinews on them, and flesh had grown, and skin had formed over them

. . . the breath entered them, and they came to life and stood on their feet, a vast multitude."[102]

All of these passages may have been metaphorical originally, but Jews came to understand them literally. God would revive the dead, reconstitute them as a nation, and provide for their well-being. The innocent, the righteous, martyrs and victims of injustice, Jews slaughtered through the ages by the regiments of Assyria, Babylonia, Persia, Greece, Syria, and Rome would all return to life. "Your sun shall set no more, your moon nor more withdraw; for the Lord will be a light to you forever, and your days of mourning shall be ended. Your people, all of them righteous, shall possess the land for all time."[103]

These images coalesced and congealed within Jewish tradition, so that by the beginning of the second century BCE, the writer of Daniel could predict with certainty that "many of those who sleep in the dust of the earth will awake, some to eternal life, others to reproach and everlasting contempt. The wise shall shine like the bright expanse of the sky; and those who lead many to righteousness will be like the stars forever and ever."[104]

The author of 2 Maccabees expressed the same understanding. "The King of the world will raise us, who died for His laws, to an everlasting renewal of life."[105] Those who maltreated and punished the righteous would experience no resurrection.[106]

Enoch described how he was transported over seven splendid mountains where he encountered a fruit tree emitting a marvelous fragrance. The angel Michael explained to him that God would rule from the summit of the seventh mountain and that the fruit of the tree would feed the resurrected. "The sweet odor shall enter into their bones, and they shall live a long life on the earth . . . in their days, sorrow, distress, trouble and punishment shall not afflict them." During that "period of the great judgment," the righteous and the humble shall be returned to life; sinners will be punished and consumed forever.[107]

In the Testament of the Twelve Patriarchs, the resurrection was extended back to include the patriarchs and their offspring. "Then you shall see Enoch, Noah, Shem, Abraham, Isaac and Jacob rising up on the right hand in exultation. Then we shall also rise, each over his own tribe, worshipping the King of heaven."[108]

By the first century, resurrection was a cardinal belief among Jews, but it was a relatively new principle and one still resisted by some of Jesus' contemporaries. There were Jews who disavowed resurrection.

According to Josephus, the Essenes believed in the immortality of souls but not in a physical resurrection. The souls of the righteous ascended to heaven, where they survived in eternal bliss. The souls of sinners suffered eternal pain and torment.[109]

Ben Sirach denied resurrection. "When a man dies, reptiles, animals and worms become his portion."[110] This life was all there was. Death extinguished any further human experience.

Job presented the same image. "My life is but wind; I shall never see happiness again. . . . As a cloud dissolves and is gone, so is one who goes down to Sheol. He does not come up."[111]

The reality of resurrection was an area of significant dispute between the Sadducees and the Pharisees. The Sadducees categorically denied the resurrection of the dead.[112] For the Pharisees, the resurrection of the dead was a reality about which they had no doubts, and they made it a cardinal principle of their teachings. Rabbi Phineas ben Jair used to say, "Heedfulness leads to cleanliness, cleanliness to purity, purity to abstinence,[113] abstinence to holiness, holiness to humility, humility to the shunning of sin, the shunning of sin to saintliness, saintliness to [the gift of] the Holy Spirit, and [the gift of] the Holy Spirit leads to the resurrection of the dead."[114]

The list of reprehensible people who had no share in the World to Come included the generation of the Flood, the residents of Sodom, the supporters of Korah's rebellion, and reprobates who claimed "there is no resurrection of the dead prescribed in the Law."[115]

Jesus stood squarely with the Pharisees in this regard and accepted physical resurrection as a cardinal principle.

In the next chapter, in two well-known parables Jesus explores further the relationships between father and sons.

Notes

1. For example, Isaiah 6:11–13; 43:27–28; 51:19; Jeremiah 4:6–8, 23–27; Ezekiel 5:15–17; Hosea 7:13; Joel 1:15–20.

2. Jeremiah 20:7–10; Matthew 13:57; Mark 6:3–4; Luke 4:24, 28–29.

3. Matthew 23:34–39, Luke 11:47–51. See also Matthew 14:1–12 regarding the execution of John the Baptist.

4. Matthew 10:16–17, 23; 23:34–36, 38; Luke 11:49–51.

5. Isaiah 25:6; 2 Esdras 2:37–41; Louis Ginzburg, *Legends of the Jews* (Philadelphia: Jewish Publication Society of America, 1956), vol. 1, 27–29. For images of the banquet, see Matthew 8:11; Luke 22:30. For images of God espousing Israel, see Isaiah 54:5, 62:1–5.

6. Rabbi Eliezer contended only Jews had a share in the World to Come. His col-

league Rabbi Joshua affirmed there were righteous non-Jews who would enjoy the World to Come. See the discussions in George Foot Moore, *Judaism in the First Centuries of the Christian Era* (Cambridge, Mass.: Harvard University Press, 1927), vol. 2, 385–86; and Claude G. Montefiore and H. Loewe, *A Rabbinic Anthology* (London: Macmillan, 1938), 604.

7. Matthew 8:11–12; Luke 13:28–29.

8. See Jeremias, *The Parables of Jesus*, 64–65, 67–69; Hultgren, *The Parables of Jesus*, 344–45.

9. See "Son of God," below 160–61.

10. Genesis 2:18, 24.

11. Genesis 16:3; 25:1; 29:21–28; 30:4, 9; Judges 8:30; 2 Samuel 5:13; 1 Kings 11:1–8.

12. Genesis 2:24.

13. Psalm 128; Proverbs 12:4, 18:22, 19:14, 31:10–31. The prophets' use of marriage as a metaphor for God's commitment to the people of Israel implied monogamy. See Isaiah 61:10, 62:5; Ezekiel 16; Hosea 2:21–22; and also the Song of Songs.

14. Genesis Rabbah 17:2, as presented in Moore, *Judaism in the First Centuries of the Christian Era*, vol. 2, 119.

15. Genesis 1:28.

16. Kiddushin 29b.

17. Josephus, *The Jewish Wars*, 2.120.

18. Some married couples entered the community after they were married. See Raphael Posner, "Marriage," in *Encyclopedia Judaica*, ed. Cecil Roth (Jerusalem: Macmillan, 1971–1972), 1027.

19. Some scholars suggest this was the reason Qumran was eventually abandoned.

20. Matthew 19:12.

21. 1 Corinthians 7:1.

22. 1 Corinthians 7:8–9. See also verse 2.

23. Genesis 29:22.

24. Judges 14:12. See also Genesis 29:27.

25. Psalms 78:63; 1 Maccabees 9:39.

26. Deuteronomy 22:23–24, 28; 28:30; 2 Samuel 3:14; Matthew 1:18, 20, 24–25; M. Yebamoth 2:6–7. There was no engagement in Jewish tradition. Legally, a person was either married or not married.

27. Tosefta Ketuboth 4.9. According to the Talmud, "the law of Moses" meant the Torah and "of Israel" referred to the rules established by the sages.

28. Baraita Ketuboth 7b.

29. Ketuboth 7b–8a.

30. Jeremiah 7:34, 1 Maccabees 9:37–41, Matthew 25:1–12.

31. Ketuboth 16b–17a.

32. Ketuboth 17a.

33. Berakhot 6b; Ketuboth 17a.

34. Pesikta 11b–12a; Genesis Rabbah 68:4, as presented in Moore, *Judaism in the First Centuries of the Christian Era*, vol. 1, 439–40.

35. John 2:1–10. See also John 4:46.

36. Matthew 25:1–12.

37. Matthew 9:14–15; Mark 2:19–20; Luke 5:34–35, 12:35–36, 14:8.

38. Exodus 4:22.

39. Hosea 11:1.

40. Exodus 4:22–23.

41. Deuteronomy 14:1.

42. Isaiah 43:6–7.

43. Hosea 2:1 (= Greek Hosea 1:10).

44. Ben Sirach 36:12; Wisdom of Solomon 18:13; Jubilees 2:20, 19:29; 2 Esdras 6:58.

45. Jubilees 1:24–25, 19:29.

46. Wisdom of Solomon 12:19–21; Ben Sirach 4:10.

47. Psalms of Solomon 17:28–30.

48. 2 Samuel 7:14.

49. Psalm 2:2–7, 89:26–27.

50. Enoch 105:2; 2 Esdras 7:28–29; 13:32, 37, 52; 14:19.

51. Psalm 2:2–7.

52. For example, Matthew 2:15, quoting Hosea 11:1.

53. See "The Son of Man" in 84–86 above.

54. Most scholars agree that the Parable of the Misdressed Wedding Guest was originally a separate metaphor and not part of the Parable of the Royal Wedding Feast. See Joachim Jeremias, *The Parables of Jesus*, rev. ed. (New York: Charles Scribner's Sons, 1963), 64.

55. John 10:1.

56. Matthew 3:2, 4:17, 7:21–23.

57. Shabbat 153a, as presented in Jeremias, *The Parables of Jesus*, 188.

58. Jesus alluded to this chapter in Isaiah on at least four other occasions: Matthew 5:3–4, 11:5; and Luke 4:18–19, 7:22.

59. Ethiopian Enoch 62:15–16, as presented in Jeremias, *The Parables of Jesus*, 189.

60. Matthew 9:16–17, Mark 2:21–22, Luke 5:36–38.

61. Luke 15:21–23.

62. Ben Sirach 17:15, reported in Moore, *Judaism in the First Centuries of the Christian Era*, vol. 1, 516.

63. Genesis Rabba 21.6, as presented in Moore, *Judaism in the First Centuries of the Christian Era*, vol. 1, 530.

64. Genesis Rabba 21.6.

65. Pesikta 162ab; Leviticus Rabba 30.3, as presented in Moore, *Judaism in the First Centuries of the Christian Era*, vol. 1, 524.

66. Isaiah 25:6–8. See also Psalms 36:7–8, Song of Songs 2:4–5.

67. Matthew 8:11. See also Luke 13:29.

68. Jeremiah 31:13–14.

69. Jeremias, *The Parables of Jesus*, 64. See also *The New American Bible*, 1118, note to Luke 14:15–24.

70. Matthew 8:10–12.

71. For the image of God as Israel's husband, see Isaiah 54:5–8; 62:5; Jeremiah 31:32; Ezekiel 16:8–14; Hosea 2:1–23.

72. Flood: Matthew 24:38–39; Luke 17:26–29. See also Matthew 7:24–28; Luke 6:47–49. Thief: Matthew 24:43; Luke 12:39. See also Luke 12:33; John 10:1, 10. Estate Owner: Matthew 18:23–34, 24:45–51, 25:14–30; Mark 13:34–36; Luke 12:43–47; 19:12–24.

73. Matthew 24:44.

74. Matthew 7:21.

75. Matthew 7:22–23. See also Luke 13:25–27.

76. Luke 13:23–24.

77. Matthew 7:13–14.

78. Matthew 7:13.

79. Matthew 25:11–12.

80. Luke 13:25–27. Though similar, the Parable of the Neighbor at Midnight (Luke 11:5–10) has a different message. See below, pp. 201–204.

81. Matthew 24:33; Mark 13:29.

82. Mark 6:13.

83. Luke 10:34.

84. Luke 7:46.

85. Matthew 7:24, 27.

86. Matthew 25:13.

87. Jeremias, *The Parables of Jesus*, 52.

88. See Arland J. Hultgren, *The Parables of Jesus: A Commentary* (Grand Rapids, Mich.: William B. Eerdmans, 2000), 169.

89. Proverbs 25:6–7.

90. Both sages appointed to try a case and disciples awaiting appointment sat in their appropriate seats (M. Sanhedrin 4:4).

91. M. Sanhedrin 4:2.

92. James 2:2–3.

93. Luke 11:43.

94. Luke 20:46.

95. Luke 20:47.

96. Luke 14:11.

97. Luke 14:12–13.

98. Deuteronomy 32:39.

99. 1 Samuel 2:6. See also 2 Kings 5:7.

100. 1 Samuel 28:8–24.

101. Isaiah 26:19.

102. Ezekiel 37:1–10.

103. Isaiah 60:20–21.

104. Daniel 12:2–3.

105. 2 Maccabees 7:9.

106. 2 Maccabees 7:14.

107. Enoch 24:1–11.

108. Testament of Benjamin, chapter 10, as presented in Moore, *Judaism in the First Centuries of the Christian Era*, vol. 2, 307.

109. Josephus, *Antiquities*, 18.1.5, and *The Jewish Wars*, 2.8.11. These ideas were also expressed in the Wisdom of Solomon, 3:1–8, 5:16. No direct expression of these ideas has been found yet in the various Dead Sea Scrolls.

110. Ben Sirach 10:11. See also Ben Sirach 17:27–28 and possibly 17:32.

111. Job 7:7–9. Later rabbinic tradition understood this passage as a denial of physical resurrection (Baba Batra 16a).

112. Josephus, *Antiquities*, 18.1.4; *The Jewish Wars*, 2.8.14; Acts 23:8, 26:8.

113. *Perishut* ("abstinence, separation")—a possible Hebrew wordplay supporting Pharisaic interpretations and rulings.

114. M. Sotah 9:15.

115. M. Sanhedrin 10:3, 1.

CHAPTER FOURTEEN

Parables about Fathers and Sons

The Parable of the Two Sons and the Vineyard

A man had two sons. When he asked one son to work in his vineyard, the son refused. Afterward he repented and obeyed. When he asked the other son to work in his vineyard, the son agreed but did not go.

Then Jesus asked the priests and elders who challenged him: "Which of the two did the will of his father?" They said the first son did what his father wanted. Jesus retorted. "Truly, I say to you, the tax collectors and the harlots go into the kingdom of God before you."

> What do you think? A man had two sons; and he went to the first and said, "Son, go and work in the vineyard today." And he answered, "I will not"; but afterward he repented and went. And he went to the second and said the same; and he answered, "'I go, sir," but did not go. Which of the two did the will of his father? They said, "The first." Jesus said to them, "Truly, I say to you, the tax collectors and the harlots go into the kingdom of God before you." (Matthew 21:28–31)

According to the teachings of the sages, the first son sinned but repented. He was eligible to enter the World to Come. The second son sinned and did not repent. Still a sinner, he was not eligible to participate in the World to Come.

Did Jesus disagree?

What Secrets Did the Parable Convey?
Jesus disagreed not with the doctrine but with its application.

The priests and elders saw themselves as the first son—occasional sinners who repented of their sins—but Jesus accused them of being like the second son. They said they knew and did the will of God, but they did not. They didn't understand what God demanded, and they didn't do what God intended. If they did, they would help the infirm and reach out to sinners.

On the other hand, Jesus taught that repentant sinners—former publicans and harlots—are like the first son. Having sinned egregiously, they repented. Now they spent their time trying to undo the harm they had created and to fulfill God's demands.

By What Authority Did Jesus Teach?

According to Matthew, the confrontation had begun much earlier. While Jesus taught in the sacred area of the Temple, preaching to all who would hear, a number of priests, scribes, and elders approached him. They had been debating about him and resolved to test his authority for what he had done the previous day. "By what authority do you do these things?" they asked. "And who gave you this authority?"

Jesus countered their question with a question. "If you answer," he said, "I will tell you by what authority I do these things. On what authority was John's baptism? Divine or human?"

If they answered that God was the source of John's baptism, Jesus would then demand of them why then they didn't believe in the Baptist—and why they didn't accept John's testimony about Jesus.

If they averred that John had no authority to preach and baptize, the people would turn against them, for the martyred Baptist was revered by many as a prophet.

"We cannot say," they answered. To which Jesus said, "Neither do I tell you by what authority I do these things."[1]

Without further interruption or comment, Jesus then proceeded to relate the Parable of the Two Sons and the Vineyard. He concluded the parable with this reproof, reinforcing the secrets he had conveyed in the story itself: "For John came to you in the way of righteousness and you did not believe him, but the tax collectors and the harlots believed him. Even when you saw it, you did not afterward repent and believe him."[2]

Jesus answered his own question. John's baptism was from God—because so many sinners earnestly repented and changed their ways as a result of his teachings.

More Secrets

In the process, Jesus revealed more secrets to those willing to listen.

Priests, scribes, and elders would have access to heaven only if they also repented and changed their ways. A first step in that process would be for them to accept the teachings of John and Jesus.

Even after they repented, they would follow, not lead, in the glorious procession of the redeemed.

Repentance

In Jewish tradition, sins against God were atoned with God. But sins against other human beings were forgiven only after the transgressor had completed four steps:

- First, the sinner must recognize that he had committeed a transgression.
- Second, the sinner must confess his sin to God and seek absolution. In addition, the sinner must apologize to those against whom he sinned and seek their forgiveness.
- Third, the sinner must make restitution and undo the harm he created.
- Four, the sinner must never commit the transgression again.

For repentance to be complete, each one of these steps must be fulfilled. "If a man repents and goes back to his sins, that is no repentance."[3]

Forgiveness was absolute. Save for the lessons learned and the insights gained, nothing of the sins remained after repentance. The transgressions were gone. "If your sins be like scarlet, they shall become white as snow."[4]

There was no time limit to repentance. God kept the gates of repentance open and removed every obstacle that might hinder a sinner's penitence from reaching Him. As Rabbi Simeon ben Yochai taught, "If a man has been completely wicked all his days and repents at the end, God receives him."[5] Even the atheist and the apostate who repented had a share in the World to Come.

Not only did each person's destiny depend upon righting his relationship with God, but there were Jews who believed proper penitence would save Israel. "Great is repentance," said Rabbi Jonathan, "for it brings the deliverance, as it is said, 'A deliverer will come to Zion and to those in Jacob who turn from transgression.'[6] How is to be understood? 'A deliverer will come to Zion *because of* those in Jacob who turn from transgression.'"[7]

John the Baptist and Jesus had these images in mind when they exhorted their listeners to repent.

Honor Your Father and Your Mother

According to Philo, "the weightiest of the weighty" of God's commandments was "Honor your father and your mother."[8] In Exodus, the father was listed first; in Leviticus, the mother was listed first—the difference indicating that neither parent had priority and that both parents should be honored equally.[9]

According to Rabbi Judah, honoring one's parents was comparable to honoring God, since the same verbs—honor, revere, and curse—were applied to both.[10] Both God and parents were partners in creating and rearing a child.[11]

A son should neither sit where his father usually sits, nor talk where his father is accustomed to speak, nor contradict him, nor disagree in public with his opinion.[12] Reverence required feeding his father, providing him with clothing and sandals, and helping him into and out of bed.[13] The same deference was extended to a person's spiritual father—his mentor or teacher or master.[14]

The court could execute a child who hit a parent or cursed him, and the elders of the town could try a stubborn or rebellious child and put him to death by stoning.[15]

It is said, "Honor the Lord with your substance." Honor Him, that is, with what He has graciously bestowed upon you [by] setting apart the forgotten sheaf and the corner of the field, [by] setting apart the priest's dues, . . . [by] making the booth and the palm branches and the ram's horn and the phylacteries and the fringes, and [by] feeding the hungry. If you have substance, you are obligated to [do] all these; if you have no [substance], you are not obligated to any of them. But when it comes to honoring father and mother, whether you have substance or not, [you must] "honor your father and your father"—even if you have to beg your living from door to door.[16]

"These are the things whose fruit a man enjoys in this world and whose capital is laid up for him in the World to Come: honoring father and mother."[17]

The Parable of the Father and His Two Sons

A man had two sons. The younger asked his father to give him his inheritance. The father agreed and gave the younger son his portion. The son sold the property, then journeyed to a far country and squandered his entire estate in loose living. To survive, he got a job feeding slops to swine. He determined to return home and apologize to his father.

When his father saw him, he embraced and kissed him. The son begged his father's forgiveness and said he was unworthy to be his son, but the father dressed him in an expensive robe, gave him a jeweled ring, and prepared a great feast.

On his way home after finishing his work in the field, the elder son heard music. When he discovered that the household was celebrating his brother's return, he grew angry and refused to enter the house. He complained to his father that in all the years he had served his father, his father had never once made a feast in his honor. But for his younger brother, who had wasted his father's property on prostitutes, his father had prepared a sumptuous celebration.

His father replied, "Son, you are always with me, and all that is mine is yours. It was fitting to make merry and be glad, for this your brother was dead, and is alive; he was lost, and is found."

He said, "There was a man who had two sons; and the younger of them said to his father, 'Father, give me the share of property that falls to me.' And he divided his living between them. Not many days later, the younger son gathered all he had and took his journey into a far country, and there he squandered his property in loose living. And when he had spent everything, a great famine arose in that country, and he began to be in want. So he went and joined himself to one of the citizens of that country, who sent him into his fields to feed swine. And he would gladly have fed on the pods that the swine ate; and no one gave him anything. But when he came to himself he said, 'How many of my father's hired servants have bread enough and to spare, but I perish here with hunger! I will arise and go to my father, and I will say to him, "Father, I have sinned against heaven and before you; I am no longer worthy to be called your son; treat me as one of your hired servants."' And he arose and came to his father. But while he was yet at a distance, his father saw him and had compassion, and ran and embraced him and kissed him. And the son said to him, 'Father, I have sinned against heaven and before you; I am no longer worthy to be called your son.' But the father said to his servants, 'Bring quickly the best robe, and put it on him; and put a ring on his hand, and shoes on his feet; and bring the fatted calf and kill it, and let us eat and make merry; for this my son was dead, and is alive again; he was lost, and is found.' And they began to make merry.

"Now his elder son was in the field; and as he came and drew near to the house, he heard music and dancing. And he called one of the servants and asked what this meant. And he said to him, 'Your brother has come, and your father has killed the fatted calf, because he has received him safe and sound.' But he was angry and refused to go in. His father came out and entreated him, but he answered his father, 'Lo, these many years I have served you, and I never disobeyed your command; yet you never gave me a kid, that I might make merry with my friends. But when this son of yours came, who has devoured your living with harlots, you killed for him the fatted calf!' And he said to him, 'Son, you are always with me, and all that is mine is yours. It was fitting to make merry and be glad, for this your brother was dead, and is alive; he was lost, and is found.' " (Luke 15:11–32)

The parable contains two interrelated sections. The first (verses 12–24) focused on the younger son; the second (verses 25–32) on the older child. Who were these sons? Why did Jesus present them? What did his audience learn from their actions and those of their father?

Jewish Notions about Inheritance

To understand Jesus' portrayal, we need to explore what his audience knew about Jewish inheritance in the first century. The following rules applied to the Parable of the Father and His Two Sons:

- A man's property belonged to him throughout his lifetime. He could use it, abuse it, enlarge it, or waste it—and its products and benefits—as he saw fit. Neither his wife, children, siblings, nor other relatives had any claim on them. Upon his death, his property passed to his sons, and if there were no sons, to his daughters. Wives, siblings, grandchildren, and other relatives received no inheritance when there were living children.[18]
- The first-born son received a double portion of his father's property. All the remaining sons of the same father received equal shares of their father's property. In a family with five sons, the first-born son would receive two-sixths of his father's estate. His siblings would each receive one-sixth.[19]
- A man could not deny the first-born son his double portion, withhold equal shares from his remaining sons, or disinherit a son. To do so would contradict God's law.[20]
- A man could assign his property to his son. In this circumstance, the father could not sell that portion, since it was assigned; similarly, the son could not sell it, since the father was still alive. If the father sold it, it reverted back to the son when the father died. If the son sold it, the buyer could claim it only after the father's death.[21]
- If a man died and left sons and daughters and the property was insufficient to provide both an inheritance for the sons and maintenance for the daughters, the daughters received their maintenance and the sons went begging. The maintenance needs of the daughters took precedence over the inheritance rights of the sons.[22]

- If he left elder and younger sons, the older males could not care for themselves (out of their inheritance) at the cost of the younger males, nor could the younger sons claim maintenance (from their inheritance) at a cost to their older siblings. They must all share alike.[23]

In the current parable, upon the father's death, the older son would have received two-thirds of the estate and the younger son one-third. At the younger son's request, the father assigned him one-third of his property. Even under these circumstances, the father would normally have use of all his property. He could plant and harvest it himself, rent it to tenant farmers, hire sharecroppers to farm it, build warehouses and workshops on it, or let it lie fallow. If he increased its value, his sons would inherit that. If he diminished its value, they would suffer the loss when he died.

But the younger son sold property—not just the right to use the property but the ownership—then took the money, journeyed to a far land, and squandered it in profligate living. In the process, he broke Jewish law, dishonored his father, left his father to work the property without his assistance, and forced his father to support himself and his family on two-thirds of what he had formerly possessed.[24] The father could have contested the sale. Had he won, his younger son would have been branded a thief and a fraud. The father chose instead to honor his son's contract and vacate the property.

The father was profoundly affected by his son's rash and wild behavior. His "living" was compromised.

At this point in the story, most of Jesus' listeners must have despised the younger son and felt a great deal of sympathy for the father. Jesus fueled their misgivings further.

The son spent every last coin he owned drinking and carousing. He had no money for food, so he bartered himself to a non-Jewish family for a place to sleep and something to eat; they sent him into the fields to feed their swine.[25] So desperate was he for food that he was willing to eat the slops the pigs ate.[26]

Jesus' listeners must have thought the younger son depraved. He had degraded himself, dispatched his inheritance, and denied his heritage.

The story called to mind the saying in Proverbs, "A man who loves wisdom makes his father glad, but he who keeps company with harlots squanders his substance."[27] The younger son was a sinner of the worst order—and a fool as well. He had sunk about as low as a Jew could go.

Repentance

At his nadir, the son "came to himself."[28] Hultgren suggests the son now realized how foolish he had been and decided to return to his home and family.[29] Others assert that the son repented.[30] I agree. The son *repented*. He was no longer a sinner.

Having returned to God, the son longed to return to his family—not just to find food and lodging but to make things right with his father, to apologize and make amends. "I will arise and go to my father, and I will say to him, 'Father, I have sinned against heaven and before you; I am no longer worthy to be called your son; treat me as one of your hired servants.'"

He journeyed home. Since he had no money, it must have been an arduous trip. Much of it probably was on foot.

His father saw him in the distance as he approached, recognized him immediately, ran toward him, and embraced him. Before the son could recite his apology, his father welcomed him and kissed him.

Not to be deterred, the son apologized. "Father, I have sinned against heaven and before you; I am no longer worthy to be called your son." But the father disregarded the son's contention. He ordered his servants to "bring the best robe, and put it on him; and put a ring on his hand, and shoes on his feet." In short, he honored him and restored him immediately to a position of status and power within the family. As far as the servants were concerned, he was once again their master.

The story reminded Jesus' audience of how Pharaoh rewarded Joseph. "Then Pharaoh took his signet ring from his hand and put it on Joseph's hand, and arrayed him in garments of fine linen, and put a gold chain about his neck and . . . set him over all the land of Egypt."[31] And how God restored Joshua, the High Priest: "'Behold, I have taken your iniquity away from you, and I will clothe you with rich apparel.' . . . So they put a clean turban on his head and clothed him with garments."[32]

The father ordered his servants to prepare a feast. The killing and cooking of a "fatted calf" indicated a large banquet involving invited guests, possibly from the extended family and estates nearby. This portion of the parable ended with the father's joyous exclamation, "My son was dead, and is alive again; he was lost, and is found"—a realization worth celebrating.

The Elder Son

The story shifted to the second son. Coming home from hard work in his father's fields, the elder son heard "music and dancing." He asked a servant the reason for such a celebration and discovered that (1) his younger brother had returned; (2) his father was making a feast in his brother's honor to which many guests had been invited; and (3) he hadn't been informed or invited himself. Furious, the older brother refused to join the festivities.

The father left his guests, met with his older son outdoors, and urged him to join the celebration. The son refused. Bitterly he complained that he had served his father diligently for years and never disobeyed one of his commands, yet not once had the father made a feast in his honor. But the son who wasted his father's assets whoring received a hero's welcome.

The elder son's outburst belied his claims. In contrast to the younger son, he did not address his father respectfully. He spoke of his brother contemptuously as "this son of yours." And he berated his father for wasting precious resources feting the son who "devoured your living." His tone was defiant and angry, his complaint filled with scorn for his father and his brother.

Deliberately choosing contrasting language, the father reminded his elder son that "this brother of yours" did not displace him in his father's affection, that the older son was "always" with him, and that he was still heir to all that remained of his father's estate. "All that is mine is yours."

But the father had suffered a terrible loss when he thought his younger son was dead. Having him return alive—hugging him and kissing him—gladdened the father's heart. He wanted to celebrate and share his joy with his neighbors.

The parable ended with the father's words. We don't know if the elder son acceded and joined the celebration, if the younger prospered, or if the brothers reconciled. Unlike the two parables that preceded it, no application or interpretation was given. Having finished the longest parable in his repertoire, Jesus stopped talking and let the images speak for themselves.

What Secrets Did the Parable Convey?

What was Jesus teaching?

While the parable was a single unit, I believe each character in the parable illustrated a different aspect of Jesus' instruction.

Let's explore the profligate son first.

In this portion of the parable, Jesus emphasized the power of repentance and reaffirmed many of the ideas he shared in other parables. The younger son had committed heinous offenses and reached the depths of depravity. He had indentured himself to gentiles, fed their swine, and longed to eat their slops.

Somehow he came to his senses and repented. He righted his relationship with God and determined to conduct himself in accordance with God's will. No more drinking and carousing. No more swine and swill.

Having returned to God, he decided to return home. He didn't expect to be accepted by his father. He was willing to serve as serf under his father's servants. Regardless of the outcome, he needed to confess his sins and restore his relationship with his father and family.

To Jesus, the younger son was saved. A transgressor who had repented of his sins and sought to undo the harm he had inflicted on his family, the younger child now lived his life in compliance with God's demands. Though his former sins were deplorable, he would be among the righteous welcomed into the kingdom of heaven.

According to Jesus, even the most depraved sinner could repent and live in the World to Come after the apocalypse.

So Jesus welcomed tax collectors and harlots to his speeches and ate with them at the same table.[33] These sinners desperately needed encouragement and support if they were going to change their ways and be saved.

What did his listeners learn from the father?

At first, they thought the father was a fool. He had indulged his son, given in to his whim, and assigned him one-third of his property before he died. Contrary to Jewish law, the son sold his inheritance and squandered the money carousing among the gentiles.

The father should have known better. Almost two centuries earlier, Ben Sirakh advised: "In all that you do retain control. . . . When the days of your life reach their end, at the time of your death distribute your property."[34]

He could have contested the sale and sued his son, but he had chosen not to do so. He had tightened his sash, supported his family from the remaining two-thirds of his estate, and allowed his son to play out his fantasy. Having heard nothing from his son for some time, he presumed he was dead and grieved accordingly. He was a fool.

Years later, when he saw his son coming toward him, he rejoiced. He ran to greet his son with hugs and kisses—conduct unbecoming a man of his station. Even before his son finished his apology, he accepted him. He declined his son's offer to work as a slave; ordered his servants to bring clothes, sandals, and a ring appropriate to his reinstated status as his son and their master; and commanded them to prepare a great feast.

The father's acceptance was not dependent on anything the son did or said. It was prior to and apart from the son's apology. Whenever the son returned home, he would have found his father ready to hug him and kiss him.

According to Jesus, God greeted every repentant sinner with love and acceptance and received true penitence with unconditional forgiveness. In the World to Come, former sinners would be clothed in splendid garments. God would rejoice. And all would enjoy God's banquet together. The hard part was repenting.

What about the older son? What part of Jesus' teachings did he represent?

The older son followed all the rules. He had worked hard and served his father diligently.

But the weakness of his character erupted when he discovered that his father had not only welcomed back his sinful brother but also prepared a banquet in his honor—something he had never done in all the years the older son had served him. At that point, he grew angry and expressed his disappointment and resentment. He had worked for his father without complaint for years, obeyed his every command, and never received any reward. His younger brother had broken his father's heart, squandered a third of his father's estate, and shattered one law after another whoring among the gentiles and eating with swine, and now he received a feast.[35] The older son was not even invited to the banquet and had to inquire why there was a celebration in progress.[36]

Many in Jesus' audience probably sympathized with the elder son's complaints.

For Jesus, the son's complaints exposed his spiritual weakness. His disappointment at getting nothing for years of devoted service indicated clearly that he expected a reward. His anger showed the depths of his jealousy. The haughty and insulting words he used in his confrontation with his father betrayed how little he respected his father's decisions. To most people, he appeared to honor his father. However, when faced with his father's behavior regarding the profligate brother, the elder son expressed pent-up rage and resentment.

From Jesus' point of view, the elder son was a selfish and self-righteous sinner. He too broke God's laws, if not as flagrantly as his younger brother.

But unlike his younger brother, he had not repented. He had not confessed his transgressions and sought forgiveness. He was still too busy condemning others.

The father treated him the same way he welcomed his younger brother. He called him "son" and spoke to him affectionately. "You are always at my side," he said. "Everything that's mine is yours." He urged him to join the celebration but allowed him to make the decision. He accepted him.

At that point, Jesus stopped the parable and left unspoken its application, but his intention was clear. He wanted the older son to repent—to repair his relationships with God, with his father, and with his brother—and join the celebration. If he didn't repent, he would be left outside. The banquet would proceed without him.

Other Jewish Images

In this parable, Jesus may have drawn on images in Jewish literature familiar to his listeners: Two twins struggled in Rebecca's womb, "and the older shall serve the younger."[37]

A king had a son who had gone astray from his father on a journey of a hundred days. His friends said to him, "Return to your father." He said, "I cannot." Then his father sent to say, "Return as far as you can, and I will come the rest of the way to you." So God says, "Return to me, and I will return to you."[38]

R. Berechiah said in the name of Rabbi Jonathan: . . . "There was a king who had two sons, one grown up, the other still young. The grown up was scrubbed clean, while the little one was covered with dirt. Still the king loved the young one more than he loved the grown up."[39]

In the same regard, Hultgren notes a consistent pattern in biblical literature: Though the first-born son had a privileged position, the line of Israel's inheritance was often through the younger children. He lists the examples: Cain and Abel, Ishmael and Isaac, Esau and Jacob, Jacob's favorite sons Joseph and later Benjamin, and Aaron and Moses. Both David and Solomon were younger sons.[40]

To Whom Was the Parable Directed?

Luke strung together three parables—the Parable of the One Lost Sheep, the Parable of the One Lost Coin, and this Parable of the Father and His Two Sons—introducing the set with the following verses: "Now the tax collectors and sinners were all drawing near to hear him [Jesus]. And the Pharisees and the scribes murmured, saying 'This man receives sinners and eats with them.'"[41] As a result, most scholars suggest the parable was directed against Jesus' detractors.

I don't agree. While these verses may quote what his opponents said, and while there may have been Pharisees and scribes among those listening to

Jesus preach, all three parables contained teachings applicable to the general community. Probably the parables were delivered at different times to different audiences in different locations. Jesus may have shared the Parable of the Father and His Two Sons on more than one occasion.

The disadvantaged and needy identified with the first son and reveled in the father's immediate and unconditional acceptance of his returning child. Jesus reminded them that God would welcome them completely and unconditionally once they repented. Even the most depraved sinner would be accepted in love.

In the World to Come, a great celebration awaited every sinner who repented. But time was short. The banquet was already prepared and would begin soon. Those who didn't atone now would be left outside and destroyed.

It didn't matter how much property, wealth, or status a person possessed. They were irrelevant in the kingdom of heaven. God treated all righteous people as His sons and gave them all an equal share of His largesse.

Regardless of their good works and their diligence in maintaining the law, those who were proud or jealous or judgmental of others were sinners. By not accepting God's willingness to welcome in love even the most debased penitent, they were thwarting God's will. Like stubborn and rebellious children, they did not honor their Father and would be punished accordingly.[42]

The "scribes and Pharisees" who murmured against Jesus' dining with sinners were like the older son, who complained about his father's decisions to welcome back his wayward son unconditionally, to exalt him to a position of respect and authority, and to organize a feast in his honor. Jesus reminded these detractors of their own doctrine that God rejoiced when any sinner repented.

The father pleaded for the elder son to join the party and rejoice in the younger son's return. So Jesus urged the leaders of the Jewish people to acknowledge and rejoice in the repentance of his followers. Then they too would enter the Kingdom of God. Instead, he complained, they continued to despise his followers and dismiss his teachings.

The elder son was not rejected. He would inherit all his father's property. The younger son still had no assets. But this was a subtle reminder to Jesus' listeners that the conventional leaders of the people—who spent their energy and talents accumulating and protecting property—would not participate in the Messianic celebration to come. Their priorities were misplaced. With the advent of God's kingdom, their assets would be worthless.

The poor and infirm—who have no wealth but have truly repented and now focused their energies on living in accordance with Jesus' teachings—

would enjoy the World to Come. They would survive the death of the wealthy and enjoy abundance.

In Jewish tradition, God was called both *av harakhameem* (Compassionate Father) and *shofeyt al kol ha'aretz* (Judge of All the Earth); debate raged among the sages as to whether mercy or justice was God's predominant characteristic. In this parable, Jesus emphasized God's tender mercy. God was not the warrior king or the strict accountant. God was a parent who welcomed His frail and selfish creatures with love.

Jesus' Teachings Contradicted Conventional Wisdom

For some listeners the parable was shocking.

While the younger son may have been sufficiently contrite in his confession to his father, he still had not made up for the harm he caused, and he had not demonstrated that he would never commit the same sins again. The elder son showed little respect for his father and dishonored his brother and had yet to recognize or apologize for either sin. According to the sages, both sons were still unrepentant sinners.

Even the father was at fault, for giving away one-third of his assets to his younger son and risking his family's ability to withstand economic hardships in the future. He had set no standard for his younger son and did not punish him for his foolhardiness and disrespect. When the son returned, he required no compensation or commitment to work for the family's well-being. Instead, he gave him clothes and sandals, hugs and kisses, and threw a big party in his honor.

Jesus' teachings contradicted this conventional understanding. God's forgiveness was immediate and unconditional. No waiting was necessary, nothing more was required, for the behavior of a truly penitent person was completely changed. He would never sin again in the same way. That was the meaning of repentance. Those who were critical of and stood in judgment against penitent sinners were transgressing God's commandments. They ought to make atonement and change their own behavior if they hoped to survive in the World to Come. The great banquet was already prepared, but by their intransigence and narrow-mindedness, they were choosing to remain outside and die.

The Pharisees and scribes didn't take kindly to Jesus' assertions.

In the next chapter, Jesus continued to explore human relationships with a focus on special people—judges, tax collectors, widows, and next-door neighbors.

Notes

1. Matthew 21:23–27.

2. Matthew 21:32.

3. Pesikta Rabbati chapter 44, as reported in George Foot Moore, *Judaism in the First Centuries of the Christian Era* (Cambridge, Mass.: Harvard University Press, 1927), vol. 1, 509. See also Ben Sirakh 31:30–31.

4. Isaiah 1:18.

5. Tosefta Kiddushin 1:14ff, as presented in Moore, *Judaism in the First Centuries of the Christian Era*, vol. 1, 521.

6. Isaiah 59:20.

7. Yoma 86b.

8. Exodus 20:12; Deuteronomy 6:15; Leviticus 19:3; Philo, *De Decalogo*, chapters 22–24.

9. Mekilta, Bahodesh 8.

10. Mekilta on Exodus 20:12. The same verb applied to two different items indicated an equivalence between them.

11. Mekilta de Rabbi Simeon ben Yochai, Exodus 20:12.

12. Sifra, Kedoshim; Kiddushin 31b, as presented in Moore, *Judaism in the First Centuries of the Christian Era*, vol. 2, 132–33.

13. Sifra, Kedoshim, Kiddushin 31b.

14. Sifre on Deuteronomy 6:7.

15. Exodus 21:15, 17; Leviticus 20:9. See also Deuteronomy 27:16; Proverbs 20:20; 30:11, 17.

16. Jerusalem Talmud, Peah 15d, as presented in Moore, *Judaism in the First Centuries of the Christian Era*, vol. 2, 132.

17. M. Peah 1:1.

18. M. Baba Batra 8.2.

19. Deuteronomy 21:17, M. Baba Batra 8.4, M. Bekhorot 8:9.

20. Deuteronomy 21:17, M. Baba Batra 8.5.

21. M. Baba Batra 8.7.

22. M. Baba Batra 9.1.

23. M. Baba Batra 8:7.

24. Arland J. Hultgren suggests that the son's request was tantamount to wishing the father were already dead (*The Parables of Jesus: A Commentary* [Grand Rapids, Mich.: William B. Eerdmans, 2000], 73). Bernard Brandon Scott calls it "an attack on the father, a violation of the commandment to honor your father and mother" (*Re-Imagine the World: An Introduction to the Parables of Jesus* Santa Rosa, Calif., Polebridge, 2001], 70).

25. Pigs are unclean animals, unfit for Jewish consumption and anathema to Jews. See Leviticus 11:7; Deuteronomy 14:8; Isaiah 65:4; 66:17; 1 Maccabees 1:47; M. Baba Kama 7.7. In 2 Maccabees, Eleazar and the seven brothers chose death to eating swine (6:18; 7:1–42). This image of the younger son feeding swine indicated the extent to which he

had rejected his faith. Forced to work on the Sabbath, eat forbidden foods, and contact unclean substances without any opportunity to immerse and cleanse himself, he was thoroughly and constantly defiled.

26. The phrase in verse 16 "and no one gave him anything" could mean that since no one gave him any food, he grew desperate and was willing to eat pig's food. Or it could mean that since no one gave him permission to eat the pigs' pods, he had to *steal* whatever food he could find. See Joachim Jeremias, *The Parables of Jesus*, rev. ed. (New York: Charles Scribner's Sons, 1963), 130. Thus, in addition to all his other crimes, he also became a thief.

27. Proverbs 29:3–4.

28. Or, better, "came to his senses." See *The New American Bible, New Jerusalem Bible with Apocrypha*, and *The Living Bible*.

29. Hultgren, *The Parables of Jesus*, 76.

30. Tertellian, *On Repentance* (Whitefish, MT: Kessinger Publishing, 2004), 8; Claude G. Montefiore, *Synoptic Gospels* (London: Macmillan, 1909), vol. 2, 989; Jeremias, *The Parables of Jesus*, 130.

31. Genesis 41:42–43.

32. Zechariah 3:4–5. See also Genesis 27:15; Esther 3:10, 8:2; 1 Maccabees 6:15.

33. Luke 15:1–2.

34. Ben Sirakh 33:22–23.

35. How poignant was the son's lament, "You gave him the fatted calf and never gave me even a scrawny kid!"

36. Here again the language was poignant. The son was an elder (*presbyteros*) who had to ask a child servant (*pias*) what was going on.

37. Genesis 25:23.

38. Pesikta Rabbati 184b–185a, as presented in Claude G. Montefiore and H. Loewe, *A Rabbinic Anthology* (London: Macmillan, 1938), 321.

39. Midrash on Psalms 9, as presented in Scott, *Re-Imagine the World*, 69.

40. For a fuller discussion, see Hultgren, *The Parables of Jesus*, 112.

41. Luke 15:1–2.

42. Deuteronomy 21:18–22.

CHAPTER FIFTEEN

Special People

The Parable of the Pharisee and the Publican

A Pharisee and a tax collector went into the Temple to pray. In his prayer the Pharisee gave thanks to God and extolled his own virtues. He was not an extortionist or an adulterer or even a tax collector. He fasted more often than was required and gave tithes regularly. Standing off to the side, the tax collector beat his breast, admitted he was a sinner, and begged God for mercy.

Jesus declared that the tax collector had fulfilled God's wishes more than the Pharisee, and he concluded with this prediction: "Every one who exalts himself will be humbled, but he who humbles himself will be exalted."

> He also told this parable to some who trusted in themselves that they were righteous and despised others: "Two men went up into the temple to pray, one a Pharisee and the other a tax collector. The Pharisee stood and prayed thus with himself, 'God, I thank thee that I am not like other men, extortioners, unjust, adulterers, or even like this tax collector. I fast twice a week, I give tithes of all that I get.' But the tax collector, standing far off, would not even lift up his eyes to heaven, but beat his breast, saying, 'God, be merciful to me a sinner!' I tell you, this man went down to his house justified rather than the other; for every one who exalts himself will be humbled, but he who humbles himself will be exalted." (Luke 18:9–14)

What Secrets Did the Parable Convey?

Once again, Jesus used two men to illustrate his ideas. Not brothers this time, but two stereotypical characters at the extremes of Jewish society—the respected sage and the reviled tax collector. He used the same language to describe both men. Each came to the Temple to pray. Each offered his confession to God.

But Jesus was building on the prejudices of his audience. Sages were generally respected in Jewish society, while tax collectors were reviled and rebuffed. His listeners would automatically favor the Pharisee and discredit the publican.

The Pharisee's prayer followed a format familiar to later generations of Jews.

The Mishnah commanded Jews to pray on entering and leaving the synagogue,[1] and the Talmud provided the prayer: "I give thanks to You, O Lord my God, that You have set my portion among those who sit in the house of study and have not set my portion among those who sit on [street] corners,[2] for I rise early and they rise early, but I rise early for words of Torah and they rise early for frivolous talk. I labor and they labor, but I labor and receive a reward and they labor and do not receive a reward. I run and they run, but I run to life in the World to Come and they run to the pit of destruction."[3]

The content of the Pharisee's prayer conformed to this pattern. He gave thanks that he was not like those whom God judged to be disreputable and unworthy—swindlers, thieves, adulterers, and tax collectors.

To the contrary, his deeds proved him to be a devoted follower of the law. He fasted twice a week. Jewish tradition required him to fast only on the Day of Atonement.[4] He tithed everything he received, even items that did not require his tithe.[5] He was a pious and observant Jew.

The tax collector beat his breast and pleaded with God, "Have mercy on me." Too ashamed to look up as he admitted his sinfulness, he stared down at the floor. Other worshippers may have been nearby, but those who knew him avoided him. He felt alone and desperate.

At the close of the service (or at the end of their prayers), each man returned to his home.

To this point, listeners would have heard nothing extraordinary in Jesus' tale. Both men behaved much as the audience expected.

How shocked they must have been, then, when Jesus declared that the tax collector was the righteous man and the Pharisee was not.

According to Jesus, the publican had truly repented. He was a changed person. God had forgiven his sins completely and accepted him. Nothing more was needed.

"But what sign of repentance has the tax collector shown?" Jesus' listeners might have asked. "Has he compensated those he hurt? Has he undone the harm he created? How do we know he has truly repented?"

People were taught, as we have seen, that repentance took place in four steps. The third step demanded the penitent sinner undo the harm he created. The fourth step required him never to commit the same sin again. There was no indication that the tax collector did any of these.

Jesus was expressing a radical new idea. It started with the Parable of the Father and His Two Sons. It was even more pronounced in this parable. God accepted a truly repentant sinner immediately. His sins were wiped clean; his soul became whole and pure again. There was no doubt or hesitation. A truly repentant sinner would work hard to undo the harm he created, and he would never sin again. That was what it meant to be truly repentant. God knew that. Jesus was suggesting that Jews should act accordingly and accept the penitent immediately and unconditionally—as God did.

Jesus Contradicted the Conventional Leaders

While opposition to this radical notion might have been expressed by anyone in his audience, the sages established the standards on penitence. The parable was directed against the Pharisees.

Jesus asserted not only that the sages were wrong in their teachings about repentance but that some Pharisees were sinners. Though they appeared to follow God's law and live pious lives—giving even more than was required— they were haughty and prideful and judgmental of others. They ignored the needy; they neglected the downtrodden; they rejected those on the margin of society. As Isaiah said, " 'What need have I of all your sacrifices?' says the Lord. '. . . Seek justice; overcome oppression; defend the fatherless; plead for the widow.' "[6]

The criteria by which God judged who was worthy and who was not included not only what a man did but also what he said and (more importantly) the manner in which he related to other people. The Pharisee's tithes and fasting were worthy endeavors, but his soul was tainted by hubris. He judged others without any knowledge of their hardships and struggles. He rejected people God accepted. He lacked humility. The sage saw himself a righteous man, but he was a sinner in Jesus' eyes. Unless he repented, he would be condemned.

"If you agree and give heed," warned Isaiah, "You will eat the good things of the earth; but if you refuse and disobey, you will be devoured [by] the sword."[7]

Jesus was not attacking all Pharisees. Not all sages were sinners, any more than all publicans were penitent. The Pharisee and the tax collector in the parable were stereotypes, conventional images in people's minds on which Jesus built his tale. They didn't represent any particular Pharisee or tax collector.

Nor did Jesus suggest that the teachings of the sages promoted haughtiness, self-satisfaction, and prejudice. On the contrary, he accepted and promoted many of their ideas, but he warned his followers that some Pharisees behaved contrary to their own teachings.[8]

The lessons of this parable applied not just to wayward Pharisees but to anyone who thought himself better than others around him, to anyone who ignored the needy and neglected the poor, to anyone who despised other Jews struggling on the margins of society. Every such person—Pharisee or not—was a sinner. Unless he repented, he would be doomed in the coming apocalypse.

As Luke stated in his introduction, Jesus addressed this parable to those "who trusted in themselves that they were righteous and who despised others."[9] That included many Jews besides the Pharisees.

The Parable of the Friend at Midnight

When unexpected guests arrived and the host had no extra food to feed them, he went to a neighbor's house at midnight, woke up the family, and requested three loaves of bread. About this situation Jesus asked a rhetorical question: Can you imagine the neighbor saying, "Don't bother me. My children are asleep. I can't give you anything"? Of course, the neighbor would give him what he needed.

Jesus concluded the story with this instruction to his disciples: "Ask, and it will be given you; seek, and you will find; knock, and it will be opened to you."

> And he said to them, "Which of you who has a friend will go to him at midnight and say to him, 'Friend, lend me three loaves; for a friend of mine has arrived on a journey, and I have nothing to set before him'; and he will answer from within, 'Do not bother me; the door is now shut, and my children are with me in bed; I cannot get up and give you anything'? I tell you, though he will not get up and give him anything because he is his friend, yet because of his importunity he will rise and give him whatever he needs. And I tell you, Ask, and it will be given you; seek, and you will find; knock, and it will be opened to you." (Luke 11:5–9)

Jesus Built on Jewish Images

Once again, Jesus built his teachings on images already in the minds of his listeners. Hospitality was considered a sacred duty in the Jewish community—even when the visitor was a stranger.[10] In this case, the visitor was a friend. It was unthinkable that the neighbor would refuse the request. Even if it meant rising off the straw mat on which husband, wife, and children slept huddled together, unlocking the creaky latch, opening the door, and waking the children, the neighbor would comply.

What Secrets Did the Parable Convey?

Luke placed the parable in a setting dealing with prayer, but the original intention of the metaphor had little to do with prayer. Depending on the audience, these are some of the ideas Jesus conveyed in this parable.

Some of the disciples left their homes and gave up their livelihoods to follow Jesus. As a result they were often dependent on the generosity of others for food and shelter. Jesus assured them that people in the community would help them—if they asked.

The followers of Jesus who preached his message in distant towns and villages often experienced resistance and opposition. Jesus assured them that people would respond to their teaching—if they were persistent.

If the followers of Jesus perceived a veiled reference to God in the neighbor, the parable assured them they could depend on God to respond to their needs even under the most unexpected circumstances.

An Additional Parable in Luke

Luke attached an additional short parable, based on two rhetorical questions: "If his son asks for a fish, what father among you will give him a serpent instead? Or if he asks for an egg, will give him a scorpion?" (Luke 11:11–12).[11]

The answers were obvious to Jesus' audience. No father would deliberately hurt his son in this fashion.

If this parable was directed at his disciples, it reinforced the previous metaphor. Most people would treat Jesus' followers decently and not deliberately hurt them.

If the father in the parable was God, this also reinforced the previous image. They could rely on God not to lie to them or hurt them.

However, if verse 13 was attached to the parable, the meanings change radically. No longer addressed to Jesus' disciples, the verse applied to Jesus' opponents: "If you who are evil know how to give good gifts to your children, how much more will the heavenly father give the holy spirit to those who ask him!" (Luke 11:13).

Even misguided Pharisees gave nice gifts to their children. Surely the Compassionate Father would do the same.

Furthermore, God's gifts were not material. They were spiritual.

The Same Additional Parable in Matthew

Matthew recorded essentially the same parable, including the focus shift to the Pharisees and other opponents.

> What man of you, if his son asks him for bread, will give him a stone? Or if he asks for a fish, will give him a serpent? If you then, who are evil, know how to give good gifts to your children, how much more will your father who is in heaven give good things to those who ask him! (Matthew 7:9–11)

But Matthew attached to this parable a concluding verse that became one of the most quoted statements in the gospels: "Do unto others what you wish them to do to you."[12]

The Golden Rule was the first half of the verse. The second half was just as important: "That is the law and the prophets."[13]

The whole verse read: "Do unto others what you wish them to do to you. That is the law and the prophets."

The Golden Rule

A seeker came to Hillel and said, "Teach me Jewish tradition while standing on one foot." And Hillel said, "What is hateful to you, do not do to others." At the close of his brief response, Hillel added, "This is the entire law."[14] A generation after Jesus, a similar story was told about Rabbi Akiba. Rabbi Akiba replied, "What is hateful to you, do not to your fellowman."[15]

In Tobit 4:15, the rule read, "What you hate, do not do to anyone";[16] and the Epistle of Aristeas taught, "Our law commands to do no harm in word or deed to any man."[17] After listing several of the Ten Commandments as examples—"You shall not commit adultery. You shall not kill. You shall not steal. You shall not covet"—Paul summarized his teaching with the sentence, "Love does no wrong to a neighbor; therefore love is the fulfilling of the law."[18] Written toward the end of the first century, the Didache echoed the same principle. "Whatsoever you would not have done to yourself, do not to another."[19]

Though Jesus gave his own phrasing to the Golden Rule, the aphorism was already familiar to Jews—at least in the negative.

Jesus did not suggest that the Golden Rule superceded all the injunctions and teachings in the Hebrew Bible. Like its predecessors, the Golden Rule was a quick summary of Jewish thought.

The Parable of the Judge and the Widow

A judge who did not revere God and had no regard for people was asked by a widow to punish her adversary for the harm he did to her. He declined, then changed his mind and punished her enemy because he didn't want to be bothered by her constant nagging.

If an uncaring judge responded to the widow's pleas, God would certainly respond to the pleas of the righteous. Their vindication would come speedily and decisively.

> He told them a parable, to the effect that they ought always to pray and not lose heart. He said, "In a certain city there was a judge who neither feared God nor regarded man; and there was a widow in that city who kept coming to him and saying, 'Vindicate me against my adversary.' For a while he refused; but afterward he said to himself, 'Though I neither fear God nor regard man, yet because this widow bothers me, I will vindicate her, or she will wear me out by her continual coming.'" And the Lord said, "Hear what the unrighteous judge says. And will not God vindicate his elect, who cry to him day and night? Will he delay long over them? I tell you, he will vindicate them speedily." (Luke 18:2–8a)

What Secrets Did the Parable Convey?

What a strange parable! God was compared to an unrighteous judge who acted on the widow's behalf to get her to stop annoying him.

Is that why God would respond to the prayers of Jesus' followers—to get them to stop pestering Him?

A common form of doctrinal proof among the sages of the first century was to establish the validity of a major principle on the basis of a minor principle. The discourse usually included the phrase, "how much the more so."

Jesus employed the same reasoning. If an uncaring judge eventually yielded to supplication and granted the widow's petition, how much the more so would God—who is just and merciful—respond to the pleas of the righteous?

Jesus Built on Jewish Images

While ultimate legal authority lay with the Roman governor of Syria (and the Roman prefect in Judea) and there were Roman courts of law to which non-Jews might appeal, the parable clearly envisioned a controversy between two Jews as something to be decided by a Jewish judge.

Rabbi Ishmael used to say, "Judge not alone, for none may judge alone save God."[20] According to the Mishnah, "cases concerning property [require] three judges."[21] But this may have been the ideal, not the reality. According to Chajes, a single judge heard most cases in small villages.[22] Since many of Jesus' listeners were from rural communities and small towns, a single judge may have been their reality.

Judges were accorded respect in Jewish tradition. As Pharisees and sages, they were expected to lead exemplary lives. As judges, they were expected to execute God's law in a fair, moral, and impartial fashion. "Do not side with the powerful to do wrong . . . and do not show deference to a poor man in his dispute."[23] "You shall not render an unfair decision. Do not favor the poor nor show deference to the rich. Judge your fellowman fairly."[24] "When you judge another man, incline the balance [of justice] in his favor."[25] "Do not judge your fellow until you have come to his place."[26] "Let those who bring suit stand before you as wicked men [question them thoroughly and diligently as if to unearth their guilt], and when they have departed from before you consider them as innocent."[27] "To do justice and righteousness is better than sacrifice."[28] They set high standards for themselves and usually met them.

Not every sage fulfilled these high ideals. "Do not take a bribe," Deuteronomy warned, "for a bribe blinds the eyes of the wise."[29] "Do not take a bribe," not even to acquit the innocent or condemn the guilty.[30] "A judge who perverts justice is called unrighteous, hateful, abominable, a cursed thing and abhorred."[31] "God does not punish the unjust judge with a penalty of money; God exacts his life."[32] These statements were made because some judges catered to the rich and powerful, took bribes, and subverted justice.

Jesus selected such a disreputable judge to star in his parable. A sage who admitted he "neither feared God nor regarded man" was the opposite of what listeners believed about most traditional teachers.

What about the widow?

The Hebrew word *almana*, usually translated "widow," denoted more than a married woman whose husband died but a once-married woman who had no means of financial support and therefore needed legal protection.[33] This may have been the difficult strait in which the widow of the parable found herself. She was destitute and needed help. So she pleaded with the sage to help her—time and time again.

She was within her rights. She was entitled to the property and maintenance provisions of her marriage contract, and her husband's heirs were obligated to fulfill them out of the estate. Particularly was she entitled to the widow's maintenance, including a residence, clothing, medical expenses, and the use of household articles. The rules were complicated and often depended on local custom. In general, however, the choice lay with the widow, and the heirs could not deprive her of her maintenance against her wishes.[34]

Biblical tradition buttressed her position. Isaiah railed against those who "subvert the cause of the poor and rob the needy of my people of their rights, that widows may be their spoil, and fatherless children their booty."[35] The psalmist lamented, "They slay the widow and the sojourner; they murder the fatherless."[36] "Thus says the Lord of hosts[:] . . . do not oppress the widow, the fatherless, the sojourner, or the poor."[37]

Jesus supported this biblical view. He excoriated those "who devour widows' houses and for a pretense make long prayers."[38] His audiences sympathized with and understood clearly the plight of the widow.

Once again, Jesus established a conflict between two well-known characters at the extremes of Jewish society—an insensitive and uncaring judge and a poor widow. It was the Pharisee and the tax collector in another guise. However, this time there were no shocking revelations. The judge remained insensitive, and the widow defenseless.

The Efficacy of Prayer

The parable was not about what to pray or how often to pray. It was about the efficacy of prayer. Jesus was responding to those in his own fellowship who wondered why their prayers were not being answered. Why were there no signs? Why did the unjust prosper still and the downtrodden still suffer? Why was the expected kingdom not apparent?

Jesus reassured his supporters that God answered all pleas and prayers. If the uncaring judge, who refused to take the widow's case, finally responded to her pleas, God, who cares for and protects His people, would respond to their heartfelt petitions all the more.

God was "the Father of the orphans" and "the Protector of widows" who "restores the lonely to their homes" and "sets free the imprisoned."[39]

God would deliver Israel and protect him. "When he calls to me, I will answer him; I will be with him in trouble, I will rescue him and honor him."[40] Jeremiah declared, "I will restore you to health and cure you of your wounds."[41] Isaiah promised, "The Lord of hosts will protect Jerusalem. He will protect and deliver it."[42] Jeremiah concurred, "I will restore the fortunes of the tents of Jacob and have compassion on his dwellings. The city shall be rebuilt on its mound, and the palace shall stand where it used to be."[43] Zechariah affirmed, "On that day the Lord their God will save them. [He shall pasture] His people like sheep. [They shall be] like crown jewels glittering on His land."[44]

God would act on their behalf—but in His own good time. He had saved the Israelites enslaved in Egypt and led them through the desert to freedom after years of hard labor, deprivation, and suffering. He had rescued the exiles, returned them to their ancient homeland, and rebuilt the Temple after several generations in Babylonia. He had allowed the Maccabees to achieve both religious and then political independence from Syria after a decade of fighting. God would save the righteous, punish the wicked, and establish His kingdom of heaven—in His own time. There was no accelerating His timetable. He had already set the final events in motion.

What was needed, then, was not more frequent petitions or more intense prayers but faith, patience, and persistence. What was exemplary about the widow was not that she hounded and pestered the sage until he finally responded but that she was so certain of her cause that she never gave up. Her faith never wavered. She knew the system would respond eventually and rescue her.

That's what Jesus demanded of his followers. In times of distress, in the face of denunciation and persecution, whenever they felt tested and pushed to the limits of their endurance, they must maintain the certitude that God would hear their pleas and respond. The kingdom was coming soon. The apocalypse had already begun.

The Parable Concerning Going before the Judge

A Jew, engaged in a dispute with another, contemplated going to court to settle the matter. He wasn't sure. Things didn't always work out right in court. Jesus offered the following advice:

> Make friends quickly with your accuser, while you are going with him to court, lest your accuser hand you over to the judge, and the judge to the guard, and you be put in prison. Truly, I say to you, you will never get out till you have paid the last penny. (Matthew 5:25–26)

What Secrets Did the Parable Convey?
Matthew included this parable in the Sermon on the Mount. Though that may not have been its original context, it fits the content of Jesus' speech at that point very well. Jesus shared his understandings of Jewish law.

With respect to the commandment "You shall not murder,"[45] the law noted that any person who murdered would be liable to judgment. Jesus went farther. "But I say to you that every one who is angry with his brother shall be liable to judgment."[46] Jesus declared that being angry with another person invoked the same consequences as murdering him.

In fact, Jesus and the teachers were talking about different kinds of "judgment." The sages declared that a murderer must be brought to trial and found guilty by a court of law before he could be punished.[47] If in the court's *judgment* the man was guilty, he could be executed. The sages were discussing the requirements of the Jewish legal system and how human judges might determine a person's guilt or innocence. In that context, there was no trial, judgment, or punishment for getting angry with another person.

Jesus was talking about divine *judgment*. Each human being was destined to appear before God in a heavenly tribunal where his life would be reviewed and judged. In that context, a person's anger, jealousy, and hatred would be considered. Jesus warned that God would punish anyone who insulted, belittled, or rejected his fellow man.[48]

Therefore, Jesus encouraged people to reconcile—to put aside their enmities and resolve their differences now before the Final Judgment was made and they suffered the consequences of their hesitancies.

In his description of the trial in this parable, Jesus evoked a double entendre. On the human level, Jesus reminded his listeners that arguing disputes in court didn't always settle matters appropriately. There were sometimes untoward consequences. People got hurt. They could be thrown in jail; they could be left penniless.

Not so in the divine tribunal. There would be no secrets, no false testimony. God knew everything. Everyone would be judged fairly, and each person would receive his just desserts. The righteous would be saved; sinners would suffer.

But in heaven the standards were more stringent. Hatred, calumny, and disrespect were sins. Just being angry with another person made one liable for punishment. We're all on our way to court, Jesus taught, a heavenly court. Reconcile now, he advised, or suffer God's adverse judgment against you.

The Same Parable Occurred in Luke
A judgement parable in Luke:

> As you go with your accuser before the magistrate, make an effort to settle with
> him on the way, lest he drag you to the judge, and the judge hand you over to the

officer, and the officer put you in prison. I tell you, you will never get out till you have paid the very last copper. (Luke 12:58–59)

However, Luke set the parable in an entirely different context. Many of the speeches that preceded it dealt with the approaching holocaust and the devastation, destruction, and death that would result. As a consequence, the emphasis of the metaphor in that setting was on the harm the defendant might experience.

Jesus warned his listeners that they were all defendants on their way to God's court and that they were in danger. Unless they changed their behavior and reconciled with those against whom they had controversies, God would condemn them, remove them from His presence, and cause them to languish in prison (hell).

Reconcile now, while you're still alive and can do something about it, Jesus taught, before the Final Judgment, when it would be too late.

Jesus used characters in his parables already in the minds of his audiences, and he got his listeners thinking by having these stereotypical characters act in unexpected ways. In the next chapter, we explore one of Jesus' most controversial and enduring metaphors—the Parable of the Priest, the Levite, and the Samaritan.

Notes

1. M. Berakhot 4:2.

2. Referring to riffraff loitering on street corners, engaged in no meaningful work, or possibly to ignorant people.

3. Berakhot 28b, as presented in Bernard Brandon Scott, *Hear Then the Parable: A Commentary on the Parables of Jesus* (Minneapolis, Minn.: Fortress, 1990), 95. Scott notes a similar prayer in Tosefta Berakhot 7:18; and Joachim Jeremias, *The Parables of Jesus*, rev. ed. (New York: Charles Scribner's Sons, 1963), 142, note 55, presents a similar prayer from the Dead Sea Scrolls (IQH7:34).

4. Leviticus 16:29–31, 23:27–32; Numbers 29:7. In each of these passages, "afflict your souls" was interpreted to mean a full twenty-four-hour fast. Postbiblical Jewish literature reported many instances of people choosing to fast as a personal penitence for sin or as part of their mourning ritual, but these fasts were not imposed by law and were opposed by some rabbis. One New Testament tradition indicated that the disciples of John and the Pharisees "fasted often" and that Jesus and his disciples deviated from their fasting standards (Matthew 9:14, Mark 2:18, Luke 5:33).

5. In addition to the tithes prescribed by Jewish law (see especially the following

tractates in the Mishnah: Demai, Ma'aserot, and Ma'aser Sheni), he probably paid tithes voluntarily on foods and other goods he purchased—even though the tithe should have been paid by their producers.

6. Isaiah 1:11–17.

7. Isaiah 1:18–20.

8. Matthew 23:2–3.

9. Luke 18:9.

10. Note the vivid tales of Abraham receiving the three messengers (Genesis 18:1–8) and of the old man in Gibeah going to great lengths to protect his visitor (Judges 19:16–28). The following statement occurred in the Midrash on Psalms (18:29): "Giving hospitality is greater than paying homage to the Lord's Presence."

11. Some manuscripts read *asks for bread, will give him a stone; or if he asks for a fish.*

12. Matthew 7:12a. The Golden Rule was reported also in Luke 6:31.

13. Matthew 7:12b.

14. Shabbat 31a.

15. As recorded in Claude G. Montefiore and H. Loewe, *A Rabbinic Anthology* (London: Macmillan, 1938), 172–73.

16. As quoted in D. M. Beck, "The Golden Rule," in *The Interpreter's Dictionary of the Bible: An Illustrated Encyclopedia*, ed. George A. Buttrick (New York: Abingdon, 1962), vol. 2, 438–39.

17. As presented in George Foot Moore, *Judaism in the First Centuries of the Christian Era* (Cambridge, Mass.: Harvard University Press, 1927), vol. 2, 87, note 4.

18. Romans 13:8–10.

19. Didache 1:2.

20. M. Avot 4:8. The Hebrew contained a wonderful wordplay. Quoting Deuteronomy 6:4, Rabbi Ishmael referred to God as "One."

21. M. Sanhedrin 3:1.

22. Chajes, "Les juges juifs," 52, as presented in Scott, *Hear Then the Parable*, 184. Scott cautions that Chajes' study drew on material after 70 CE and needs to be updated. Drawing on a later precedent, Jeremias (*The Parables of Jesus*, 153) suggests the controversy involved money. Perhaps a debt or a pledge or a portion of an inheritance was being withheld from her. "One authorized scholar sitting alone may decide money cases" (Sanhedrin 4b).

23. Exodus 23:2.

24. Leviticus 19:15.

25. Avot 1:6.

26. Avot 2:5.

27. Abot 1:8.

28. Proverbs 21:3.

29. Deuteronomy 16:19.

30. Sifre Deuteronomy, Shoftim, §144, as presented in Montefiore and Lowe, *A Rabbinic Anthology*, 384.

31. Sifra 88d. Each of these terms of opprobrium was supported by biblical references.

32. Sifre Deuteronomy, Devarim, §9, as presented in Montefiore and Lowe, *A Rabbinic Anthology*, 387.

33. Chayim Cohen, "Widow: Biblical Period," in *Encyclopedia Judaica*, ed. Cecil Roth (Jerusalem: Macmillan, 1971–1972), vol. 16, cols. 487–88. There was no indication that the widow was an older woman. Women married in their early teens and could be widowed any time thereafter. Some widows were quite young.

34. Ben Zion Schereschewsky, "Widow: In Jewish Law," in *Encyclopedia Judaica*, ed. Cecil Roth (Jerusalem: Macmillan, 1971–1972), vol. 16, cols. 491–95.

35. Isaiah 10:2–3. See also Isaiah 1:13–17, 23; Malachi 3:5.

36. Psalm 94:6.

37. Zechariah 7:9–10.

38. Luke 20:47.

39. Psalms 68:6–7 (= Greek Psalm 68:5–6). See also Deuteronomy 10:18, Jeremiah 49:11, Psalm 146:9.

40. Psalms 91:14–15.

41. Jeremiah 30:17.

42. Isaiah 31:5.

43. Jeremiah 30:18.

44. Zechariah 9:16.

45. Exodus 20:13, Deuteronomy 5:17.

46. Matthew 5:22.

47. The Hebrew Bible established that a person accused of homicide could not be put to death "unless he stood trial before the assembly" (Numbers 35:12b). In the first century, the assembly before which the accused was tried for a capital offense was a Sanhedrin of twenty-three judges (M. Sanhedrin 1:4).

48. Matthew 5:22 suggested they would burn in hell.

CHAPTER SIXTEEN

The Parable of the Priest, the Levite, and the Samaritan

The Parable of the Priest, the Levite, and the Samaritan

A lawyer challenged Jesus. "What do I have to do to attain immortal life?" the lawyer asked. Jesus answered, "What is written in the Law?"

By responding with a question, Jesus was not evading the challenge. He was engaging the lawyer in debate on terms the sage understood—exploring what the Torah said.

The lawyer quoted Deuteronomy 6:5, "Love the Lord your God with all your heart and soul and strength"; and Leviticus 19:18, "Love your neighbor as yourself."

Jesus agreed. At this point, there was no difference between the two.

Pressing Jesus, the lawyer asked, "Who is my neighbor?" Jesus' answer would either support or contradict the traditional views.

Jesus responded with a parable: A man was robbed and beaten on the road from Jerusalem to Jericho. A priest came along, noticed the injured man, and passed him by. A Levite came by, noticed the injured man, and moved on. But a Samaritan stopped, bound up the man's wounds, carried him to a nearby inn, and treated his injuries. Before he left the next morning, the Samaritan paid the innkeeper two days' charges in advance to care for the injured stranger and promised to pay any additional costs when he returned a few days later.

Behold, a lawyer stood up to put him to the test, saying, "Teacher, what shall I do to inherit eternal life?" He said to him, "What is written in the law? How do you read?" And he answered, "You shall love the Lord your God with all your heart, and with all your soul, and with all your strength, and with all your mind; and your neighbor as yourself." And he said to him, "You have answered right; do this, and you will live." But he, desiring to justify himself, said to Jesus, "And who is my neighbor?" Jesus replied, "A man was going down from Jerusalem to Jericho, and he fell among robbers, who stripped him and beat him, and departed, leaving him half dead. Now by chance a priest was going down that road; and when he saw him he passed by on the other side. So likewise a Levite, when he came to the place and saw him, passed by on the other side. But a Samaritan, as he journeyed, came to where he was; and when he saw him, he had compassion, and went to him and bound up his wounds, pouring on oil and wine; then he set him on his own beast and brought him to an inn, and took care of him. And the next day he took out two denarii and gave them to the innkeeper, saying, 'Take care of him; and whatever more you spend, I will repay you when I come back.'" (Luke 10:25–35)

Jesus asked the lawyer, "Which of these three, do you think, proved neighbor to the man who fell among the robbers?" The lawyer admitted that the non-Jew was the neighbor. Neither Jew in the parable had displayed the love that Leviticus demanded:

> Which of these three, do you think, proved neighbor to the man who fell among the robbers?' He said, 'The one who showed mercy on him.' (Luke 10:36–37a)

Jesus won the debate—and contradicted popular beliefs—without declaring his own ideas and teachings directly.

Jesus' listeners understood his many implications, because they accepted traditions that are no longer part of our lives.

A Neglected Corpse

According to the Torah, both the *koheyn* (priest) and the Levite were prohibited from touching a human corpse in any fashion.[1] They could not lift it, prepare it for burial, or even to accompany it to the funeral site. The rules were even more stringent for the high priest. He could not care for or accompany even the dead body of his mother or father.[2]

After discussing this prohibition, the Mishnah concluded that "a high priest or Nazarite may not contact uncleanliness because of their [dead] kin, but they may contact uncleanliness because of a neglected corpse."[3] Specifically, according to Rabbi Eliezer, "If they were on a journey and found a neglected corpse . . . the high priest may contact uncleanliness, but the Nazarite may not."[4] If the high priest could draw near to deal with a neglected corpse, so could all lesser priests.

Sadducees, who did not recognize the teachings of the Mishnah and followed their own interpretations of the Mosaic law, would have approved the actions of the priest and the Levite in Jesus' parable. They were fulfilling God's commands, avoiding contamination as Leviticus demanded, and maintaining their ritual purity. Even an ordinary Jew who touched a human corpse was unclean for seven days. He could not have intercourse with his wife, hug his children, or use the same utensils they used, since his contact would spread the impurity to others. On the third day and the seventh day, he underwent a complicated cleansing ritual to remove the impurity. On the completion of his ritual cleansing, he could rejoin his family and community.[5] The consequences of touching a corpse were enormous for a priest or Levite.

Most Jews, however, followed the teachings of the Pharisees and accepted the Mishnah as their guide. Imagining the victim unconscious and abandoned on that lonely road, Jesus' listeners would have condemned the priest and the Levite for not stopping for what they presumed was a human corpse. If they had examined the injured man, they would have discovered he was breathing and needed attention. They might have saved his life. According to the sages, every Jewish law could be broken to save a human life.[6] Even if he were dead, they could have covered his nakedness, brought his body to safe place, and searched for his relatives.

For the Jews in Jesus' audience, the priest and the Levite had broken the very laws they were expected to uphold.

Samaritans

At one time, Samaria was the capital of the kingdom of Israel. Founded in the ninth century BCE by King Omri, it remained the center of northern Jewish life for two hundred years until the Assyrians conquered the city and deported most of its inhabitants. In their place Sargon II settled colonists from Babylon, Cutha, and Hamath. As a consequence, the Samaritans became a mixed population of Jews and foreigners.

The Samaritans rebelled during the reign of Alexander the Great. As punishment, a colony of Macedonians was settled there, and the capital was turned into a Greek city. Recaptured by the John Hyrcanus in 107 BCE, the region came under Jewish rule again. Herod rebuilt the city in 25 BCE and renamed it Sebaste, in honor of the Roman Emperor Augustus.

Samaritans and Jews shared many religious ideas, but the Samaritans understood them differently. They acknowledged Moses as their lawgiver, but they had their own Torah, and they recognized Mount Gerizim as their spiritual center (not Mount Zion) and the sanctuary they constructed there as the true temple (not Solomon's Temple in Jerusalem). Over the centuries, they developed their own priesthood, their own rituals, and their own laws. They didn't accept the authority or the ideas of the Pharisees and the Sadducees. On the contrary, the Samaritan leaders claimed they were the true bearers of the ancient faith of Moses.

This rivalry reached its climax a hundred years before Jesus' birth, when the armies of John Hyrcanus obliterated the Samaritan temple on Mount Gerizim and killed thousands of Samaritan fighters. After that, each community viewed the other as apostates. Some twenty years before Jesus' ministry, a group of Samaritans defiled the Jerusalem Temple by strewing it with human bones.[7]

The enmity and mistrust Jews felt were expressed in a series of laws. Jews normally said "Amen" after an Israelite recited a blessing, but Jews were commanded not to say "Amen" after a Samaritan said a blessing.[8] Two witnesses normally certified a document. However, if one of the two witnesses was a Samaritan, the document was invalid.[9] Samaritans routinely married gentiles. This alone made them suspect to Jews. Rabbi Eliezer ruled that Jews should not marry Samaritans.[10] A man who had intercourse with a Samaritan woman (even though he could marry her) paid a fifty-shekel fine.[11] Samaritan women were unclean, and Samaritan men defiled whatever they touched.[12] The half-shekel tax to support the Temple was not accepted from a Samaritan even when he offered it voluntarily.[13] Rabbi Eliezer used to say, "Who eats the bread of the Samaritans is like [a Jew] who eats swine."[14]

These antipathies and prejudices filled the minds of Jesus' listeners the moment he mentioned that the third passer-by was a Samaritan.

Priests, Levites, and Israelites

According to Jewish tradition at the time of Jesus, Levi was Leah's child, Jacob's third son, and the progenitor of the Israelite tribe that bore his name.[15] Moses and Aaron were members of the tribe of Levi.[16] During the Exodus, Aaron served as chief priest of the Israelite people. His sons and various members of the tribe of Levi assisted him. They cared for, maintained, used, preserved, and transported all the objects used in Jewish worship during that wilderness journey.[17] Following the conquest, the land of Canaan was divided among eleven tribes. The tribe of Levi received no specific territory. Instead, its members settled among the other tribes to continue to serve them as priests.[18]

The structure that emerged under Aaron during the Exodus recognized

three levels of priests. Aaron served as high priest. All other priests were subservient to him and under his jurisdiction. Aaron's sons, their families, and
their descendents constituted the next level of priesthood. Like Aaron they
were consecrated for the sacred office of priest, and they alone offered sacrifices on the altar in the tabernacle. The lowest and largest cadre was the
Levites. They set up the tabernacle in each encampment, prepared the animals for sacrifice, shared the special portions, cleaned up afterward, and
wrapped and carried the tabernacle with its furnishings and appurtenances
to the next location.

Solomon built a central sanctuary. Eventually all local shrines and places
of worship were abolished, and the three-tiered priestly system operated only
at the Temple in Jerusalem. Under the monarchy, priestly traditions
expanded. The high priest and the priests who served under him became part
of the aristocracy. They were among the captives conquered by the Babylonians and sent into exile.

Under the Hasmoneans and especially under the Romans, the high
priest's office increased in power and splendor. The priests under him
belonged to twenty-four priestly families, all descendents of Aaron.[19] Each
family provided priests to serve the Temple for one week, rotating through
twenty-four weeks. On major festivals, they all officiated together. Only these
priests offered sacrifices.[20] In addition, they cared for the vessels of the sanctuary.[21]

The Levites assisted the priests. They cleaned and maintained the Temple
courts and chambers, polished and protected the sacred vessels, prepared the
cereal offering and the service of praise.[22] Some were porters or gatekeepers;
some recorded and guarded the Temple treasures; others served as members
of the choir or as Temple musicians.[23]

In the time of Jesus, Jews were used to thinking in terms of a common
triad of priest, Levite, and Israelite. For example, "a priest takes precedence
over a Levite, a Levite over an Israelite, and an Israelite over a *mamzeyr*."[24]
This tripartite division had been part of their social structure for centuries
and an indelible part of their personal experiences.

Jesus' listeners expected someone to help the beaten victim. When the
priest and the Levite neglected to do so, they anticipated that the caregiver
would be an Israelite. In that case, the parable would reinforce Jesus' teachings that (1) status had nothing to do with righteousness; (2) ordinary people—even people on the margins of Jewish society—could be righteous; and
(3) many conventional leaders did not obey God's commands and were sin-

ners. This would have been a powerful story, much in keeping with his other lessons.

It would have buttressed biblical tradition and supported Jesus' contention that ordinary Jews must look to God and not to priests for guidance and inspiration. God's covenant called upon the entire nation to be a "kingdom of priests and a holy people."[25]

The fact that Jesus selected a Samaritan as the caregiver and not an Israelite caught them by surprise.

Love and Law

Through Moses, God articulated 613 commandments. In their efforts to understand the full meanings of each law, sages amplified and expanded the requirements until—by the time of Jesus—thousands of rules existed, and it took a lawyer to explain them all. So condensations developed, popular sayings to help people remember the essential ideas.

Rabbi Simlai said that David took the 613 commandments and condensed them into the eleven principles noted in Psalm 15. Isaiah compressed them into six.[26] Micah comprehended them in three: "To do justice, to love goodness, and to walk humbly with your God."[27] Isaiah compressed them into two: "Observe what is right and do what is just."[28] Amos compressed them further: "Seek Me and live."[29] Another sage found the one all-encompassing statement in Habakkuk: "The righteous man shall live by his faith."[30] Rabbi Akiba declared that the most comprehensive rule in the Torah was "You shall love your neighbor as yourself."[31] Two generations later, Paul said the same thing. "For the whole law is fulfilled in one word, 'You shall love your neighbor as yourself.'"[32]

The two images were conjoined in the Testaments of the Twelve Patriarchs. Isaachar said, "Love the Lord and your neighbor," and "I loved the Lord with all my strength, and I loved every man with all my heart." Daniel advised, "Love the Lord with all your life, and one another with a sincere heart."[33]

Jesus may have said it first. More likely, it was a popular saying in his time. A lawyer asked Jesus, "What is the most essential commandment?" Jesus said to love God and love your neighbor.[34] In the current parable Jesus questioned the lawyer, and the sage mentioned the same two commandments.

Both men understood the Jewish context of the question, and both men responded by quoting Torah to justify their contentions. The first quote (to love God with all your heart, soul, and might) was embedded in a section of Deuteronomy that included dozens of other commandments as well: teach these words to your children, recite them in your home and when you are away, and inscribe them on the doorposts of your house and on your gates.[35] Loving God didn't supersede the other commandments. It was merely a condensation of what was required. Loving God meant fulfilling the other commandments.

The same was true for the second quotation (to love our neighbor). The Holiness Code contained many other commandments: do not steal; do not deceive one another; do not insult the deaf or place a stumbling block before the blind, and do not stand idle while your neighbor bleeds. Loving your neighbor didn't mean neglecting these other demands. On the contrary, a Jew loved his neighbor precisely by fulfilling these commandments.

A proselyte came to Rabbi Hillel and asked, "Teach me the entire Torah while standing on one foot." Rabbi Hillel said, "Do to no other person what is hateful to you. That is the whole Torah. All the rest is commentary. Now go and study it."[36] Jesus and the lawyer would have concurred with Rabbi Hillel's response. Jesus said as much in his response to the sage, "On these two commandments depends all the law."[37]

To Whom Was the Parable Addressed?

Scott notes correctly that Jesus' listeners may have identified differently with the people in the parable depending on their ethnic background. If they were Jewish, they would have identified with the priest and the Levite. If they were non-Jews, they would have identified with the Samaritan.

For Jews, the story would be wrenching—forcing them to reevaluate their images of the Temple leaders as exemplars of morality and followers of the law and to revise their thinking about Samaritans. The wall in their minds dividing Jews from gentiles was shattered once they accepted the idea that a non-Jew might respond to a Jew suffering with greater compassion than members of his own people. The result of this realization for some Jews would be a major shift in their understanding. A "neighbor" was not just another Jew but any person needing assistance.

For non-Jews, no such shift occurred. From the outset, they identified with the Samaritan.[38]

To whom, then, was the parable addressed? Was Jesus speaking to an audience of Jews? Or was this parable addressed to a non-Jewish audience, possibly during one of Jesus' visits to Samaria?

Scott suggests Jesus was talking to a gentile audience.[39]

I disagree. I believe Jesus addressed the parable to Jewish listeners—to convey ideas Jesus wanted Jews to consider, in order to overcome their antipathy to Samaritans and others traditionally despised in Jewish society, and to broaden their understandings of the biblical commandment "Love your neighbor."

What Secrets Did the Parable Convey?
In Jesus' parable, a despised Samaritan treated the injured Jew with love, whereas a respected priest and Levite neglected and endangered him—leading his listeners to consider two significant affirmations:

- Some respected Jewish leaders disregarded the very instructions they taught to others and neglected members of their community desperately in need of help.
- Some people despised and defined by the Jewish community as non-Jews upheld God's Law and provided better care to Jews in need than some Jewish leaders did.

Traditional interpretations that deprecated Samaritans and elevated priests and Levites were wrong. Jesus' teachings were correct. Any person—Jew or gentile—who responded to the needs of his fellow man with love would inherit eternal life.

Then Jesus invited the lawyer to behave in accordance with his new understanding of God's Law. Jesus said to him, "Go and do likewise."[40]

Who Acted as a Neighbor?
Jesus' question at the end of the parable was significantly different from the lawyer's question at the beginning. The sage asked, "Who is my neighbor?" His concern was to determine which people must he love in order to fulfill God's commandment.

In asking, "Who acted as a neighbor?" Jesus shifted the concern from the object to the subject. The man hurt and dying was not the focus; the three travelers were. Which of the three men, each intent on his journey, behaved like a neighbor?

According to Jesus, we don't fulfill the commandment to love a neighbor by looking for the right person under the proper circumstances to love. We're the *neighbor*, and we remain a *neighbor* only as long as we continue to act toward our fellow men with love. When we show compassion, we fulfill God's demand. When we cease caring—no matter the circumstances or the persons involved—we sin.

Who Needs My Help?

The account of the Good Samaritan emphasized ideas central to Jesus' teaching. The lawyer was thinking: How far must I extend myself to treat people like a neighbor? Who was my neighbor, anyway?

Jesus shifted the focus. The real question was, "Who needs my help?" Anyone nearby and needy has a claim on us—as Spoto suggests, "even a despised half-breed, a heretic, a killer and sworn enemy of my people."[41]

Jesus emphasized this notion in his teachings about the poor, the despised, and the helpless and in his activities among the ill, the downtrodden, and the oppressed. It was a very significant part of his mission.

From Jerusalem to Jericho

Jerusalem stands on mountains some 2,700 feet above sea level. Jericho lay 3,500 feet below in a plain formed over millennia by the Jordan River nearby. The road connecting the two cities was steep and treacherous and often deserted. There were many caves in the surrounding hills in which to hide, and the road was notorious for bandits. One of the surprising aspects of the parable was that all the travelers journeyed alone. Usually, people traveled this highway in groups. When the Essenes passed through, they carried weapons to protect themselves from robbers.[42]

Jericho was a beautiful city, well irrigated and lush, which Josephus called the "City of a Thousand Palm Trees." Herod built a winter palace there and visited often. Many priests had their homes in Jericho. But the area surrounding the city was arid and inhospitable, and the mountains nearby were rugged and harsh.

Jesus knew the region well. Baptized by John a few miles east of Jericho, he had struggled with temptation in the wilderness northwest of the city. On his way to Jerusalem from Galilee, he had traversed the Jordan Valley and passed through Jericho. The healing of Bartimaeus and his meeting with Zacchaeus had been in Jericho.[43]

The Greek text clearly noted that the man who was robbed and the priest were going *down* from Jerusalem to Jericho. The direction in which the Levite and the Samaritan were traveling was not reported. Either or both could have been journeying from Jericho *uphill* toward Jerusalem when they encountered the unconscious victim on the side of the road. That might intensify the story for Jesus' listeners and explain a few loose ends. Going toward Jerusalem might have implied that the Levite was on his way to the Temple to participate with other Levites in preparing the sacrificial service.

In order to participate (and to receive the special portions), he would have to be ritually clean. It was a bit unusual for a Samaritan to be traveling toward Jericho and the Jordan Valley, far less unusual to be heading toward Jerusalem.

The Caring Samaritan

The fact that Jesus selected a Samaritan as the caregiver not only caught his listeners by surprise, it shocked them. The image of a Samaritan as a model of profound and loving compassion was as astonishing to Jews then as a Nazi becoming the hero of a story today.

The gospels described caring Samaritans on two other occasions.

On the way to Jerusalem, passing between Samaria and Galilee, Jesus entered a village and encountered ten lepers who begged him to cure them. Jesus healed all of their affliction, but only one—a Samaritan—came back to praise God and thank Jesus. The other nine disappeared without expressing their gratitude to God or to Jesus.[44]

On another journey, Jesus rested beside a well just outside the village of Sychar. A Samaritan woman drew water for him and gave him drink. In the course of their conversation, she became convinced that Jesus was a prophet. When his disciples returned and she saw that Jesus was safe, the woman rushed to the village to prepare its residents for Jesus' visit. As a consequence, "many Samaritans from that city believed in him because of the woman's testimony."[45]

These encounters with well-intentioned and helpful Samaritans may have provided the background for Jesus' teachings in the current parable.

Not only were Samaritans despised, but Jews often neglected and rejected members of their own community—the diseased and the impoverished. In the next chapter, we explore what Jesus taught about people suffering on the margins of society.

Notes

1. Leviticus 21:1–2, 6. See also Numbers 6:6, where the same rules applied to the Nazarite.
2. Leviticus 21:11.
3. M. Nazir 7.1.
4. M. Nazir 7.1.
5. Numbers 19:11–19.

6. M. Yoma 8.6, Yoma 82a.

7. Josephus, *Antiquities*, 18.30.

8. M. Berakhot 8.6.

9. M. Gittin 1.5.

10. M. Kiddushin 4.3.

11. M. Ketubot 3.1.

12. Niddah 4.1, 2.

13. Shekalim 1.5.

14. Shevi'it 8.10.

15. Genesis 29:34, 35:23.

16. Exodus 2:1–10, 4:14, 6:20.

17. Numbers 3:6–8, 4:50–53.

18. Deuteronomy 12:12; 14:27, 29; 18:1–2.

19. 1 Chronicles 24:1–4.

20. Numbers 18:5, 7.

21. Numbers 18:5, 7.

22. 1 Chronicles 23:28–32.

23. 1 Chronicles 9:19; 26:1, 19–20; 2 Chronicles 8:14; Ezra 3:10; Nehemiah 12:27.

24. M. Horayot 3.8. A *mamzeyr* is the offspring of a forbidden marriage.

25. Exodus 19:6. See also Leviticus 44–45, Numbers 15:40.

26. Isaiah 33:15.

27. Micah 6:8.

28. Isaiah 56:1.

29. Amos 5:4.

30. Habbakuk 5:4. This Midrash was found in Makkot 24a, as presented in George Foot Moore, *Judaism in the First Centuries of the Christian Era* (Cambridge, Mass.: Harvard University Press, 1927), vol. 2, 83–84.

31. Sifra Kedoshim, Perek 4, as presented in Moore, *Judaism in the First Centuries of the Christian Era*, vol. 2, 85.

32. Galatians 5:14. See also Romans 13:8, James 2:8.

33. Isaachar 5.2, 7.6; Daniel 5.3; as presented in Moore, *Judaism in the First Centuries of the Christian Era*, vol. 2, 86.

34. Matthew 22:35–39, Mark 12:28–31.

35. Deuteronomy 6:5–8. This section of Deuteronomy was very familiar to Jews of the first century. They recited it as part of their daily worship.

36. Shabbat 31a.

37. Matthew 22:40.

38. Bernard Brandon Scott, *Hear Then the Parable: A Commentary on the Parables of Jesus* (Minneapolis, Minn.: Fortress, 1990), 192.

39. Scott, *Hear Then the Parable*, 192.

40. Luke 10:37b.

41. Donald Spoto, *The Hidden Jesus: A New Life* (New York: St. Martin's, 1998), 131.
42. Josephus, *The Jewish Wars*, 2.8.4.
43. Matthew 20:29–34; Mark 10:46–52; Luke 18:35–43, 19:1–11.
44. Luke 17:11–19.
45. John 4:5–39.

CHAPTER SEVENTEEN

The Rich Man, the Beggar, and the Unclean Spirit

The Parable of the Unclean Spirit

Often in first-century Palestine, diseased people were thought to be possessed by an evil spirit, and the way to cure such people was to chase away the offending demon. All four gospels noted that Jesus was skilled at such healing.

In the Parable of the Unclean Spirit, Jesus described the dangers a person encountered after such an exorcism.

> When the unclean spirit has gone out of a man, he passes through waterless places seeking rest; and finding none he says, 'I will return to my house from which I came.' And when he comes he finds it swept and put in order. Then he goes and brings seven other spirits more evil than himself, and they enter and dwell there; and the last state of that man becomes worse than the first. (Luke 11:24–26)

What Secrets Did the Parable Convey?

Jesus suggested a parallel between the dwelling place of the evil demon within the human psyche and an actual home. Chasing out the unclean spirit was like leaving a home unoccupied. Unless the owner took proper care to maintain and guard his home, intruders would enter and occupy it.

The same warning applied to a person's psyche. Driving out an evil demon left a spiritual vacuum. Unless a person filled the empty space with commitment to God and observance of His commandments, the unclean spirit would return. The consequent disease would be worse than before—seven times worse—and the suffering experienced even more malevolent.

The relapse was not automatic. It could be prevented. The healed person had to fill his psyche with reverence for God and His commandments. Any letup opened a space in his soul for the unclean spirit to return and wreak its havoc.

Staying Healed Was a Religious Decision

Jesus' language emphasized his belief that staying healed was a religious decision. He used irony to paint the image of the dispossessed psyche as a house "empty, swept and set in order"—that is, a house the owner prepared for occupation, an empty house ready and waiting for someone to move in. Unless the owner did what was necessary to secure the premises, unwelcome demons would occupy it.[1]

The Same Parable in Matthew

Matthew presented the same parable.

> When the unclean spirit has gone out of a man, he passes through waterless places seeking rest, but he finds none. Then he says, 'I will return to my house from which I came.' And when he comes he finds it empty, swept, and put in order. Then he goes and brings with him seven other spirits more evil than himself, and they enter and dwell there; and the last state of that man becomes worse than the first. So shall it be also with this evil generation. (Matthew 12:43–45)

The only significant difference between the two versions was the ending. Matthew included a half-verse missing in Luke.

According to Matthew, in this half-verse Jesus repeated his beliefs that the cataclysm would occur in this generation. Sometime during the next twenty-five years unrepentant sinners would suffer unprecedented destruction, disease, and devastation. In that sense, their "last state" would be worse than anything they previously experienced.

Jesus was not suggesting that the entire current generation was evil but only that the evil members of the generation would perish. His own followers would escape. Of course, any supporter who lapsed opened his psyche to malevolent consequences and would suffer the same fate as other sinners.

Demons and Other Unclean Spirits

In the biblical story of Creation, God sculpted a human body from the dust of the earth, breathed into it, and brought to life the first human being.[2] That "spirit"—the breath of God—was the life force resident in all living beings.[3]

Mentioned some ninety-four times in the Hebrew Bible, the "spirit of God" inspired prophets,[4] drove people to frenzied behavior,[5] provided energy and power to the leaders of ancient Israel,[6] and gave the coming Messianic redeemer his strength.[7] The "spirit of God" that hovered over the deep at the Creation still hovered over the earth in the first century.[8] According to Psalm 139:7, that "Spirit" was the universal presence of God.

Every human has a spirit. "The spirit of man is the lamp of the Lord."[9] God created man's spirit and preserved it.[10] In fact, God created all spirits. Even the malevolent spirits were formed by God and served His purposes.

In Jewish tradition, there were good and evil, clean and unclean spirits.[11] A demon was an "unclean spirit." Guidance through danger was credited to an angel or to a spirit.[12] A gifted man was "filled with the spirit of God."[13] Sickness was blamed on a demon.[14]

In the Dead Sea Scrolls and other intertestamental books, the struggle between good and evil often took place on the battlefield of the human soul. Demons tempted people and enticed them to wrongdoing.[15]

The sages taught that "harmful angels" were created just before God rested on the Sabbath.[16] Both Hillel and his disciple Rabbi Yohanan ben Zakkai understood "the speech of the demons."[17] Ben Zakkai once explained to a non-Jew the laws of the red heifer using the analogy of how a demon entered a man's body, caused him to go mad, and had to be exorcised.[18]

These images of demons continued in the New Testament, where they were regarded as ministers of Satan or Belial.[19] Demons were noxious or unclean spirits[20] that "enter into a man"[21] and caused him to suffer physical or psychic disorders.[22]

Demons were expelled through prayer and fasting—but only when these outward behaviors reflected a sincere and complete repentance within. Ben Sirakh wrote: "If a man washes himself after touching a corpse and then touches it again, what good has his bath done him? The same is true for a man who fasts for his sins and goes again and does the same thing. Who will listen to his prayer? And what has he gained by humbling himself?"[23] Of such vain fasting the Testament of Asher noted, "Another commits adultery and fornication, and abstains from food; and (even) while fasting does evil to others."[24] Jesus' disciples asked why they failed in an exorcism, and he explained that the demon with which they were dealing could only be expelled through prayer and fasting.[25]

According to this view, sickness was essentially a spiritual matter and healing occurred only after the diseased person reestablished his relationship with God. On several occasions after successfully healing a person, Jesus affirmed, "Your faith has made you well."[26] Faith was a necessary condition of healing.

Special substances and incantations sometimes exorcised demons. The author of Tobit reported that the daughter of Raguel in Acbatana married seven times but that the wicked demon Asmodeus killed all her husbands before they could cohabit with her. When Tobias went to her (on their wedding night), he took the ashes of incense and put the heart and liver of the fish on them and made smoke, whereupon the demon fled to Upper Egypt.[27] Rabbi Akiba warned that any person who utters charms to heal would lose his place in the World to Come.[28]

One might expel demons by invoking God's ineffable name against them.[29] The conviction that Jesus used the name of God to heal or taught his followers to speak God's name would have provided another reason for traditional Jewish leaders to oppose him.[30] The sage Abba Saul went so far as to suggest that any ordinary person who pronounced the divine Name would have no afterlife.[31]

While demons had the power to tempt humans and seduce them to sin, in the future they would have no such power.[32] God's kingdom would be free of sin.

From the beginning of his ministry, Jesus healed.[33] His opponents attributed his gift to Satan.[34] His supporters claimed his power came from God.[35]

The Seven Other Demons
In Deuteronomy, Moses warned the Israelites that if they disobeyed the commandments of God, He would smite them with seven disasters—consumption, fever, inflammation, fiery heat, drought, blasting, and mildew.[36] These may have been the "seven other demons" Jesus had in mind in this parable.[37]

The Parable of the Rich Man
and the Beggar Lazarus

Poor, ulcerated Lazarus lay among the dogs at the gate of an enormous villa and begged to eat the scraps that fell on the floor beneath the owner's table. Inside, the owner, who dressed in the finest garments and ate sumptuously every day, paid no attention. Eventually both men died.

Angels carried Lazarus to heaven, to a place of honor near the patriarch Abraham. The rich man was consigned to suffer searing pain and torment in hell. Through the flames, the wealthy man begged Father Abraham to send

Lazarus with just a few drops of water to cool his parched tongue. Abraham rejected his request. Justice required that Lazarus receive the proper rewards for his undeserved suffering in life and that the rich man receive appropriate punishment for his abuse and neglect of others.

Then the rich man asked Abraham to send Lazarus to the home of his five brothers to warn them of the suffering that awaited them in hell after they died. Abraham denied this request also. They had already been warned many times by Moses and the prophets. The rich man pleaded that someone resurrected from the dead would surely convince them. To that Abraham replied, "If they do not hear Moses and the prophets, they will not be convinced if someone should rise from the dead."

> There was a rich man, who was clothed in purple and fine linen and who feasted sumptuously every day. And at his gate lay a poor man named Lazarus, full of sores, who desired to be fed with what fell from the rich man's table; moreover the dogs came and licked his sores. The poor man died and was carried by the angels to Abraham's bosom. The rich man also died and was buried; and in Hades, being in torment, he lifted up his eyes, and saw Abraham far off and Lazarus in his bosom. And he called out, "Father Abraham, have mercy upon me, and send Lazarus to dip the end of his finger in water and cool my tongue; for I am in anguish in this flame." But Abraham said, "Son, remember that you in your lifetime received your good things, and Lazarus in like manner evil things; but now he is comforted here, and you are in anguish. And besides all this, between us and you a great chasm has been fixed, in order that those who would pass from here to you may not be able, and none may cross from there to us." And he said, "Then I beg you, father, to send him to my father's house, for I have five brothers, so that he may warn them, lest they also come into this place of torment." But Abraham said, "They have Moses and the prophets; let them hear them." And he said, "No, father Abraham; but if some one goes to them from the dead, they will repent." He said to him, "If they do not hear Moses and the prophets, neither will they be convinced if some one should rise from the dead." (Luke 16:19–31)

Resurrection and Redemption

Jesus again built on specific understandings in the minds of his Jewish listeners.

To counteract the impression that the good suffer on earth and the wicked often succeed, the Wisdom of Solomon taught, "In the eyes of foolish people they seemed to die, and their demise was thought to be an affliction and their departure from us their ruin, but . . . their hope is in full immortality. . . . God has tried them and found them worthy . . . but the ungodly will be punished according to their reasonings."[38] Death was not the end, but the beginning of a new existence in which divine justice prevailed. No matter how much they suffered in life, the faithful would receive God's blessings. The wicked would be punished.

The book of Daniel envisioned a time of turmoil and great deliverance when "many of those who sleep in the dust of the earth shall awake, some to everlasting life and some to shame and everlasting contempt. Those who are wise shall shine like the brightness of the firmament; those who turn many to righteousness [will sparkle] like the stars for ever and ever."[39] Though they suffered and died on earth, the good would be redeemed to life eternal. The wicked would suffer shame and contempt forever.

Seven brothers and their mother were arrested and tortured in the presence of King Antiochus to force them to eat swine. "We are ready to die," said one brother for them all, "rather than transgress the laws of our forefathers."[40] So the king killed them, one by one.

With his last breath, the second son declared, "You release us from the present life, but the King of the world will raise us up . . . to an everlasting renewal of life."[41] The sixth said, "Do not think that you will go unpunished for having attempted to fight against God."[42] And the last son, the youngest, declared, "Our brothers, after enduring a brief suffering, will drink everlasting life. . . . But you, by the judgment of God, will receive the rightful penalty of your arrogance."[43]

The war continued, and Jews were slain on the battlefield fighting the Syrian forces. So Judas Maccabeus took up a collection and sent two thousand drachmas to Jerusalem to provide a sin offering to expiate the transgressions of their fallen martyrs and prepare for their eventual resurrection. Judas provided the Temple sacrifice "through regard for the splendid reward destined for those who fall asleep in godliness."[44]

In the Testaments of the Twelve Patriarchs, the resurrection was extended back in time to include the very first Jews and their descendants. Judah predicted, "After these things, Abraham, Isaac and Jacob will rise up to life, and I and my brothers will be chiefs of the tribes."[45]

A description of the place of punishment for sinners was given in Second Esdras. "The lake of torment will appear, and opposite it will be a place of rest; the furnace of Hell will appear, and opposite it is the Paradise of delight."[46]

The Testament of Benjamin presented a good summary of the beliefs fostered by Jewish literature in the first century. "Those who died in grief will rise up in joy, and those in poverty for the Lord's sake will be enriched, and those in want will be fully fed, and those in weakness will be made strong, and those who died for the Lord's sake will awaken in life."[47]

Jesus' listeners had these images in mind the day they first heard the Parable of the Rich Man and the Beggar Lazarus.

God Helps Me

Like names in any language, Hebrew names are words with meaning. Daniel means "God is my Judge." Ezekiel means "God is my strength."

Lazarus was the only person in any parable whose name was published. In Hebrew, his name was *Eli'ezer*—which means "God helps me." Though it was not described, some listeners may have received a hint at Lazarus' character and commitment from the meaning of his name.[48]

Discarded Pieces of Bread

In Jesus' day, people ate with their fingers, picking up pieces of fruit or cake, dipping bits of bread into condiments and relishes, and drinking soups or stews from small bowls. According to Jeremias, in addition to using bread to scoop up items in a dish, the custom among diners in Palestine was to use pieces of bread to wipe off their hands or their mouths—much as we would use a napkin today—and to toss these dirty pieces of bread on the floor.[49] Lazarus longed to eat these discarded slops.

What Secrets Did the Parable Convey?

In this parable Jesus reiterated a number of key teachings.

- Wealth and status were not the criteria that determined who entered God's kingdom. In God's kingdom, divine justice prevailed. Those who suffered undeservedly in this life would be rewarded in the World to Come, and those who abused their wealth and neglected to respond to the needs of others would suffer anguish and pain. Things would even out in the world beyond death.
- Death was the end of the process. No further reprieves were possible. Now was the time to make changes.
- The people of Israel had been warned many times in the past by Moses and the prophets—and were still being warned by Jesus. Sages and aristocrats affirmed they upheld and practiced God's laws. Jesus negated that conviction and asserted they had, in fact, rejected the warnings and denied the consequences.

There is considerable scholarly debate about whether Jesus spoke this sentence at the end of the parable: "If they do not hear Moses and the prophets, neither will they be convinced if some one should rise from the dead."[50]

Crossan suggests that the concluding words reflected "the Jewish refusal to accept either Moses or the prophets as witnesses to the resurrection of Jesus or even to accept the risen Jesus himself" and, therefore, represented the situation of the early Christian community in Palestine *after* the death of Jesus.[51] They could not have been original to Jesus.

Hultgren agrees. "Unmistakably, the present wording ('if someone should rise from the dead') has been conformed to Christian language concerning the resurrection of Jesus." Though he used the present tense, I think Hultgren meant to say, "If persons [were] not converted to belief in Jesus as the Messiah on the basis of Moses and the prophets, neither will they be on the basis of the preaching of the resurrection of Jesus."[52] Such teaching about Jesus' resurrection was characteristic of the church *after* his death.

These scholars agree that Jesus would have asserted, "They [the people, the sages, the Pharisees] do not hear Moses and the prophets." But they question whether he would have said, "Neither will they be convinced if someone should rise from the dead."

There was no indication in the statement Jesus was referring to himself. Nowhere did he say when *I* am resurrected. The statement merely stated "if *someone* should rise from the dead." Later Christian tradition read into the phrase a reference to Jesus.

According to Jewish tradition, people had been revived from death in the past. Elijah stayed at the home of a widow who fed and cared for him. One day the widow's son became ill and died, and Elijah revived the child.[53] The same thing happened a generation later. Occasionally Elisha lodged and dined at the home of a wealthy Shunamite woman. Her son became ill and died, and Elisha brought him back to life.[54] Still the people of Israel sinned.

Jesus healed time and time again. People still resisted his teachings and condemned his behavior. Jesus could have been saying that some Jews were so intransigent in their beliefs and so arrogant that, even if Ezekiel's and Isaiah's prophecies came to pass[55] and an army of resurrected Jews marched through the streets before them, these Jews would still not reconsider. Though they would suffer eternally in hell, they would go to their graves convinced they were right.

Jesus could have said that.

I agree with Jeremias. "Jesus does not want to comment on a social problem, nor does he intend to give teaching about the afterlife, but he relates the parable to warn men who resemble the brothers of the rich man of the impending danger."[56] The people to whom Jesus preached were like those who witnessed Noah building the Ark, heard his warning about the impending flood, and disregarded what he said. They drowned.[57]

Though sages and scholars affirmed the doctrine of the resurrection of the dead, encountering a resurrected person would not dissuade them of their misunderstandings. They studied continually and discussed the Law of Moses and the prophets endlessly among themselves, and still they didn't understand. And when they taught the people, they led them astray.

Jesus was not hinting that he would die and appear again. He was telling the people once again they had been given all the warnings they needed. The holocaust had been set in motion. The disaster was on its way. They needed no more signs. Their very request was a sign of their intransigence and unwillingness to change. Now was the time to repent.

In the next chapter, we consider one of Jesus' most popular metaphors—the Parable of the Good Shepherd.

Notes

1. Some scholars suggest even greater irony when they translate the Greek word in verse 44 (*kekosmeemenon*) as "decorated," "adorned," or "garnished." The owner actually decorated the house as if he were preparing for a welcome guest, then left the house unattended. As a consequence of his neglect, seven demons moved in. See the following Bible translations: King James, American Standard, Young, Darby, and Webster.

2. Genesis 2:7.

3. "Wind," "breath," and "spirit" are all proper translations of the Hebrew word *ru'akh.*

4. Numbers 11:17–29; 22:38; 23:3, 4; 24:2; 1 Samuel 10:6–10; 19:20–23; 2 Samuel 23:2.

5. 1 Samuel 16:15–16, 23; 18:10; 19:9; 1 Kings 22:21.

6. Judges 3:10; 11:29; 1 Samuel 11:6; for example.

7. Isaiah 11:2; 42:1.

8. Genesis 1:1ff.

9. Proverbs 20:27.

10. Isaiah 42:5; Zechariah 12:1; Job 27:3, 10:12.

11. For example, the souls of the dead (Daniel 3:86 LXX, Hebrews 12:23); angels and demons (1 Samuel 16:14); and God and the Devil.

12. Exodus 23:23, 32:23; Isaiah 63:14; Psalm 143:10.

13. Exodus 31:3, 35:31.

14. 1 Samuel 16:14–23.

15. Erubim 4:1, Shabbat 2:5.

16. M. Avot 5:6.

17. M. Sof 16:9, Sukkot 28a.

18. PR40a; Numbers Rabba 19:4 (19:8??).

19. Matthew 10:25; 12:24, 27; Mark 3:22; Luke 11:15, 18–19.

20. Luke 8:29; Acts 5:16, 8:7.

21. Mark 9:18, Luke 8:30, Acts 5:16.

22. Matthew 4:24; 8:16, 28; 9:32; 11:18; 12:22; Mark 5:3, 5; 9:18; Luke 4:33; 8:27; 11:14; 13:11; John 10:19–21. There was no clear distinction between demonic and diseased, though in some passages demonic was specified in addition to disease (Matthew 4:24; Mark 1:32; Acts 5:16, 8:7, 10:38).

23. Ben Sirakh 34:25–26. See also Ben Sirakh 35:3.

24. Testament of the Twelve Patriarchs, Asher 2:8f., as presented in George Foot Moore, *Judaism in the First Centuries of the Christian Era* (Cambridge, Mass.: Harvard University Press, 1927), vol. 2, 259.

25. Matthew 17:21, Mark 9:29.

26. Matthew 9:29; Luke 17:19, 18:42.

27. Tobit 3:8, 8:2. The High Priest may have performed a comparable rite on Yom Kippur. See M. Yoma 5:1.

28. M. Sanhedrin 10:1.

29. Matthew 7:22. See also Numbers 6:27—"I put My name upon the people of Israel and I will bless them." See earlier anticipations in Psalms 118:12 (*b'sheym adonai*) and 20:6 (*b'sheym eloheynu*).

30. In Sanhedrin 7:5, an ordinary person who pronounced God's Name was a blasphemer.

31. M. Sanhedrin 10:1. Only the High Priest could pronounce God's ineffable name and only once a year during the sacrificial ceremonies on Yom Kippur. See M. Yoma 3:8; 6:2.

32. Testament of the Judah, chapter 25, as presented in Moore, *Judaism in the First Centuries of the Christian Era*, vol. 2, 316.

33. Mark 1:29–32, 40–45.

34. Mark 3:22.

35. Matthew 12:28; Luke 5:17, 11:20.

36. Deuteronomy 28:22.

37. Luke 11:26, Matthew 12:45.

38. Wisdom of Solomon 3:1–10.

39. Daniel 12:1–3.

40. 2 Maccabees 7:2.

41. 2 Maccabees 7:9. See also 2 Maccabees 7:11, 14.

42. 2 Maccabees 7:19.

43. 2 Maccabees 7:36.

44. 2 Maccabees 12:43–45.

45. Testament of Judah, chapter 25, as presented in Moore, *Judaism in the First Centuries of the Christian Era*, vol. 2, 307.

46. 2 Esdras 7:36.

47. Testament of Judah, chapter 25, as presented in Moore, *Judaism in the First Centuries of the Christian Era*, vol. 2, 307.

48. This Lazarus has no relation to brother of Mary and Martha (John 11:1–44, 12:1–11). Eleazar was a popular Jewish name. Many men were named Lazarus. In contrast to Lazarus, the rich man has no name, but popular tradition often called him Dives. *Dives* is a Latin adjective meaning "rich."

49. Joachim Jeremias, *The Parables of Jesus* (New York: Charles Scribner's Sons, 1963), 184, both the text and note 53 indicating Talmudic sources buttressing this practice.

50. Luke 16:31.

51. John Dominic Crossan, *In Parables: The Challenge of the Historical Jesus* (New York: Harper and Row, 1973), 67.

52. Arland J. Hultgren, *The Parables of Jesus: A Commentary* (Grand Rapids, Mich.: William B. Eerdmans, 2000), 114–15.

53. 1 Kings 17:10–24.

54. 2 Kings 4:8–37.

55. Ezekiel 37:1–10, Isaiah 26:19.

56. Jeremias, *The Parables of Jesus*, 186–87.

57. Matthew 24:37–39.

CHAPTER EIGHTEEN

Two Parables in John

John and The Synoptic Gospels

The parables we've studied so far were recorded in the first three gospels. All of them were imbedded in a literary and theological context that reflected both the understandings of the gospel writer and the traditions he inherited. None of these stories appeared pristine and unvarnished. All were edited. But the narration flowed smoothly, and the parable was usually distinct from its explanation.

In the fourth gospel, two parables and a good deal of metaphorical material were intrinsically enmeshed in John's theological understandings. John wove Jesus' teachings into his own framework and recast (or created) dialogue to fit his literary and religious structure. It's difficult, therefore, to determine where Jesus ends and John begins.

To complicate matters further, the gospel of John was written decades after the destruction of the Temple and the decline of Jerusalem, for a Christian community growing in the Roman world. It is the gospel farthest removed from Jewish tradition and the one most antagonistic to the Jewish community.

The Parable of the Good Shepherd

At night, in order to guard their sheep from predators and rustlers, shepherds would pen several flocks together inside a protected sheepfold. One shepherd would stand guard. The others would go to sleep and return in the morning to reclaim their flocks. The returning shepherds would enter by the gate, pass the watchman, and cull their own sheep from the intermingled herd. Walking in front of his flock, each shepherd would lead his sheep through the gate and out to pasture.

Jesus used all these images in the Parable of the Good Shepherd.

> "Truly, truly, I say to you, he who does not enter the sheepfold by the door but climbs in by another way, that man is a thief and a robber; but he who enters by the door is the shepherd of the sheep. To him the gatekeeper opens; the sheep hear his voice, and he calls his own sheep by name and leads them out. When he has brought out all his own, he goes before them, and the sheep follow him, for they know his voice. A stranger they will not follow, but they will flee from him, for they do not know the voice of strangers." This figure Jesus used with them, but they did not understand what he was saying to them. (John 10:1–6)

What Secrets Did the Parable Convey?

Though the images were familiar, his listeners didn't understand the parable. So Jesus explained it to them.

Four different explanations were included in the text. The first two explained verses 1–3a. Jesus was the *door* of the sheepfold.

> So Jesus again said to them, "Truly, truly, I say to you, I am the door of the sheep. All who came before me are thieves and robbers; but the sheep did not heed them. I am the door; if any one enters by me, he will be saved, and will go in and out and find pasture. The thief comes only to steal and kill and destroy; I came that they may have life, and have it abundantly. (John 10:7–10)

Two different explanations were given, each based on the statement "I am the door."

There was a proper way to enter the sheepfold and claim the sheep. A legitimate shepherd entered through the gate, where the gatekeeper identified him, permitted him to pass, and noted the sheep he took out with him. A thief climbed over the wall, entered the sheepfold surreptitiously, and tried to lead away sheep he didn't own. In this first explanation, Jesus accused those who preceded him of being like thieves sneaking into the sheepfold to lead the sheep astray.

The sheep were the Jews; the sheepfold was the world in which they lived; and those who preceded Jesus were the conventional leaders and teachers of the people. Once again, this time using blatantly insulting and degrading language, Jesus accused the authorities of leading people astray. Their way was the wrong way. They were using the wrong gate. By declaring, "I am the door," Jesus challenged both the people and the authorities to accept his ideas.[1]

The second explanation amplified the first and focused on what might happen when the flock left the sheepfold. Peril lurked outside, and a shepherd who didn't know the land or who didn't properly guard his herd endangered their lives.

Jesus declared that his teachings offered salvation—not only in this world but also in the World to Come. Like thieves, the acknowledged authorities were leading the people toward destruction and death. Redemption was possible only by adopting Jesus' ideas and behaving as Jesus taught. His way alone would guarantee eternal life, abundance, and joy.[2]

Jesus' listeners heard Psalm 118 recited occasionally in Jerusalem at the Temple. It may have been part of their synagogue worship. The psalm was filled with eschatological allusions: "I shall not die, but I shall live, and recount the deeds of the Lord" and "The Lord has chastened me sorely, but he has not given me over to death," and included the following petition: "Open to me the gates of righteousness that I may enter through them and give thanks to the Lord."[3] The path to God was through the gates of righteousness. Those who entered attained spiritual abundance and eternal life. The psalm included this affirmation: "This is the gate of the Lord, the righteous shall enter through it."[4]

In declaring, "I am the door," Jesus may have been applying the psalm to himself—as he did on a different occasion to a verse toward the end of another psalm: "The stone that the builders rejected has become the chief cornerstone."[5]

A third commentary explained verses 3b–5. The emphasis in these verses was on the close relationship between the sheep and the shepherd. Jesus was the *good shepherd,* who knew and cared for his flock:[6] "I am the good shepherd; I know my own and my own know me, as the Father knows me and I know the Father" (John 10:14–15a).[7]

On hearing these words, Jesus' listeners who knew the Bible may have recalled Moses' plea at the close of his life for a proper successor. "Let the Lord, Source of the breath of all flesh, appoint someone over the community, who shall go out before them and come in before them, who shall lead them out and bring them in, so that the Lord's community may not be like sheep that have no shepherd." And God said to Moses, "Take Joshua the son of Nun, a man in whom is the spirit, and lay your hand upon him. Have him to stand before Eleazar the priest and all the community, and commission him in their sight. Invest him with some of your authority, so that the whole

Israelite community may obey."[8] Joshua was God's choice to succeed Moses. Joshua was the proper shepherd to lead God's flock from the wilderness into the Promised Land.

Because Jesus' Hebrew name was Joshua, his listeners may have heard in this parable Jesus' intimation that he was Moses' true successor, invested with the same authority, the Good Shepherd who would lead the Israelite community to their ultimate redemption.

They may even have heard echoes of Micah's messianic promise. "I will assemble all of you, Jacob, I will gather together the remnant of Israel; I will set them together like sheep in a pasture, like a flock in a fold. . . . One will open the breach and go before them; they will enlarge the gate and leave by it. Their king will march before them, the Lord at their head."[9] Though Jesus didn't say it directly, some may have imagined Jesus as that messianic leader.

For those who knew the Bible, allusion tumbled on allusion. Moses and David were both shepherds, and Jesus was the spiritual successor to the first and a descendent of the second. No prophet was greater than Moses. "Never again did there arise in Israel a prophet like Moses"—at least not up to that point—because no other prophet had the same intimate relationship with God. Moses knew God "face to face." As a consequence, Moses performed "the various signs and wonders which the Lord sent him to do."[10]

Jesus taught that (1) he was a prophet; (2) as authentic as Hosea, Isaiah, and Ezekiel; (3) the chosen successor by name to Moses; (4) who interpreted his law with greater insight and authenticity than the acknowledged sages and teachers of his time; (5) shared information with his disciples even former prophets didn't know; and (6) performed miracles, marvels, and wonders. Like Moses, Jesus claimed a special relationship with God. God was the Father; Jesus was the son; and their union was as intimate and compelling as that of a father and son on earth.

Jesus was the good shepherd because he knew the members of his fellowship as intimately "as the Father knows me and I know the Father." He knew their ultimate destiny. "Fear not, little flock, for it is your Father's good pleasure to give you the kingdom."[11] He understood what they needed to learn to fulfill that destiny. "He saw a great throng and had compassion on them, because they were like sheep without a shepherd. So he began to teach them many things."[12]

The third explanation reinforced the second. The only way into God's kingdom was through Jesus, because only Jesus understood God's will. And that understanding flowed from the intimate and supportive relationship

God and Jesus shared. Jesus encountered and experienced God as a son encountered and experienced his father.

The fourth explanation added characters not in the original parable: a hired caretaker and an attacking wolf. The hired hand fled before the wolf's onslaught, leaving the sheep unprotected. Jesus was the *good shepherd* who protected his sheep even at the risk of his own life.

> I am the good shepherd. The good shepherd lays down his life for the sheep. He who is a hireling and not a shepherd, whose own the sheep are not, sees the wolf coming and leaves the sheep and flees; and the wolf snatches them and scatters them. He flees because he is a hireling and cares nothing for the sheep. (John 10:11–13)

Verses 3b–5 emphasized the intimate relationship between the shepherd and his sheep. The sheep recognized their owner's voice and followed him. They fled the voice of a stranger and refused to obey him. In the initial parable, there was no mention of wolves or danger, and no indication that the shepherd was a hired caretaker. It seems likely that this fourth explanation was not part of the original parable. If Jesus spoke the words in verses 11–13, it was in some other (unknown) context.[13]

Knowledge Involved Experiencing

Beasley-Murray notes correctly that, in Greek tradition, knowledge was analogous to *seeing*, as a way to comprehend the nature of an object. In Hebrew culture, knowledge involved *experiencing* something. For example, knowledge of God for Greeks meant contemplating of the divine reality. For Jews, it meant entering into a relationship with God.[14]

This parable reflected that Jewish understanding. The mutual knowledge of the shepherd and his sheep denoted an intimate relationship in which there was shared loyalty, respect, and affection. Jesus compared that relationship to the love between father and child—and, specifically, to the love between God and Jesus.

Ezekiel and Jesus

In Jewish tradition, God was often depicted as a farmer and grower of grapes. He was also pictured as a shepherd. God "led forth his people like sheep and guided them in the wilderness like a flock."[15] The Rock of Israel, the Mighty One of Jacob was also "the Shepherd," the Source of all blessings.[16] "The Lord is my shepherd, I lack nothing. He makes me lie down in green pastures; He leads me to still waters; He renews my life."[17]

God was the Shepherd, and the Jews were His sheep. Though His flock had been conquered and scattered throughout the Near East, Ezekiel assured Israel God would not abandon them. "As I live, declares the Lord God, because my flock has become a spoil and my sheep have become prey for all the wild beasts, . . . I Myself will search for my sheep and will seek them out. . . . I will rescue them from all places where they have been scattered . . . I will bring them into their own land and will pasture them on the mountains of Israel, by the watercourses and in all the settled places of the country. I will feed them on good grazing land, and the lofty hills of Israel shall be their pasture. . . . I myself will be the Shepherd of my sheep."[18]

Jesus drew heavily on these words by Ezekiel. The prophet denounced foreign kings for plundering his flock and for neglecting the weak, the sick, and the confused among them. God would rescue his people and punish these kings for their neglect. Since they had no shepherd to care for them, God Himself would become their Shepherd. "I will search for the lost and bring back the strayed; I will bandage the injured and strengthen the weak. . . . I will tend them properly."[19] As Jesus applied these images against the leaders and teachers of his own era for their neglect, his listeners could hear the words of Ezekiel thundering in the background.[20]

Other Shepherds

God was not the only shepherd depicted in Jewish tradition. The king, the priests, and the leaders were to serve as shepherds to the people of Israel. They failed. As a consequence, God's people suffered defeat and exile. "Thus says the Lord, the God of Israel, concerning the shepherds who should care for my people: It is you who let My flock scatter and go astray."[21]

"Son of man, prophesy against the shepherds of Israel. . . . You have not strengthened the weak, healed the sick, or bandaged the injured; you have not brought back the strayed, or searched for the lost; but you have ruled them with rigor and force. So they were scattered, because there was no shepherd; and they became food for every wild beast."[22]

Woe, cried Jeremiah, "Woe to the shepherds who destroy and scatter the sheep of my pasture! declares the Lord."[23] God would punish the leaders of the Jews and rescue the Jewish people from their suffering. "Behold, I am against the shepherds; and I will . . . rescue my sheep from their mouths, that they may not be food for them."[24] "I will attend to you for your wicked acts, says the Lord."[25]

Jeremiah announced that God would appoint new leaders to protect His people. "I will set shepherds over them who will tend them. They shall no longer fear or be dismayed, and none of them shall be missing, declares the Lord."[26]

Ezekiel envisioned just one shepherd. "And I will set up over them one shepherd, my servant David, and he shall feed them."[27] Micah and Zechariah agreed: one shepherd.[28] Ezekiel described him. "My servant David shall be king over them; they shall all have one shepherd. They shall follow My rules and faithfully obey My laws."[29]

When Jesus said, "I am the *good* shepherd," he was reminding his listeners of the *bad* shepherds who failed them. Many of their current leaders behaved as immorally as did the kings, priests, and leaders of the past, and their teachings imperiled the people. Only Jesus knew the path to salvation. He was the Good Shepherd the prophets had predicted.

This Parable and Hanuka

According to the gospel, Jesus shared this parable in winter shortly before the Feast of Dedication.[30] Brown suggests that, in the cycle of synagogue readings, all the regular readings on the Sabbath nearest Hanuka were concerned with the topics of sheep and shepherds and posits a connection between this parable and Hanuka. He asserts that Ezekiel 34 was the *haftara* reading at Hanuka in the second year of the cycle.[31]

The Parable of the Vine and the Branches

Viticulture was pervasive in Palestine. In addition to farmland, most farmers owned trees and vines; and much of their time was devoted to protecting, pruning, and harvesting fruit, nuts, and grapes. From the grapes, they made wine.

At the end of winter, sometime in February and March, the farmer inspected his vines and cut off branches he determined would no longer bear fruit. Later in August, when the vines sprouted leaves, the vinedresser pinched off little shoots so that the main fruit-bearing branches received all the nourishment. If he was successful, clusters of grapes would dangle from each branch.

Jesus built on these images in the Parable of the Vine and the Branches.

> I am the true vine, and my Father is the vinedresser. Every branch of mine that bears no fruit, he takes away, and every branch that does bear fruit he prunes, that it may bear more fruit. You are already made clean by the word which I have spoken to you. Abide in me, and I in you. As the branch cannot bear fruit by itself, unless

it abides in the vine, neither can you, unless you abide in me. I am the vine, you are the branches. He who abides in me, and I in him, he it is that bears much fruit, for apart from me you can do nothing. If a man does not abide in me, he is cast forth as a branch and withers; and the branches are gathered, thrown into the fire and burned. (John 15:1–6)

What Secrets Did the Parable Convey?

Jesus addressed this parable to his followers and supporters. Jesus was the vine—the *true* vine; God was the vinedresser; and the members of Jesus' fellowship were the branches.

Like every good farmer, God explored his vine and destroyed all those branches He determined would not bear fruit. There would be members of his fellowship who wouldn't succeed, Jesus declared; disciples (or groups of disciples) whom God would destroy as fruitless or, even worse, as harmful to the survival of the vine.

Who might these followers be?

John had already determined that Judas served the devil.[32] The Iscariot was one of Jesus' followers who would not survive. In his letter, John wrote about the antichrist, a group that "went out from us, but they were not of us"[33]—possibly a group of dissident Christians who were preaching a different message. These breakaway followers also would be destroyed.

While these might have been John's understandings two generations after Jesus' trial and crucifixion, were they Jesus' understandings? Who among his contemporaries did Jesus' have in mind when he declared that God would break off and discard any branch that couldn't bear fruit?

We don't know, in part, because Jesus' words were so well integrated into John's own literary and theological framework. Perhaps Jesus had no specific people in mind. As he had done before, he was reminding his disciples that their salvation wasn't automatic. They needed to maintain their relationship with God and their commitment to obey His will. Their faith would be tested; they could stray. Then God would prune them from the vine.

That's why most scholars believe that the next verse, "You are already made clean by the word which I have spoken to you," was not original to this parable.[34] The words undo the warning and undermine its significance. If we delete verse 3 and continue the parable with verse 4, the natural flow is maintained. The warning precedes the remedy. "Abide in me, and I in you" became the way to avoid the peril, since "the branch cannot bear fruit by itself, unless it abides in the vine."

This was an audacious new suggestion. Relationship was the key to their salvation, not just obeying the commandments or doing righteous deeds. One could not be redeemed outside the community; one could not be saved without Jesus.

In Jewish tradition, salvation was not dependent upon following any one sage or teacher, but on thoroughly comprehending the will of God and applying that understanding to life experiences and relationships. There was not one path of access to God's will; there were myriads. A person could begin with the study of the Jewish dietary laws or the laws governing ritual purity, or contemplate the ethics of Amos and Isaiah, or explore the Psalms, or probe the mysteries of Daniel and Lamentations. God revealed His wishes in them all, and each one ultimately led to the other. That's why the most important part of Hillel's response was not the maxim he recited while standing on one foot, but his instruction: *zil gmar*—"Go and study." To fully understand the implications of his one-statement summary entailed a commitment to further education.

Jesus was establishing a new standard for his followers. There was no other access to the will of God. Jesus alone was the way.

Jesus insisted that he was the only teacher with the correct understanding of God's will. All other sages were wrong. They led people astray. As a result, they endangered their current lives and jeopardized their afterlives. The consequence of following other teachers would be death and devastation.

The next two verses of the parable reinforced that image. "If a man does not abide in me, he is cast forth as a branch and withers; and the branches are gathered, thrown into the fire and burned."

The language may have evoked Ezekiel's warnings in the minds of Jesus' listeners. "Like the wood of the grapevine among the trees of the forest, which I have designated to be fuel for fire, so will I treat the inhabitants of Jerusalem. I will set my face against them; though they escape from the fire, the fire shall yet consume them."[35] "The vine was plucked up in fury and hurled to the ground. The east wind withered her branches; they broke apart and dried up; her strong stem was consumed by fire. . . . Fire has issued from her twig-laden branch and consumed her boughs. She is left without a mighty stem, [without] a scepter to rule with."[36]

Ezekiel's dire predictions were fulfilled. The monarchy was overthrown; the House of God ransacked; Jerusalem burned; and the people were exiled across the desert to a parched and forbidding land. Jesus warned the same sad end awaited his contemporaries, unless they accepted his teachings and changed their behavior. Even that wouldn't suffice. Since they could not survive detached and on their own, Jesus added one more requirement. They needed to join his fellowship. Otherwise, they would suffer and die in the conflagration soon to come.

Israel as a Vine or Vineyard

Isaiah described how God tenderly planted and nurtured His vine. "My beloved had a vineyard on a very fertile hill. He digged it and cleared it of stones, and planted it with choice vines; he built a watchtower in the midst of it, and hewed out a wine vat in it."[37] Hosea called Israel "a luxuriant vine that yields its fruit."[38] Jeremiah, Ezekiel, and Psalms all portrayed Israel as a vine.[39] The vine was a frequent image on coins and pottery during the Maccabean era and beyond. Josephus described a large golden vine that decorated the sanctuary entrance of Herod's Temple.[40] By the first century, the prophetic image had become a national symbol for the people of Israel, God's goodly vine.

However, in each instance where the prophets portrayed Israel as a vine, they spoke of its corruption. In Hosea, Israel forsook its special relationship with God and turned to idolatry. "The more his fruit increased the more altars he built."[41] In Isaiah, God appeared to harvest His vine and found its yield inedible.[42] As a consequence, God, the Vinedresser who planted and tended His vine, would do what any good farmer would do: pluck out the malevolent vine and destroy it for its wickedness.

Hosea predicted it. "Their heart is false; now they must bear their guilt. The Lord will break down their altars, and destroy their pillars."[43] Isaiah affirmed it. "Now I will tell you what I will do to my vineyard. I will remove its hedge, and it shall be devoured; I will break down its wall, and it shall be trampled down."[44] Ezekiel warned them again and again.[45]

Isaiah summed it best. "Now, O inhabitants of Jerusalem and men of Judah, I pray you, judge between me and my vineyard. What more was there to do for my vineyard that I have not done? When I looked for it to yield grapes, why did it yield wild grapes?"[46]

Jesus implied the same questions. Why did the Jews continue to sin against God? What could they do to avert the impending catastrophe? The answers he provided were clear: join his fellowship, follow his teachings, repent and repair your relationship with God. There was no other way.

Jesus Was the True Vine

In this parable, Jesus transformed the image. He was the true vine—not the people of Israel. Israel was a dead vine, plucked and discarded by the Vinedresser for failing to fulfill its promise to be fruitful for God. God now tended

Jesus. As a consequence of their special relationship, access to God was possible only through Jesus.

Jesus suggested that the transformation in belief and behavior necessary to achieve salvation derived from relationship—not from a set of rules or system of teachings. Jesus understood God's will because of his special union with God. And Jesus could transmit that understanding to others by their establishing the same kind of relationship to him.[47]

Verses 7–11

Filled with allusions to the Last Supper, the explanation in verses 7–11 reflected a time after Jesus' trial and crucifixion. Though they amplified Jesus' ideas of relationship and love, at least in their present form, Jesus did not speak them.[48]

In the next chapter, we explore two final parables and discover more secrets about Jesus' views of the Final Judgment.

Notes

1. Jesus conveyed the same message later in Jerusalem: "I am the way, and the truth, and the life; no one comes to the Father, but by me" (John 14:6).

2. All of Matthew 23 also excoriated the Pharisees and scribes, but this verse was particularly telling: "Woe to you, scribes and Pharisees, hypocrites! because you shut the kingdom of heaven against men; for you neither enter yourselves, nor allow those who would enter to go in" (v 13).

3. Psalms 118:17–19.

4. Psalms 118:20.

5. Psalm 27:22. See Mark 12:10.

6. Translated here as the *good* shepherd, the Greek word *kalos* might be translated better as the *noble* shepherd, *exemplary* shepherd, or *ideal* shepherd.

7. The phrase at the close of verse 15b ("and I lay down my life for the sheep") referred back to the earlier explanation in verses 10–13 and was not originally part of this explanation.

8. Numbers 27:15–20.

9. Micah 2:12–13. See also Jeremiah 23:1–4, 1 Kings 22:1.

10. Deuteronomy 34:10–11.

11. Luke 12:32.

12. Mark 6:34.

13. Matthew may have supplied the context. Jesus sent forth his disciples with the following warning: "Behold, I send you out as sheep in the midst of wolves; so be wise as serpents and innocent as doves" (Matthew 10:16). Or John may have included verses

11–13 (from an entirely different context) to reinforce the statements he imputed to Jesus a few verses later: "For this reason the Father loves me, because I lay down my life, that I may take it again. No one takes it from me, but I lay it down of my own accord. I have power to lay it down, and I have power to take it again" (John 10:17–18).

14. George R. Beasley-Murray, "John," in *Word Bible Commentary*, ed. David A. Hubbard and Glenn W. Barker (Waco, Tex.: Word Books, 1987), vol. 36, 170.

15. Psalms 78:52.

16. Genesis 49:24–25.

17. Psalm 23:1–3. See also Psalms 80:1.

18. Ezekiel 34:8–15.

19. Ezekiel 34:16.

20. Compare Matthew 18:12–13 to Ezekiel 34:16 and Matthew 25:32–33 to Ezekiel 34:20.

21. Jeremiah 23:2.

22. Ezekiel 34:2–5.

23. Jeremiah 23:1.

24. Ezekiel 34:10.

25. Jeremiah 23:2.

26. Jeremiah 23:4.

27. Ezekiel 34:23.

28. Isaiah, Micah 2:13, Zechariah 11:16.

29. Ezekiel 37:24.

30. John 10:22–23.

31. Raymond E. Brown, "The Gospel According to John I–XII," in *The Anchor Bible*, ed. William Foxwell Albright and David Noel Freedman (Garden City, N.Y.: Doubleday, 1966), vol. 29, 389.

32. John 13:2, 26–27.

33. 1 John 2:18–19, possibly 4:1–6.

34. Brown, "The Gospel According to John XIII–XXI," *The Anchor Bible*, 676.

35. Ezekiel 15:6–7.

36. Ezekiel 19:12–14.

37. Isaiah 5:1–2.

38. Hosea 10:1.

39. Jeremiah 2:21; Ezekiel 17:7–8, 19:10–11; Psalms 80:8–11.

40. Josephus, *Antiquities*, 15.395.

41. Hosea 10:1.

42. Isaiah 5:2.

43. Hosea 10:2.

44. Isaiah 5:5–6.

45. Ezekiel 15:6–7, 19:12–14.

46. Isaiah 5:3–4.

47. After Jesus died and was no longer physically available, his successors taught that

this redemptive relationship with Jesus continued in the Christian community and began to interpret the vine in the parable as the Church.

48. Raymond E. Brown, "The Gospel According to John XIII–XXI," in *The Anchor Bible*, ed. William Foxwell Albright and David Noel Freedman (Garden City, N.Y.: Doubleday, 1970), vol. 29a, 666–68, 672–74; Beasley-Murray, "John," *Word Biblical Commentary*, 273; C. H. Dodd, *The Interpretation of the Fourth Gospel* (Cambridge: Cambridge University Press, 1960), 411–15; Joachim Jeremias, *The Parables of Jesus*, rev. ed. (New York: Charles Scribner's Sons, 1963), *The Parables of Jesus*, 86.

CHAPTER NINETEEN

Two Last Parables

The Parable of the Children in the Marketplace

If Matthew's chronology was accurate, Jesus shared this parable while John the Baptist was still alive, though in prison. The authorities were increasing their harassment of Jesus and his disciples as he preached and healed from one Galilean community to the next. The Parable of the Children in the Marketplace was Jesus' response to their criticism.

> To what shall I compare this generation? It is like children sitting in the market places and calling to their playmates, "We piped to you, and you did not dance; we wailed, and you did not mourn." For John came neither eating nor drinking, and they say, "He has a demon." The son of man came eating and drinking, and they say, "Behold, a glutton and a drunkard, a friend of tax collectors and sinners!" (Matthew 11:16–19a)

What Secrets Did the Parable Convey?

In addition to condemning Jesus for eating with "tax collectors and sinners," some sages were calling him "a glutton and a drunkard." The phrase derived from the discussion in Deuteronomy regarding a child who refused to listen to his parents.

> If a man has a wayward and defiant son, who will not heed his father or mother and does not obey them even after they discipline him, then his father and his mother shall take hold of him and bring him out to the elders of his city at the public place of his community. They shall say to the elders of his city, "This son of ours is stubborn and rebellious. He does not obey us. He is a glutton and a drunkard." Then the men of his town shall stone him to death. In this manner, you shall purge the evil from your midst. (Deuteronomy 21:18–21)

By using the phrase "a drunkard and a glutton," the Pharisees who opposed Jesus were warning him that he was behaving like a rebellious child. If he didn't cease his activities and conform, they might invoke the biblical injunction, bring him to trial, and punish him—not literally by stoning him to death, but by ostracizing him.

They were also reminding his listeners that they were associating with a person who had no regard for God's law, who behaved like "a wayward and defiant" child, showing no respect for his parents and refusing to accept their instructions and directions. Jesus was not to be admired. On the contrary, people should oppose and condemn him.

Jesus responded to their accusations by calling them children in return. They were just like the children people saw every day playing in the streets and whining because no one would play the game their way. "We played on the flute, but you would not dance; we sang the funeral dirge, but you refused to mourn."

Jesus was denigrating their teachings and denying their instructions. The leaders and teachers determined when and how to rejoice and when and how to mourn, but they were wrong. They often condemned when they should have rejoiced; they often applauded when they should have feared. They didn't understand what God wanted, and they were leading His people toward destruction. The people who refused to play their way would be saved.

The conventional authorities commanded people to fast on specific occasions and to refrain from eating specific foods, yet they condemned John the Baptist for fasting and disregarded the good work he was doing in saving souls.[1]

In the same way, the sages paid no attention to Jesus' ideas or to the fact that Jesus healed people of their suffering. They taught about doing good to others but neglected the very people who needed their help. Instead of reaching out to the weak and the confused, they occupied themselves with the strictures of Jewish dietary law and condemned Jesus for associating with those sinners who needed their assistance most. They called him "a drunkard and a glutton" because he ate with people they denigrated. Jesus called them "hypocrites."

The Same Parable in Luke
Luke reported the same parable.

> To what then shall I compare the men of this generation, and what are they like? They are like children sitting in the market place and calling to one another, "We

piped to you, and you did not dance; we wailed, and you did not weep." For John the Baptist has come eating no bread and drinking no wine; and you say, "He has a demon." The Son of man has come eating and drinking; and you say, "Behold, a glutton and a drunkard, a friend of tax collectors and sinners!" (Luke 7:31–34)

The Parable of the Last Judgment

It is fitting that we conclude our exploration of Jesus' teachings with the Parable of the Last Judgment, for this last parable summarized many of the ideas Jesus taught throughout his mission.

> When the son of man comes in his glory, and all the angels with him, then he will sit on his glorious throne. Before him will be gathered all the nations, and he will separate them one from another as a shepherd separates the sheep from the goats, and he will place the sheep at his right hand, but the goats at the left. Then the king will say to those at his right hand, "Come, O blessed of my Father, inherit the kingdom prepared for you from the foundation of the world; for I was hungry and you gave me food, I was thirsty and you gave me drink, I was a stranger and you welcomed me, I was naked and you clothed me, I was sick and you visited me, I was in prison and you came to me." Then the righteous will answer him, "Lord, when did we see thee hungry and feed thee, or thirsty and give thee drink? And when did we see thee a stranger and welcome thee, or naked and clothe thee? And when did we see thee sick or in prison and visit thee?" And the king will answer them, "Truly, I say to you, as you did it to one of the least of these my brethren, you did it to me." Then he will say to those at his left hand, "Depart from me, you cursed, into the eternal fire prepared for the devil and his angels; for I was hungry and you gave me no food, I was thirsty and you gave me no drink, I was a stranger and you did not welcome me, naked and you did not clothe me, sick and in prison and you did not visit me." Then they also will answer, "Lord, when did we see thee hungry or thirsty or a stranger or naked or sick or in prison, and did not minister to thee?" Then he will answer them, "Truly, I say to you, as you did it not to one of the least of these, you did it not to me." And they will go away into eternal punishment, but the righteous into eternal life. (Matthew 25:31–46)

Jesus' Images of the Final Judgment

Jewish tradition presented the following vision of the Final Judgment: God would sit on His throne of glory. All souls would pass before Him. As a consequence of His review of each person's life, God would determine each soul's ultimate destiny. God would separate all humans into two groups—one destined for eternal life, the other destined for suffering and punishment. Watching (witnessing, possibly assisting) would be God's messengers, the angels, and other heavenly beings. Standing at God's right hand would be Enoch, the Patriarchs, Moses, Elijah, and Elisha.

Present also was another figure. Enoch called him the son of man. "From eternity was the *son of man* concealed, whom the Most High preserved in the presence of His power and revealed to the elect." At the Last Judgment, all souls "shall fix their hopes on this son of man. They shall pray to him and petition him for mercy." In vain, for "the Lord of all spirits will expel them from His presence. . . . The angels shall take them to punishment." The righteous "have arisen from the earth [to be] clothed with the garment of life . . . [which] garment shall never wax old or diminish in glory." These elect shall "dwell, eat, lie down and rise up forever with this son of man."[2]

The same vision was presented in Daniel. "One like a son of man came with the clouds of heaven; he reached the Ancient of Days and was presented to him. Dominion, glory and kingship were given to him; all peoples and nations of every language must serve him. His dominion is an everlasting dominion that shall not pass away, and his kingship one that shall not be destroyed."[3]

Jesus presented the same image. "Then will appear the sign of the son of man in heaven, and then all the tribes of the earth will mourn, and they will see the son of man coming on the clouds of heaven with power and great glory; and he will send out his angels with a loud trumpet call, and they will gather his elect from the four winds, from one end of heaven to the other."[4] He portrayed the son of man seated on a glorious throne.[5]

Then Jesus went farther than Jewish tradition had gone before. He intimated that he was the son of man. As the good shepherd, who knew and cared for his flock, he would separate the sheep from the goats, placing the righteous on his right and condemning the wicked on his left. As the king, sitting on his throne, he would judge "all the nations"[6] and mete out appropriate rewards and punishments.

It was an astonishing assertion. The leaders and teachers of the Jewish community were bound to react aggressively.

Jesus Challenged the Conventional Criteria of Righteousness

Jesus pushed farther and challenged the conventional criteria of righteousness. Those standing on the right, who would enjoy eternal life in God's kingdom, were blessed because they alleviated the distress of people in need. They fed the hungry, slaked the thirst of the parched, befriended the stranger, provided garments to the poor, cared for people who were ill, and assisted those in prison. These acts expressed explicitly what the sages called *g'milut khasadim*—"deeds of lovingkindness." According to Simeon, "The world is sustained by three things: by Torah, by Temple worship and by deeds of lovingkindness."[7]

All six acts were encouraged in Jewish literature.[8] Neglecting them was tantamount to apostasy. "Hospitality to wayfarers is more important than welcoming the *shekhina*."[9] "A person who neglects to visit the sick is like one who sheds blood."[10] And a passage that echoed the statement of Jesus in our parable: "My children," God said to Israel, "whenever you give food to the poor, I impute it to you as though you gave Me food."[11]

Jesus knew sick people the Pharisees never visited, poor people the sages never noticed, and prisoners the lawyers ignored. For Jesus, such persistent neglect on the part of many of the leaders and teachers of Israel was a clear indication that they didn't care. The anguish and suffering of the poor and disadvantaged didn't move them. He felt they were heartless and lacked compassion. They would be surprised, Jesus warned, when they found themselves on the left side, doomed to destruction.

Jesus' repetitive use of the personal pronoun emphasized another complaint. Not only had the scribes and lawyers ignored the pressing needs of disadvantaged Jews, but they had harassed, belittled, and besmirched Jesus, his fellowship, and his teachings. The righteous "gave *me* food," "gave *me* drink," "clothed *me*," and "welcomed *me*." The conventional leaders opposed his teachings and tried to thwart the activities of his disciples. "You gave me no food. You gave me no drink. You did not clothe me." They would suffer for their intransigence. At the Final Reckoning, they would be condemned to die. "Depart from me, you cursed ones, into the eternal fire prepared for the devil and his angels."[12]

Even the righteous were surprised. "When did we feed you?" they asked. "When did we clothe you or see you sick or visit you in prison?" They understood the personal pronoun to refer specifically to Jesus—and by extension to his disciples.

In his final comments, Jesus emphasized once again his concern for the downtrodden and disadvantaged. "I say to you, because you did it to one of the least of these my brethren, you did it to me."[13]

Who Were the Brethren?

Who were these "brethren" whom the righteous helped?[14]

Biblical commentators provided three different answers. The first response suggested that the judgment would be determined by how well people treated

Jesus' disciples. Jesus called his disciples "brethren." "Stretching out his hand toward his disciples, he said, 'Here are my mother and my brothers!'"[15]

Jesus' disciples were dependent on the good will of others to provide lodging, food and drink, clothing, and provisions for travel. The first answer declared that those who treated the disciples well would receive their reward at the Final Reckoning.

Jesus applied the term "brethren" to anyone in his fellowship—not just to the disciples. "Whoever does the will of my Father in heaven is my brother and sister and mother."[16] This second response broadened the judgment to include anyone who protected, succored, or defended members of Jesus' community of believers.

Jesus also applied the term universally to refer to any human being. "I say to you that every one who is angry with his brother shall be liable to judgment; whoever insults his brother shall be liable to the council."[17] "If you are offering your gift at the altar, and there remember that your brother has something against you, leave your gift there before the altar and go. First be reconciled to your brother, and then come and offer your gift."[18] "Why do you see the speck that is in your brother's eye, but do not notice the log that is in your own eye?"[19]

Every human is your "brother," just as every person in need is your "neighbor."[20] The third answer declared that judgment would be based on how people responded to those in their midst suffering misfortune—the hungry, the thirsty, the naked, the neglected, the infirm, and the imprisoned. This applied not only to Jews but to non-Jews as well, for "all the nations" would array themselves before the throne of glory on Judgment Day, and all would be evaluated by the same criterion.

This was what Jesus meant when he said "Because you did it to one of the least of these my brethren, you did it to me." It reinforced the lessons of the Parable of the Priest, the Levite, and the Samaritan. It applied universally to all people. It agreed with his use of the term "brethren" in other contexts. Most of all, it focused the attention of his listeners on the group of people Jesus believed was the most neglected—the poor and the disadvantaged.

For Jesus, to do God's will meant to reach out with compassion to any other person suffering. Not only did Jewish law prescribe it, but love demanded it.

Jesus as King of the Jews

In Enoch, God sat on His throne of glory and judged "all the kings, the princes, the exalted and those who possess the earth." In the course of His judgment, God revealed the son of man, whom He had concealed, and declared that the son of man would have "dominion over all things."[21] For Enoch, God and the son of man were distinct; God reviewed the souls arrayed before Him and determined who would enjoy eternal life and who would suffer the eternal flames.

Daniel also described how the son of man was revealed. One like a son of man came with the clouds of heaven; he reached the Ancient of Days and was presented to him. Dominion, glory, and kingship were given to him; all peoples and nations of every language must serve him. His dominion is an everlasting dominion that shall not pass away, and his kingship one that shall not be destroyed.[22] The son of man was to rule in the World to Come.

Jesus often identified himself as the son of man, but nowhere did he designate himself as king. Was Jesus now announcing that he was the king in this parable? That he would rule in God's kingdom over kings and princes?

Apparently he was.

Jesus blurred the distinction between God and the son of man when he depicted the son of man as the shepherd separating the sheep from the goats, granting eternal life to the sheep and punishing the goats.[23]

Jesus envisioned the son of man sitting on a throne.

Jesus depicted the king answering the questions of the blessed and the cursed, saying, "Because you did it to one of the least of these my brethren, you did it to me."

The king was not God but an entirely separate person. How else could the king say, "Come, O blessed of my Father, inherit the kingdom of the world"? The Father was God; the one who spoke was the king, the son of man—Jesus.

This teaching, spoken late in his career, provided the excuse for bringing Jesus to trial before the Roman authorities. In all four gospels Pilate asked Jesus, "Are you the king of the Jews?"[24] The *titulus* that indicated Jesus' crime which the Romans affixed to the column of the cross provided the answer: "Jesus of Nazareth, king of the Jews."[25]

Jesus Established a Universal Moral Standard

With this parable, Jesus established a universal standard by which all humans would be judged. People who lived in distant lands, who never heard Jesus preach and never met a disciple, nonetheless encountered members of their communities who were distressed and needed assistance. How they responded to the needs of the hungry, the poor, the infirm, the stranger, and the imprisoned would determine their fate on Judgment Day. If they reached out with compassion to provide food to the malnourished, clothing to the naked, and friendship to the stranger, if they tried to heal the afflicted and aid the neglected, they would enjoy eternal life among the blessed in God's kingdom. For Jesus, every person was a "brother." According to him, if "you did it to one of the least of these my brethren, you did it to me."

With the Parable of the Last Judgment we conclude our review of Jesus' parables. The next two chapters present a summary of the teachings Jesus conveyed through his parables—including the secrets.

Notes

1. John ate locusts and drank wild honey and water (Matthew 3:4, Mark 1:6). Luke 1:15 predicted John would drink no wine.

2. 1 Enoch 61:9–18.

3. Daniel 7:13–14.

4. Matthew 24:30–31. See also Matthew 16:27–28.

5. Matthew 25:31. See also Matthew 19:28, where the son of man and *all twelve disciples* sit on thrones.

6. The cataclysm was universal; all human life ceased. Though nations were mentioned, the judgment was still individual and not by country or groups.

7. M. Avot 1:2.

8. See Arland J. Hultgren, *The Parables of Jesus: A Commentary* (Grand Rapids, Mich.: William B. Eerdmans, 2000), 315–17, for an excellent review of the Jewish sources for each of the six helpful acts.

9. Shabbat 127a.

10. Nedarim 40a.

11. Midrash Tannaim on Deuteronomy 15:9, as reported in George Foot Moore, *Judaism in the First Centuries of the Christian Era* (Cambridge, Mass.: Harvard University Press, 1927), vol. 2, 169; and in Joachim Jeremias, *The Parables of Jesus*, rev. ed. (New York: Charles Scribner's Sons, 1963), 207.

12. Matthew 25:41.

13. Matthew 25:40, and its opposite in 25:45.

14. The Greek word *adelphos* meant "brother," but the plural (v 40) referred both to groups of men and to mixed groups of men and women. Some texts print "brothers and sisters," but that can confuse the English reader into thinking siblings were meant. "Brethren" is a better translation.

15. Matthew 12:49. See also Matthew 23:8, 28:10.

16. Matthew 12:50.

17. Matthew 5:22.

18. Matthew 5:23–24.

19. Matthew 7:3. See also Matthew 7:4–5; 18:15, 21, 35.

20. See the discussion above (pp. 212–222) regarding the Parable of the Priest, the Levite, and the Samaritan.

21. 1 Enoch 61.

22. Daniel 7:13–14.

23. Contrast Jesus' image in verses 32–33 with Ezekiel 34:17.

24. Matthew 27:11, Mark 15:2, Luke 23:2, John 18:33.

25. John 19:19.

CHAPTER TWENTY

Conclusions

Why Jesus Spoke in Parables

Jesus built his parables on the experiences of his listeners. Since most Jews in first-century Palestine were farmers, many parables included allusions to plowing, seeding, and harvesting crops. The most frequent crops were grains, fruit, vegetables, and nuts. From wheat, they baked their daily bread. From flax, Galileans produced fine linens. From grapes, they made wine. Jesus' parables were filled with allusions to grain fields, orchards, and vineyards, as well as to the everyday demands of running a farm.

In addition, most farmers tended sheep, goats, and a few cattle. In that sense, they were shepherds also, and Jesus included references in his parables to herding as well.

The Parable of the Sower demonstrated how Jesus based his parables on the ordinary experiences of his audience. Though a good farmer sowed his seeds carefully, some seeds spilled into the rocks, and some the birds carried away. Most farmers disregarded the resulting sprouts and concentrated on nurturing the seeds rooted in good soil. From each such seed planted and harvested might come thirty, sixty, or even a hundred more seeds. Because they had experienced similar circumstances, Jesus' listeners immediately understood his images and identified quickly with the characters in the story and their struggles.

Bible stories and Jewish allusions were also part of the mindset of his audiences. Isaiah's image of God's vineyard, Hosea's references to Israel as an unfaithful wife, and Ezekiel's dazzling portrayal of God's throne of glory were familiar images. Most shared a common vision of the coming apocalypse, the Final Judgment, and the World to Come. Most believed in angels and demons, and also in the struggle between the forces of good and evil over each human's soul. Jesus used his listeners' understandings of Jewish tradition as a platform on which to build his own teachings.

The goal of his preaching was to change his audiences' perceptions of these traditional images and to infuse them with new meaning. Once he set the scene and established the characters, he often had his protagonists behave in surprising and unconventional ways. That forced his listeners to reevaluate their understandings.

Jesus often got his listeners to accept his ideas by showing the incongruities of their conventional thinking and by reinterpreting traditional characters. The abused and neglected became the heroes of his stories; the acknowledged leaders and teachers became the villains.

Nothing better illustrated this technique than the Parable of the Priest, the Levite, and the Samaritan. As Jesus developed the tale, his audience expected the priest and the Levite to assist the beaten traveler—at least to the extent of determining whether he was alive and of getting him help once they saw he was living. That neither the priest nor the Levite stopped was surprising, but not entirely unanticipated. Both were concerned with observing the laws of ritual purity.

His listeners then expected a third Jew to help the man lying on the ground. This would have completed the traditional triad of priest, Levite, and Israelite, reinforced Jesus' assertions that the acknowledged leaders of the people were not fulfilling their own moral precepts, and made it an antiestablishment parable. They were surprised when the third passerby turned out to be a Samaritan, and shocked to hear that he responded compassionately to the hurt man's plight. Jesus had confounded their expectations and forced them to consider the notion that a Samaritan could be a role model for their own behavior.

Though the settings were familiar to his listeners, Jesus' explanations and insights were not. They often presented images and ideas that his audiences had never before considered and in a manner that confounded their expectations. Often his listeners were confused. Sometimes, even Jesus' disciples didn't understand. They asked Jesus why he spoke in parables. Why didn't he convey his ideas clearly and directly?

Matthew recorded Jesus' answer to the disciples' question.

Jesus saw many Jews behaving as the prophet Isaiah had predicted. They heard but did not comprehend; they saw but did not perceive. Though alert and successful, they did not understand that God was waiting for them to turn and be healed. So Jesus spoke in parables that they might understand.

According to Matthew, Jesus used metaphors to help people comprehend what God intended. Perhaps these stories would provide insights not given through their own experiences or in the instructions of other teachers.

A significantly different answer was reported in Mark. Asked why he spoke in parables, Jesus explained that true believers possessed information most Jews did not—secret information. The parable form hinted at these secrets but did not express them explicitly.

According to Mark, the parable form permitted everyone to hear the secrets, but only the members of Jesus' fellowship understood them. Those "outside" didn't comprehend.

Mark reversed Matthew. Matthew suggested that the parables were designed to help those who didn't understand to comprehend the secrets, while Mark observed that the parables were designed to hide the secrets from the uninitiated.

Why hide the secrets at all? Jesus encouraged his disciples to share everything. Why not broadcast the secrets loudly and clearly?

Most Jews were not scholars. They accepted as their own the beliefs and practices of the acknowledged leaders and teachers of the community. Jesus' mission was to change people's understandings. To do so, he needed to challenge the instructions of the authorities and bring their teachings into question. Jesus shared ideas the sages found offensive and encouraged his followers to behave in ways the scribes condemned. The more outspoken he became, the more their resistance would grow.

Knowing the leaders of the Jewish community had beaten and killed former prophets, including eventually John the Baptist, Jesus hid his secrets in metaphors to protect himself. Outsiders wouldn't attack him physically if they didn't understand the secrets.

Jesus also wanted to protect the members of his fellowship. People in their towns and villages would notice their changed behavior. Authorities in communities where they preached and healed would take exception to their activities. Metaphors that contained secrets inaccessible to the uninitiated would limit the responses of "outsiders" and protect his followers from harm.

Who were these "outsiders" whose resistance or opposition to Jesus' activities might have created problems for Jesus and his supporters?

The gospel writers assigned them various titles—Sadducees, Pharisees, scribes, lawyers, chief priests, and ordinary priests—and made some of them responsible for Jesus' trial and crucifixion. Jesus called them hypocrites, fools, blind guides, and a brood of vipers.

First, *Pharisees*, *sages*, *scribes*, and *lawyers* were synonymous terms. They did not refer to different groups. In postbiblical Jewish literature and in the gospels, they described scholars within the Jewish community concerned primarily with understanding the nuances of biblical revelation and teaching their findings to others. Though widely recognized, they were only loosely organized. Some established academies and led disciples, but the head and disciples of one circle often disagreed with their counterparts in other schools. Some served as judges and worked together in various trials, but the composition of the Sanhedrin and the lower courts changed frequently and never included all sages and teachers. At no time, either before, during, or after Jesus' lifetime, did all the lawyers, all the sages, or all the Pharisees assemble to consider an item or render a decision. Wherever the gospels reported "the Pharisees," readers must understand that as *some* Pharisees— not even most Pharisees, just *some* Pharisees.

Second, *high priest, chief priests, ordinary priests,* and *Levites* were terms used to describe officials functioning in the Holy Temple in Jerusalem. The high priest was the head, and all other priests were subordinate to him. He appointed chief priests over key departments; ordinary priests and Levites were assigned to specific tasks under their jurisdiction. Some priests resided in Jerusalem and worked at the Temple year-round. Most priests and Levites lived in family groups scattered throughout the Land of Israel and resided in or near Jerusalem only during the weeks or festivals in which their respective communities were called to work at the Temple. Rarely was a majority of all priests and Levites in Jerusalem. Never did all priests gather in Jerusalem or anywhere else. Therefore, wherever the gospels reported the "chief priests" or the "priests and Levites" did something, readers must understand that *some* chief priests or *some* ordinary priests and Levites were involved. Many were still at home with their families in towns scattered throughout Palestine. Even in Jerusalem, most were busy doing their assigned tasks in the Temple.

Third, not all sages, scribes, lawyers, priests, or Levites opposed Jesus' teachings or condemned his activities. Jesus taught some Pharisees, engaged in conversation with others, and even dined in one Pharisee's home. Scribes and Pharisees were among his followers, and some Pharisees may have saved his life. In every instance where the gospels reported "lawyers" opposed him or "Pharisees" questioned him, readers must understand that as *some* lawyers or *some* Pharisees, since not all lawyers or Pharisees opposed Jesus.

Fourth, many of Jesus' essential beliefs were Pharisaic. Life after death, heaven and hell, the World to Come, resurrection, Final Judgment, the Messiah, the Apocalypse, the banquet of the righteous, and eternal life were grounded in the teachings of the Pharisees and opposed by the Sadducees. Jesus may have colored these beliefs differently on the basis of his own insights, but he never rejected them (as did the Sadducees). In this regard, Jesus was within Pharisaic tradition, for sages differed among themselves in their descriptions of these great ideas. Jesus' debates with the Pharisees were arguments over significant details between proponents of the same system.

Finally, while most lawyers, scribes, priests, and Levites were accorded respect and status, many were not among the leaders of the Jewish community. Some sages were poor and lacking in influence. Most priests lived outside Jerusalem and performed tasks at the Temple under the supervision of other priests. Leadership in the Jewish community rested in the hands of the descendents of Herod the Great, the high priest, certain priestly families, some Pharisees, some wealthy merchants, some large estate owners, a few members of the Hasmonean family, and some people appointed to serve the rulers of Judea, Galilee, and Perea. All of them were subservient to the prefect in Judea, the Roman legate in Syria, and the Emperor in Rome.

Who, then, were the resisters from whom the secrets of heaven had to be hidden?

They included some Pharisees; some Sadducees; some lawyers, scribes, priests and Levites; some wealthy merchants and landowners; and many of the people attached to and dependent upon the Roman authorities. Once mobilized, they had the power to harm him and his supporters.

The Secrets Jesus Taught

What were these potentially dangerous secrets?

Jesus affirmed the Jewish idea that God was fair, just, good, and (above all) merciful. Therefore, the righteous and the innocent who hadn't received their proper due during their lives would be rewarded in the World to Come, and the wicked who were not appropriately chastised in this life would be punished in the World to Come. On these affirmations Jesus built his teachings about the Final Judgment, the Kingdom of Heaven, the struggle of good and evil, and the ultimate destiny of every righteous and wicked person.

The Righteous

In the Parable of the Wheat and the Weeds, the "wheat" were the righteous, true believers who accepted Jesus' teachings. The "weeds" were the wicked, those who rejected Jesus' teachings.

At the Final Judgment, the righteous and the wicked would be separated.

Only the righteous would survive. All organizations, communities, and societies that did not adopt Jesus' teachings would be destroyed. Among the Jewish people, those priests, sages, merchants, and farmers who rejected Jesus' ideas would perish.

Until that Final Judgment, God allowed evildoers to live among the righteous and tolerated their inequity temporarily. In the long run, however, justice would prevail. Those who perverted God's law would be punished; the faithful would be rewarded.

In the meantime, the righteous and the wicked battled for survival. The "weeds" hoped to choke off and destroy the "wheat."

According to Matthew, the "sons of the kingdom" and the "sons of the evil one" were opposing armies, the former affirming God and the latter obeying Satan. Regardless of how things seemed at present—that is, regardless of how many weeds were sprouting and growing—ultimately God would win. The wicked would suffer pain and death; the righteous would live on in God's glorious kingdom.

While many of his teachings about the righteous were familiar to first-century Jews, Jesus did assert one unique idea. He defined the righteous as those who accepted *his* teachings, not the teachings of the acknowledged sages and leaders of the Jewish people. Only his followers would survive the Final Judgment.

Jesus' disciples instructed others. And they taught others. Jesus called these teachers "the children of light." They included both men and women.[1] Women provided support and sustenance to Jesus and his followers; they were an essential part of his fellowship. Women as well as men could be effective in spreading Jesus' message to others.

Paul instructed the Ephesians to "walk as children of light" and encouraged the Philippians to "shine as lights in the world."[2] In his letters he explained what he meant. "Look to the interests of others," Paul wrote. "Do nothing from selfishness or conceit. Do all things without grumbling or questioning. Do not be foolish. Do not get drunk with wine. God is at work in you."[3] Paul urged these early Christians to behave in accordance with the teachings of their faith and to set an example for others. That's what he meant by *light*.[4]

This was what Jesus meant when he said, "I am the light of the world; he who follows me will not walk in darkness, but will have the light of life."[5] Whoever behaved as Jesus behaved and followed his teachings would evidence his enlightenment. He would be wise and righteous, no longer living in confusion and sin, no longer unrepentant and condemned. His mind and body would be healthy; his soul would be integrated, and his life would be complete.

The righteous (or faithful or wise) person became a light himself and set an example for others to follow.

In the Parable of the Last Judgment, Jesus challenged the conventional criteria of righteousness. The "blessed" would survive the Final Judgment because they had alleviated the distress of people in need. They fed the hungry, slaked the thirst of the parched, befriended the stranger, provided garments to the poor, cared for people who were ill, and assisted those in prison. Constantly and repeatedly, they performed "deeds of lovingkindness."

Jesus knew sick people the Pharisees never visited, poor people the sages never noticed, and prisoners the lawyers ignored. For Jesus, such persistent neglect was a clear indication that many of the leaders and teachers of Israel didn't care. They would be surprised, he warned, when they found themselves doomed to destruction.

In the Parable of the Wheat and the Weeds, the workers asked if they should remove the weeds. The owner told them not to, "lest in gathering the weeds you root up the wheat along with them."[6] The owner was afraid the workers would not be able to distinguish the wheat from the weeds and would not carry out the separation effectively.

Jesus reminded both his followers and detractors not to judge who was righteous and who was wicked. Since they could not discern a person's intentions or observe a person's total behavior, inevitably they would err, applaud evildoers, and condemn the faithful. Only God could determine who was worthy of being saved and who should be condemned to death.

These teachings coalesced in the Parable of the Priest, the Levite, and the Samaritan. The priest and the Levite disregarded the very instructions they taught to others and neglected the battered roadside victim desperately in need of help, while the Samaritan upheld God's Law and provided better care to a Jew in need than some Jewish leaders did.

Traditional interpretations that deprecated Samaritans and elevated priests and Levites were wrong. Jesus' teachings were correct. Any person— Jew or gentile—who responded to the needs of his fellow man with love would inherit eternal life.

Jesus taught that a Jew didn't fulfill the commandment to love a neighbor by looking for the right person under the proper circumstances to love. He was the *neighbor*. When he showed compassion, he fulfilled God's demand. When he ceased caring—no matter the circumstances or the persons involved—he sinned.

Jesus wanted to break down Jewish stereotypes about gentiles and to loosen the constraints on who is a neighbor. Any person in need deserved our assistance. It didn't matter whether the injured was a Jew, a Roman, or a Samaritan. Any person—Jew or gentile—who responded to someone in distress was a *neighbor*.

To Jesus, every human being was "brother," just as every person in need was "neighbor." Final Judgment would be based on how people responded to those in their midst suffering misfortune—the hungry, the thirsty, the naked, the neglected, the infirm, and the imprisoned. This applied not only to Jews but to non-Jews as well. On Judgment Day, "all the nations" would array themselves before the throne of glory, and all would be evaluated by the same criteria.

For Jesus, to do God's will meant to reach out with compassion to any other person suffering. Not only did Jewish law prescribe it, but love demanded it.

The Wicked

The Pharisees and Jesus agreed—false prophets continued to misguide people. To avoid any misunderstanding, some sages declared that prophecy had ended hundreds of years earlier. According to this tradition, Malachi was the last authentic prophet.

Jesus denied this assertion and insisted that he was as much a prophet as Elijah, Elisha, and Isaiah. He had access to secrets about God's kingdom some of these biblical prophets hadn't known.

His parables were filled with allusions to the prophecies of Isaiah, Jeremiah, and Ezekiel. His teachings echoed their dire predictions of death, destruction, and exile. He applied their warnings to the Jews of his own time. Like their forebears, they were neglecting their covenant with God and transgressing His commandments. This time, they would suffer an upheaval from which there would be no return. Unless they reconciled with God and changed their behavior, they would be condemned to searing flames in the World to Come as punishment for their sins.

John the Baptist warned them, but they had rejected his teachings. Now they had one last chance. In the Parable of the Barren Fig Tree, Jesus told his listeners that God was ready to destroy His unresponsive people. The intercession of the gardener (Jesus) stayed the execution for one more season. It was their final reprieve. Through Jesus' solicitous care, the Jewish people might yet bear fruit and survive. However, if the Jewish people did not respond to Jesus' ministrations, it would be destroyed.

Especially wicked were the leaders of the people. They denied John's and Jesus' authenticity as prophets and led people astray with their false teachings. Like their ancestors, they would suffer devastation and destruction.

Though invited to the Banquet, the leaders and teachers snubbed God's invitation.

In the Parable of the Great Banquet and the Parable of the Royal Wedding Feast, the banquet depicted the glorious experiences of the redeemed in God's kingdom after the impending apocalypse. The members of the Jewish aristocracy were invited to celebrate the marriage of the king's son. They refused and murdered the king's messengers. They were replaced by the very people they neglected—"the poor and maimed and blind and lame."

God would not recognize the leaders and teachers or acknowledge their good work.

In the Parable of the Ten Maidens, the maidens stood outside in the dark and pounded on the door, pleading with the master of the house, "Lord, lord, open to us." But he replied, "Truly, I say to you, I do not know you."[7]

Jesus presented the same idea in a different metaphor. Having finished his work, the homeowner locked the door. People stood outside, pounded on the door, and pleaded to be let in. "We ate and drank in your presence, and you taught in our streets." The homeowner rejected them and denied their request. "I tell you, I do not know where you come from. Depart from me, all you workers of iniquity!"[8]

At the Final Judgment, God would reject the "workers of iniquity" among the Jewish people. They would be left out of the kingdom of heaven and condemned to suffer darkness, devastation, and death. Foremost among them would be the leaders and teachers of Israel.

Those who saw themselves as righteous but despised others were doomed.

Jesus chastised Pharisees for accepting seats of honor in synagogues and at public feasts. Not only did they lack humility and a sense of social propriety, but these Pharisees were immoral hypocrites as well. They "devour widows' houses and for a pretense make long prayers." They deserved and would receive "the greater condemnation."[9]

In the Parable of the Pharisee and the Publican, a sage and a tax collector went into the Temple to pray. In his prayer the Pharisee gave thanks to God and extolled his own virtues. He was not an extortionist, an adulterer, or a tax collector. He fasted more often than was required and gave tithes regularly. Standing off to the side, the tax collector beat his breast, admitted he was a sinner, and begged God for mercy.

Jesus declared that the reviled tax collector had fulfilled God's wishes more than the sage, and he concluded with this prediction: "Every one who exalts himself will be humbled, but he who humbles himself will be exalted."[10]

The lessons of this parable applied not just to wayward Pharisees but to anyone who thought himself better than others around him, to anyone who ignored the needy and neglected the poor, to anyone who despised fellow Jews struggling on the margins of society. Every such person—Pharisee or not—was a sinner. Unless he repented, he would be doomed in the coming apocalypse.

The same emphasis was presented in the Parable of the Misdressed Wedding Guest. What the guest lacked was not a physical garment but an attitude. He had not repented. His behavior reflected no change of heart, no new understanding. As a consequence, he was ineligible for God's kingdom.

Normal expectations would be completely overturned with the coming of God's kingdom, and persons of exalted status in contemporary society—sages, priests, and aristocrats—would be humiliated. People who acted humbly and considered others would be honored.

As if to reinforce this image, after the Parable of the Place of Honor Luke inserted another teaching about reaching out to the disadvantaged: "When you give a feast, invite the poor, the maimed, the lame, [and] the blind, and you will be blessed." Jesus concluded with the following statement: "They cannot repay you. You will be repaid at the resurrection of the just."[11]

The leaders and teachers of Israel used their power for their own self-aggrandizement.

The Parable of the Servant Left Alone may have been directed against the leaders and teachers of the Jewish community. They held their exalted positions at God's behest. But many of them abused their authority, used their power for their own self-aggrandizement, and led people astray. Jesus warned that, if they didn't change, they would suffer the fate of all sinners. During the cataclysm, they would be destroyed.

The leaders were to serve as shepherds to the people of Israel. They had failed.

According to Jeremiah and Ezekiel, the king, the priests, and the other leaders of Old Testament times had been supposed to serve as shepherds to the people of Israel. They had failed. As a consequence, God's people had suffered defeat and exile. Jesus asserted that many current leaders behaved as immorally as did the kings, priests, and leaders of the past and that their teachings imperiled the people.

Some Pharisees, Sadducees, scribes, priests, and lawyers were sinners.

In the Parable of the Pharisee and the Publican, Jesus asserted that some Pharisees were sinners. Though they appeared to follow God's law and live pious lives—giving even more than was required—they were haughty and prideful and judgmental of others. They ignored the needy; they neglected the downtrodden; they rejected those on the margin of society.

The criteria by which God judged who was worthy and who was not included not only what a man did but also what he said and (more importantly) the manner in which he related to other people. The Pharisee's soul was tainted by his hubris. He judged others without any knowledge of their hardships and struggles. He rejected people God accepted. He lacked humility. The sage saw himself a righteous man, but he was a sinner in Jesus' eyes.

In the Parable of the Two Sons and the Vineyard, the elders saw themselves as the first son—occasional sinners who repented of their sins—but Jesus accused them of being like the second son. They said they knew and did the will of God, but they did not. They didn't understand what God demanded, and they didn't do what God intended. If they did, they would help the infirm and reach out to sinners.

In contrast, Jesus taught that repentant sinners were like the first son. Having sinned egregiously, they repented. Now they spent their time trying to undo the harm they created and to fulfill God's demands.

The Parable of the Father and His Two Sons echoed the same principle. From Jesus' point of view, the elder son was a selfish and self-righteous sinner. Not only had he broken God's laws, but he had not repented. He was too busy condemning others.

Jesus castigated community leaders and teachers who acted sinfully. He called them to account, asked them to change their behavior, and demanded that they accurately present God's wishes to their constituencies.

Jesus concluded the Parable of the Two Sons and the Vineyard with this reproof of the sages who rejected his teachings and the teachings of John the Baptist: "I say to you, tax collectors and harlots [will] go into the kingdom of God before you."[12]

In the Parable of the Vineyard Owner and His Tenants, Jesus taught that the people had become as rebellious and destructive as wild grapes. Therefore, the vineyard needed to be destroyed—Jerusalem, the Temple, its priests, the elders of the city, the merchants, bakers, cheese makers, potters, builders, and masons. Jesus condemned everyone who disobeyed God and refused to repent.

In the Parable of the Priest, the Levite, and the Samaritan, both the priest and the Levite walked past the man suffering on the roadside without bothering to check if he was alive and if he needed help. Even if they were on their way to participate in the sacrificial service and touching the man would have defiled them, they could still have alerted others and sought assistance. Jesus taught that sacrifices that fostered the neglect of people in distress were meaningless and that cleanliness that caused human suffering and death was disgraceful.

Conventional understandings that deprecated Samaritans and elevated priests and Levites were wrong. Jesus' teachings were correct. Any person—Jew or gentile—who responded to the needs of his fellow man with love would inherit eternal life. Any person—including priests and Levites—who refused to help would die in the holocaust to come.

Zealots were sinners also.

The Parable of the Seed Growing Secretly may have been directed against Zealots and other revolutionaries who hoped to overthrow the yoke of Roman oppression and expedite the coming of the Messiah. Jesus was telling them and their supporters that their efforts were futile. The timetable was already in motion, and their activities would not influence the divine eschatology in the slightest.

According to Jesus, in their revolutionary zeal they exhibited unwarranted arrogance. He called on Jews to be patient, submit to the will of God, and accept God's plan.

Apocalypse

Jesus explained the secrets of the Parable of the Wheat and the Weeds to his disciples. Like reapers in a field of wheat ready for harvest, angels would slice through the peoples of the earth, gathering true believers together under God's love and protection and burning the rest of humanity. Following this conflagration, God's kingdom would be established on earth.

Only the righteous would survive. All others would perish, and the current epoch of human experience would come to a close.

Jesus believed the biblical period came to an end with John the Baptist. The kingdom of God had already started. Soon God would make his final determination, and the apocalypse would carry out His judgment.

This calamity would be like no other in history, and Jesus described it in parable after parable.

In the Parables of the Flood and of the Well-Built House, he warned that floods would inundate communities. In the Parable of Sodom's Destruction, fire and brimstone would destroy cities. Rainstorms would buffet the earth. Darkness would cover the skies. "The stars will fall from heaven, and the powers of the heavens will be shaken."[13]

As in Abraham's time, it would happen suddenly. The people of Sodom and Gomorrah had had no warning. They had died still believing they were righteous.

Jesus advised his listeners not to worry about homes, crops, or other assets. They would all be destroyed. Save yourselves, he urged. Commit yourselves entirely to reconciling with God. And don't hesitate or falter, Jesus warned: "Remember Lot's wife."[14]

Before he was fired and banished from his master's estate in disgrace, the steward in the Parable of the Steward and His Master's Debts approached every merchant who had not paid on his account and offered to change the amount due. As a consequence, he saved each client a considerable amount of money.

Jesus called the servant "dishonest," yet he commended him. Faced with the imminent prospect of disgrace and homelessness, the dishonest steward used his skills to construct a brighter future. Believers should do the same.

In the Parable of a Rich Man Who Decided to Enjoy Himself, Jesus encouraged his listeners to diminish their concern with profit and worldly possessions and focus their attention on their moral and spiritual behavior. It was all right to acquire wealth, but material assets were irrelevant to survival in the World to Come. At death, God judged a person not on how much wealth he attained, but on the spiritual and moral qualities of his life.

Jesus said, "If you would be perfect, go, sell what you possess and give to the poor, and you will have treasure in heaven."[15]

Jesus' focus was on the approaching holocaust and on the certain knowledge that all the people in his audience would die painfully if he couldn't change their beliefs and behavior.

Final Judgment

Eventually, every person would be called to judgment for his behavior. There was no fooling God, and there was no escaping His decision. Until the day of his death, God called on each sinner to repent. Echoing Jewish tradition, Jesus said, repent now, as if this were the last day of your life.

There was an urgency to Jesus' preaching. Once God's kingdom began, there would no time to repent. Judgment would follow swiftly, and those who were sinners would be condemned to suffering and death. People had just a short window of time in which to become true servants of God before the devastation began.

Since the righteous had no shepherd to care for them, God Himself would become their Shepherd. In the Parable of One Lost Sheep, God not only waited for each person to return (repent) but went out to search for each lost soul.

In the Parable of the Father and his Two Sons, Jesus portrayed God as a parent who welcomed His frail and selfish creatures with love. In the Parable of the Judge and the Widow, Jesus asserted that God would respond to their pleas and vindicate them.

In the Parable of the Last Judgment, Jesus described for his followers his vision of the Final Judgment: God would sit on His throne of glory. All souls would pass before Him, and God would review each person's life. As a consequence of His review, God would determine each soul's destiny. God would separate all humans into two groups—one destined for eternal life, the other destined for suffering and punishment.

In the Parable of the Fishing Net, Jesus compared the Final Judgment to fishing on the Sea of Galilee. As the current age of human experience came to a close, angels would sort through all the people on earth and select only true believers to take with them into God's kingdom. All the others would be thrown into the fiery furnace and burned to death.

Some Will Survive

The image of Noah and the ark in the Parable of the Flood reminded his listeners that some people had survived the deluge. Not everyone had been killed. Those in the ark had found dry land and started life anew.

So it would be for faithful followers of God's law. They would endure the devastation without suffering and would begin life again in the New Era.

In the Parable of the Salt, Jesus reminded his listeners that they would celebrate in the kingdom of heaven. God had established an eternal covenant with them—a "covenant of salt."

In both the Parable of the Great Banquet and the Parable of the Royal Wedding Feast, Jesus indicated the time for judgment had arrived. Unless they repented and corrected their relationships with God, the acknowledged leaders and teachers of the people would suffer and die in the apocalypse to follow. Only the poor, the blind and the lame, the humble and the meek, would survive to participate in the great banquet God had prepared for the righteous.

Like the five unprepared young ladies in the Parable of the Ten Maidens, the leaders would stand outside in the dark and pound on the door. And God would reply, "Truly, I say to you, I do not know you."[16]

Wealth and status were not the criteria that determined who entered heaven. In God's kingdom, divine justice prevailed. Those who suffered undeservedly in this life would be rewarded in the World to Come, and those who abused their wealth and neglected to respond to the needs of others would suffer anguish and pain. As Jesus illustrated dramatically in the Parable of the Rich Man and the Beggar Lazarus, things would even out in the world beyond death.

The standards in God's tribunal were more stringent than those of any human court. Jesus warned that God would punish anyone who insulted, belittled, or rejected another human being. Therefore, Jesus encouraged people to put aside their enmities, resolve their differences, and be reconciled before the Final Judgment was made and they suffered the consequences of their hesitance.

In the Parable of the Vine and the Branches, Jesus extended his warning even to the members of his fellowship. Survival was not automatic. Like every good farmer, God examined his vine regularly and destroyed the branches He determined would not bear fruit. God would declare some disciples fruitless and destroy them.

In the Parable of the Last Judgment, those standing on the right would enjoy eternal life in God's kingdom, because they alleviated the distress of people in need. Scribes and lawyers had ignored the pressing needs of disadvantaged Jews. Pharisees would be surprised when they found themselves on the left, doomed to destruction.

Within This Generation

Jesus took no pleasure in announcing Jerusalem's impending devastation. On the contrary, he wanted desperately to save it from destruction. But the disaster would occur within that generation. Even as he refused to describe signs of the coming apocalypse, Jesus asserted that the signs were apparent—the sign of the prophet Jonah, the condemnation of the Queen of Sheba, and the tender leaves growing on the branches of the fig tree. "When you see these things taking place, you know that the kingdom of God is near. Truly, I say to you, this generation will not pass away till all has taken place."[17]

The next chapter presents additional conclusions drawn from Jesus' parables.

Notes

1. Most translations render the Greek phrase *huious tou fotos* as "the sons of light," but in Hebrew and Aramaic the masculine plural was always used for mixed groups. Thus *b'nai yisra'eyl* did not mean "the sons of Israel" but "the children of Israel"—men and women.

2. Ephesians 5:8, Philippians 2:15.

3. Philippians 2:3, 4, 13, 14; Ephesians 5:17, 18.

4. With the same meaning, Isaiah admonished the Israelites to be "a light to the nations" (Isaiah 42:6; 49:6; 60:3, 5; 62:1). See also Matthew 5:16, Luke 2:32, Philippians 2:15.

5. John 8:12.

6. Matthew 13:29.

7. Matthew 25:11–12.

8. Luke 13:26–27.

9. Luke 20:47.

10. Luke 18:14.

11. Luke 14:12–13.

12. Matthew 21:31.

13. Matthew 24:29. See also Mark 13:24–25.

14. Luke 17:32.

15. Matthew 19:21.

16. Matthew 25:11–12.

17. Luke 21:31–32. See also Matthew 12:38–42, 23:34–36, 24:32–34; Mark 13:28–30; Luke 11:29–32, 49–51.

CHAPTER TWENTY-ONE

The Secrets Jesus Taught

Repentance

Jesus taught in one town after another to bring God's message that if people turned away from their false beliefs and erroneous practices, they might still survive the impending disaster. His mission was to get people to repent.

God's forgiveness was not determined by the extent, quality, or duration of a person's sins. Forgiveness flowed from God's grace. In the Parable of the Two Debtors, God forgave both sinners without hesitation and by virtue of His own decision.

One act of forgiveness was no different from the other. Not bigger than or smaller than the other, each was a sublime gift. It was not the debts that were forgiven but the debtors. The sinners were cleansed and made whole.

Forgiveness Was Immediate and Unconditional

In the Parable of the King Who Settles Accounts, the sum of ten thousand talents was beyond all reasonable possibility of repaying. Out of his compassion and without hesitation, the king forgave the entire debt. Our most horrendous sin would be forgiven if we truly repented.

For some listeners the Parable of the Father and His Two Sons was shocking. While the younger son may have been sufficiently contrite in his confession to his father, he still had not made up for the harm he caused and he had not demonstrated that he would never commit the same sins again. The elder son showed little respect for his father, dishonored his brother, and had yet to recognize or apologize for either sin. He had not begun to repent. According to the sages, both sons were still unrepentant sinners.

Even the father was at fault for giving away one-third of his assets to his younger son and possibly jeopardizing his family's ability to withstand economic hardships in the future. He set no standard for his younger son and did not punish him for his foolhardiness and disrespect. When the son returned, he required no compensation and no commitment to work for the family's well-being. Instead, he gave him clothes and sandals, hugs and kisses, and prepared a celebration in his honor.

Jesus' teachings contradicted conventional understandings. God's forgiveness was immediate and unconditional. No waiting was necessary; nothing more was required, for the behavior of a truly penitent person was completely changed. He would never again sin in the same way. That was the meaning of repentance. Those who stood in judgment against penitent sinners were themselves transgressing God's commandments. If they hoped to survive in the World to Come, they needed to make atonement and change their own behavior.

At the close of the Parable of the Pharisee and the Publican, listeners must have been shocked when Jesus declared that the tax collector was the righteous man and that the Pharisee was not. According to Jesus, the publican had truly repented. God had forgiven his sins completely and accepted him.

People were taught that repentance took place in four steps. The third step demanded the penitent sinner undo the harm he wrought. The fourth step required him never to commit the same sin again. There was no indication that the tax collector accomplished any of these.

Jesus was expressing a radical new idea. It started with the Parable of the Father and His Two Sons; it was even more pronounced in the Parable of the Pharisee and the Publican. God accepted a truly repentant sinner immediately. His sins were wiped clean; his soul became whole and pure again. There was no doubt or hesitation. Jesus suggested that Jews accept the penitent immediately and unconditionally—just as God did.

In the Parable of the Father and His Two Sons, Jesus emphasized the power of repentance. The younger son had committed heinous offenses and reached the depths of depravity. He indentured himself to gentiles, fed their swine, and longed to eat their slops.

Somehow he came to his senses and repented. He righted his relationship with God and determined to conduct himself in accordance with God's will. No more drinking and carousing. No more swine and swill.

He decided to return home to confess his sins and restore his relationship with his father and family. He was willing to serve as serf to his father's servants.

To Jesus, the younger son was saved. Though his former sins were deplorable, he would be among the righteous welcomed into the kingdom of heaven.

Even the most depraved sinner could repent and live in the World to Come. So Jesus welcomed tax collectors and harlots to his speeches and ate with them at the same table. These sinners needed encouragement and support if they were going to change their ways and be saved.

You Could Tell a Truly Repentant Person by His Behavior toward Others

In the Parable of the King Who Settles Accounts, Jesus suggested that you could tell a truly repentant person not by his status or power or teaching but by his behavior toward others. While they mouthed prayers, offered proper sacrifices, and recited penitential poems, many Pharisees and priests were insincere. Like the first servant, they sounded contrite and their pleas seemed heartfelt, but their behavior belied their words. Instead of extending mercy and forgiveness, they judged others harshly, condemned them, and abused them.

A sign of true repentance was our willingness to forgive others who sinned against us.

Access to God Was Possible Only through Jesus

According to the Parable of the Good Shepherd, there was a proper way to enter a sheepfold and claim the sheep. A legitimate shepherd entered through the gate, where the gatekeeper identified him, permitted him to pass, and noted the sheep he took out with him. A thief climbed over the wall, entered the sheepfold surreptitiously, and tried to lead away sheep he didn't own. Jesus accused those who preceded him of behaving like thieves sneaking into the sheepfold to lead the sheep astray.

The sheep were the Jews; the sheepfold was the world in which they lived; and those who preceded Jesus were the leaders and teachers of the Jewish people. Their way was the wrong way. They were using the wrong gate. By declaring, "I am the door," Jesus challenged both the people and the authorities to accept his ideas.

A second explanation in the same parable focused on what might happen when the flock left the sheepfold. Peril lurked outside, and a shepherd who didn't know the land or who didn't properly guard his herd endangered their lives.

Jesus declared that his teachings alone guaranteed eternal life, abundance, and joy. Like thieves, the acknowledged authorities were leading the people toward destruction.

In Jewish tradition, salvation was not dependent on following any one sage or teacher but on thoroughly comprehending the will of God and applying that understanding to daily experiences and relationships. There was not one access to God's will; there were myriads. A person could begin with the study of the Jewish dietary laws or the laws governing ritual purity, or explore the Psalms, or probe the mysteries of Daniel and Lamentations. God revealed His wishes in them all, and each ultimately led to the other.

Jesus insisted that he was the only teacher with the correct understanding of God's will. All other sages were wrong. They led people astray. As a result, they endangered their current lives and jeopardized their afterlives.

A verse in the Parable of the Vine and the Branches reinforced that image. "If a man does not abide in me, he is cast forth as a branch and withers; and the branches are gathered, thrown into the fire and burned."[1]

Access to God Was a Consequence of the Special Relationship between Jesus and His Followers

Jesus transformed the prophetic image. In the Parable of the Vine and the Branches, Jesus was the true vine—not the people of Israel. Israel was a dead vine, plucked and discarded by the Vinedresser for failing to fulfill its promise to be fruitful. God now tended Jesus. As a consequence of their special relationship, access to God was possible only through Jesus.

The change in belief and behavior necessary to achieve salvation derived from relationship—not from a set of rules or system of teachings. Jesus understood God's will because of his special union with God. And Jesus could transmit that understanding to others by their establishing the same kind of relationship with him.

Jesus added one more requirement. Since the righteous couldn't survive detached and on their own, they needed to join his fellowship. Otherwise, they would suffer and die in the conflagration soon to come.

These were audacious new ideas. One could not be redeemed outside the community; one could not be saved without Jesus.

Jesus as the Gardener

For three years in a row, the owner found no fruit on his fig tree. So he decided to cut it down and plant something else. His gardener asked him to wait one more year while he fertilized and tended the barren tree.

The fig tree represented the Jewish people, the owner was God, and the gardener who interceded for the barren tree was Jesus. Through the Parable of the Barren Fig Tree, Jesus reminded his listeners that the penalty for disobeying God was disaster. For years, the Jewish people had neglected God's laws. As a consequence, they were unproductive and doomed to destruction. There was one more chance. Through Jesus' personal ministry and solicitous care, the Jewish people might yet bear fruit and survive. However, if the Jewish people did not respond to Jesus' ministrations, it would be destroyed.

Jesus as the Shepherd

The third commentary within the Parable of the Good Shepherd emphasized the close relationship between the shepherd and his sheep. Jesus was the *good shepherd*, who knew and cared for his flock.

On hearing these words, listeners who knew the Bible may have recalled Moses' plea at the close of his life for a proper successor. "Let the Lord, Source of the breath of all flesh, appoint someone over the community . . . who shall lead them out and bring them in, so that the Lord's community may not be like sheep that have no shepherd." And God said to Moses, "Take Joshua the son of Nun."[2] Joshua was God's choice to succeed Moses. Joshua was the proper shepherd to lead God's flock from the wilderness into the Promised Land.

Jesus' Hebrew name was Joshua, and his listeners may have heard in this parable Jesus' intimation that he was Moses' true successor, invested with the same authority, the Good Shepherd who would lead the Israelite community to their ultimate redemption.

They may even have heard echoes of Micah's messianic promise. "I will gather together the remnant of Israel; I will set them together like sheep in a pasture, like a flock in a fold. . . . One will open the breach and go before them; they will enlarge the gate and leave by it. Their king will march before them, the Lord at their head."[3] Some listeners may have imagined Jesus as that Messianic leader.

For those who knew the Bible, allusion tumbled on allusion. Moses and David were both shepherds, and Jesus was the spiritual successor to the first and a descendent of the second. Jesus affirmed that he was (1) a prophet; (2) as authentic as Hosea, Isaiah, and Ezekiel; (3) the chosen successor by name to Moses; (4) who interpreted his law with greater insight and authenticity than the acknowledged sages and teachers of his time; (5) shared information with his disciples even former prophets didn't know; and (6) performed miracles, marvels, and wonders. Like Moses, Jesus claimed a special relationship with God. God was the Father, Jesus was the son, and their union was as intimate and compelling as that of a father and son on earth.

The kings and leaders of Israel were supposed to protect and nurture the people. Instead, like malevolent shepherds, they led their people astray and caused them to suffer. Jeremiah announced that God would appoint new shepherds to protect His people.

When Jesus said, "I am the good shepherd," he reminded his listeners of the *bad* shepherds who had failed them. Their current leaders behaved as immorally as did the kings, priests, and teachers of the past.

Jesus as the Vine
Sometime in February and March, the farmer inspected his vines and cut off branches he determined would no longer bear fruit. Later in August, when the vines sprouted leaves, the vinedresser pinched off the little shoots so that the main fruit-bearing branches received all the nourishment. If he was successful, clusters of grapes would dangle from each branch.

In the Parable of the Vine and the Branches, Jesus identified himself as the vine and God as the vinedresser. The branches were the members of Jesus' fellowship of believers, offshoots of the vine. God would destroy some members of his fellowship as harmful to the vine's survival.

Jesus as the Door
At night, in order to guard their sheep from predators and rustlers, shepherds would pen several flocks together inside a protected sheepfold. One shepherd would stand guard; the others would go to sleep and return in the morning to reclaim their flocks.

In the Parable of the Good Shepherd, Jesus declared, "I am the door."

Redemption was possible only by adopting Jesus' ideas and behaving as Jesus taught. His way alone guaranteed eternal salvation and joy. "I am the way, and the truth, and the life; no one comes to the Father, but by me."[4]

Jesus as the Son of Man
In the Final Judgment, all souls would pass before God; and God would determine each person's destiny. Standing at God's right hand would be Enoch, the Patriarchs, Moses, Elijah, and Elisha.

Present also would be the "son of man." At the Last Judgment, all souls "shall fix their hopes on this son of man."[5] The elect who survived shall "dwell, eat, lie down and rise up forever with this son of man."[6]

Jesus claimed he was the son of man.

As the good shepherd, who knew and cared for his flock, he would separate the sheep from the goats, placing the righteous on his right and condemning the wicked on his left. As the king, sitting on his throne, he would judge the nations and mete out appropriate rewards and punishments.

It was an astonishing assertion. The leaders and teachers of Jewish tradition were bound to react aggressively.

Jesus Was in Charge of the Angels

The explanation of the Parable of the Wheat and the Weeds intimated that Jesus was in charge of the angels. At Jesus' command, the angels would begin their sweep through the nations to gather up the wicked and incinerate them like noxious weeds.

Those ideas—that he was in charge of the punishing angels and that they would begin their devastation at his command—were incredible assertions and accounted for more of the opposition Jesus' teachings aroused.

Jesus as the King

Then Jesus went farther than Jewish tradition had gone before.

In Enoch, God sat on His throne of glory and judged "all the kings, the princes, the exalted and those who possess the earth." In the course of His judgment, God revealed the son of man and declared that the son of man would have "dominion over all things."[7] For Enoch, God and the son of man were distinct. God reviewed the souls arrayed before Him and determined who would enjoy eternal life and who would suffer the eternal flames.

Jesus blurred the distinction between God and the son of man. He depicted the son of man as the shepherd separating the sheep from the goats, granting eternal life to the sheep and punishing the goats.

He envisioned the son of man sitting on a throne.

He depicted the king answering the questions of the blessed and the cursed, saying, "Because you did it to one of the least of these my brethren, you did it to me."[8]

The king was not God, but an entirely separate person. How else could the king say, "Come, O blessed of my Father, inherit the kingdom of the world"?[9] The Father was God; the one who spoke was the king, the son of man—Jesus.

This teaching, spoken late in his career, provided the excuse for bringing Jesus to trial before the Roman authorities. In all four gospels, Pilate asked Jesus, "Are you the king of the Jews?"[10] In three he responded, "You have said so"—not denying the accusation, but leaving the decision up to the prefect.[11] In John, he said, "My kingship is not of this world . . . My kingship is not from the world"—which Pilate heard as an affirmation. "So you are a king," Pilate said to him.[12] The *titulus* that was affixed to the column of the cross indicated Jesus' crime. All four gospels agreed. The inscription read: "King of the Jews."[13]

Through our exploration of Jesus' parables we uncovered many of his beliefs and teachings, the secrets he revealed to his disciples and supporters, the conditions of life in Palestine in the first century, and the concepts and images already in his Jewish listeners' minds when first they heard Jesus preaching. As Jeremias notes, "The parables of Jesus compel his hearers to come to a decision about his person and his mission."[14]

As his messages became more widely known and his secrets more widely revealed, more opposition emerged against both his leadership and his ideas. Pharisees, Sadducees, lawyers, scribes, priests, and Levites challenged Jesus' behavior, his teachings, and his authority. They tried to dissuade people from listening to him and to undermine the convictions of those who supported him.

As his mission progressed, Jesus became more outspoken. Sages and priests were leading people astray both by their example and their teachings. They were sinners and would burn in Hell. His way was the only path to paradise. He was the vine God now tended and protected. He was the ideal shepherd chosen to lead the people of Israel into the promised New Era. He was the son of man—concealed and now revealed—who would separate the righteous from the wicked on Judgment Day and assign to each his reward or punishment. Along with Enoch, Abraham, Elijah, and Elisha, Jesus would sit with God in heaven on a throne. Eventually, Jesus would be king—not only of the Jews but of all humankind.

These images were not accepted by most Jews. As a consequence, the Jewish and Christian communities drifted apart. Today, most Jews know little about the New Testament, and most Christians are unaware of their Jewish roots. Perhaps this book will be a bridge connecting neighbor to neighbor.

"Jesus came preaching . . . and he taught them many things in parables."[15]

Notes

1. John 15:6.
2. Numbers 27:15–20.
3. Micah 2:12–13. See also Jeremiah 23:1–4, 1 Kings 22:1.

4. John 14:6.

5. 1 Enoch 61:13.

6. 1 Enoch 61:17.

7. 1 Enoch 61:10ff.

8. Matthew 25:40.

9. Matthew 25:34.

10. Matthew 27:11, Mark 15:2, Luke 23:2, John 18:33.

11. Matthew 27:11, Mark 15:2, Luke 23:2.

12. John 18:36–37.

13. Matthew 27:37, Mark 15:26, Luke 23:38, John 19:19–22.

14. Joachim Jeremias, *The Parables of Jesus* (New York: Charles Scribner's Sons, 1963), 230.

15. Mark 1:14, 4:2.

Bibliography

The Apocrypha: An American Translation. Translated by Edgar J. Goodspeed. New York: Modern Library, 1959.

The Apocrypha and Pseudepigrapha of the Old Testament. Edited by R. H. Charles. Oxford: Clarendon, 1913.

Bamberger, Bernard J. "Tax Collector." In *The Interpreter's Dictionary of the Bible: An Illustrated Encyclopedia*. Edited by George A. Buttrick. New York: Abingdon, 1962.

Bashan, Eliezer (Sternberg). "Weights and Measures." In *Encyclopedia Judaica*. Edited by Cecil Roth. 16 vols. Jerusalem: Macmillan, 1971–1972.

Beasley-Murray, George R. "John." In *Word Bible Commentary*. Edited by David A. Hubbard and Glenn W. Barker. Vol. 36. Waco, Tex.: Word Books, 1987.

Beck, D. M. "The Golden Rule." In *The Interpreter's Dictionary of the Bible: An Illustrated Encyclopedia*. Edited by George A. Buttrick. New York: Abingdon, 1962.

Berman, Saul. "Law and Morality." In *Encyclopedia Judaica*. Edited by Cecil Roth. 16 vols. Jerusalem: Macmillan, 1971–1972.

Brandon, S. G. F. "Zealots." In *Encyclopedia Judaica*. Edited by Cecil Roth. 16 vols. Jerusalem: Macmillan, 1971–1972.

Brown, Francis, S. R. Driver, and Charles A. Briggs. *A Hebrew and English Lexicon of the Old Testament*. Oxford: Clarendon, 1907.

Brown, Raymond E. "The Gospel According to John I–XII." In *The Anchor Bible*. Edited by William Foxwell Albright and David Noel Freedman. Vol. 29. Garden City, N.Y.: Doubleday, 1966.

———. "The Gospel According to John XIII–XXI." In *The Anchor Bible*. Edited by William Foxwell Albright and David Noel Freedman. Vol. 29a. Garden City, N.Y.: Doubleday, 1970.

Cohen, Chayim. "Bet Din and Judges." In *Encyclopedia Judaica*. Edited by Cecil Roth. 16 vols. Jerusalem: Macmillan, 1971–1972.

———. "Widow: Biblical Period." In *Encyclopedia Judaica*. Edited by Cecil Roth. 16 vols. Jerusalem: Macmillan, 1971–1972.

Cohn, Haim Hermann. "Weights and Measures." In Encyclopedia Judaica. Edited by Cecil Roth. 16 vols. Jerusalem: Macmillan, 1971–1972.

Crossan, John Dominic. In Parables: The Challenge of the Historical Jesus. New York: Harper and Row, 1973.

Crossan, John Dominic, and Jonathan Reed. Excavating Jesus. San Francisco: HarperSan-Francisco, 2002.

De Breffny, Brian. The Synagogue. New York: Macmillan, 1978.

Dodd, C. H. The Interpretation of the Fourth Gospel. Cambridge: Cambridge University Press, 1960.

———. The Parables of the Kingdom. Rev. ed. New York: Charles Scribner's Sons, 1961.

Eisenman, Robert, and Michael O. Wise. The Dead Sea Scrolls Uncovered. New York: Penguin Books, 1993.

Epstein, Isadore, ed. The Babylonian Talmud. 16 vols. London: Soncino, 1961.

The Ethiopic Book of Enoch. Translated by Michael A. Knibb. 2 vols. Oxford: Oxford University Press, 1978.

Evans, O. E. "Kingdom of God, of Heaven." In The Interpreter's Dictionary of the Bible: An Illustrated Encyclopedia. Edited by George A. Buttrick. New York: Abingdon, 1962.

Farmer, W. R. "Zealot." In The Interpreter's Dictionary of the Bible: An Illustrated Encyclopedia. Edited by George A. Buttrick. New York: Abingdon, 1962.

Feldman, Asher. The Parables and Similes of the Rabbis. Cambridge: Cambridge University Press, 1927.

Fischel, H. A. "Epicureanism." In Encyclopedia Judaica. Edited by Cecil Roth. 16 vols. Jerusalem: Macmillan, 1971–1972.

Flandrin, John-Louis, and Massimo Montanari. Food: A Culinary History. New York: PenguinUSA, 1999.

Flusser, David. Jesus. Jerusalem: Magnes, 2001.

Gaster, Theodor H. "Demon, Demonology." In The Interpreter's Dictionary of the Bible: An Illustrated Encyclopedia. Edited by George A. Buttrick. New York: Abingdon, 1962.

Ginzberg, Louis. Legends of the Jews. 7 vols. Philadelphia: Jewish Publication Society of America, 1956.

Goldin, Judah, trans. The Fathers according to Rabbi Nathan. Yale Judaica Series. New Haven, Conn.: Yale University Press, 1955.

Good, Edwin M. "Fire." In The Interpreter's Dictionary of the Bible: An Illustrated Encyclopedia. Edited by George A. Buttrick. New York: Abingdon, 1962.

Grayston, K. "Sermon on the Mount." In The Interpreter's Dictionary of the Bible: An Illustrated Encyclopedia. Edited by George A. Buttrick. New York: Abingdon, 1962.

Harrison, R. K. "Healing." In The Interpreter's Dictionary of the Bible: An Illustrated Encyclopedia. Edited by George A. Buttrick. New York: Abingdon, 1962.

Hillers, Delbert Roy. "Demons, Demonology." In Encyclopedia Judaica. Edited by Cecil Roth. 16 vols. Jerusalem: Macmillan, 1971–1972.

Horsley, Richard A. Bandits, Prophets and Messiahs: Popular Movements at the Time of Jesus. San Francisco: HarperSanFrancisco, 1988.

Hultgren, Arland J. *The Parables of Jesus: A Commentary*. Grand Rapids, Mich.: William B. Eerdmans, 2000.

Jastrow, Marcus. *A Dictionary of the Targumim, the Talmud Babli and Yerushalmi, and the Midrashic Literature*. New York: Pardes, 1950.

Jeremias, Joachim. *The Parables of Jesus*. Rev. ed. New York: Charles Scribner's Sons, 1963.

———. *Unknown Sayings of Jesus*. New York: Macmillan, 1957.

Johnson, S. E. "Son of Man." In *The Interpreter's Dictionary of the Bible: An Illustrated Encyclopedia*. Edited by George A. Buttrick. New York: Abingdon, 1962.

Josephus. Flavius. *Against Apion*. In *The New Complete Works of Josephus*. Translated by William Whiston with commentaries by Paul L. Maier. Grand Rapids, Mich.: Kregel Publications Inc., 1998.

———. *Antiquities*. In *The New Complete Works of Josephus*.

———. *The Jewish Wars*. In *The New Complete Works of Josephus*.

———. *Life*. In *The New Complete Works of Josephus*.

Klausner, Joseph. *Jesus of Nazareth: His Life, Times and Teaching*. Translated by Herbert Danby. New York: Macmillan, 1944.

McCasland, S. V. "Spirit." In *The Interpreter's Dictionary of the Bible: An Illustrated Encyclopedia*. Edited by George A. Buttrick. New York: Abingdon, 1962.

Mekilta de-Rabbi Ishmael. Edited and translated by J. Z. Lauterbach. 3 vols. Philadelphia: Jewish Publication Society, 1933–1935.

Miller, Madeleine S., and J. Lane Miller. *Harper's Encyclopedia of Biblical Life*. Rev. ed. New York: Harper and Row, 1978.

The Mishnah. Translated from the Hebrew with introduction and brief explanatory notes by Herbert Danby. Oxford: Clarendon, 1933.

Montefiore, Claude G. *Synoptic Gospels*. 3 vols. London: Macmillan, 1909.

Montefiore, Claude G., and H. Loewe. *A Rabbinic Anthology*. London: Macmillan, 1938.

Moore, George Foot. *Judaism in the First Centuries of the Christian Era*. 3 vols. Cambridge, Mass.: Harvard University Press, 1927.

The New American Bible. Louis F. Hartman and Francis T. Cignac, chairmen. Canada: Catholic World Press, 1987.

The New Testament from 26 Translations. Edited by Curtis Vaughan. Grand Rapids, Mich.: Zondervan, 1967.

The Old Testament Pseudepigrapha. Edited by James Charlesworth. 2 vols. Garden City, N.Y.: Doubleday, 1983–1985.

The Oxford Annotated Bible. Edited by Herbert G. May and Bruce M. Metzger. New York: Oxford University Press, 1962.

Philo Judaeus. *De Decalogo*.

———. *II Som*.

———. *Legationem ad Gaium*.

———. *On the Account of the World's Creation*.

———. *On Execrations.*

———. *On Cherubim.*

Philo of Alexandria: The Contemplative Life, the Giants and Selections. Edited and translated by David Whiston. Mahwah, N.J.: Paulist Press, 1988.

Posner, Raphael. "Marriage." In *Encyclopedia Judaica.* Edited by Cecil Roth. 16 vols. Jerusalem: Macmillan, 1971–1972.

Preuss, Julius. *Biblical and Talmudic Medicine.* Translated by Fred Rosner. New York: Jason Aronson, 1994.

Rabinowitz, Louis I. "Demons, Demonology." In *Encyclopedia Judaica.* Edited by Cecil Roth. 16 vols. Jerusalem: Macmillan, 1971–1972.

———. "Parable: In the Talmud and Midrash." In *Encyclopedia Judaica.* Edited by Cecil Roth. 16 vols. Jerusalem: Macmillan, 1971–1972.

Rivkin, Ellis. *A Hidden Revolution: The Pharisee's Search for the Kingdom Within.* Nashville Tenn.: Abingdon, 1978.

Ross, J. F. "Salt." In *The Interpreter's Dictionary of the Bible: An Illustrated Encyclopedia.* Edited by George A. Buttrick. New York: Abingdon, 1962.

Schereschewsky, Ben Zion. "Widow: In Jewish Law." In *Encyclopedia Judaica.* Edited by Cecil Roth. 16 vols. Jerusalem: Macmillan, 1971–1972.

Scholem, Gershon. "Demons, Demonology." In *Encyclopedia Judaica.* Edited by Cecil Roth. 16 vols. Jerusalem: Macmillan, 1971–1972.

Scott, Bernard Brandon. *Hear Then the Parable: A Commentary on the Parables of Jesus.* Minneapolis, Minn.: Fortress, 1990.

———. *Re-Imagine the World: An Introduction to the Parables of Jesus.* Santa Rosa, Calif.: Polebridge, 2001.

Sellers, O. R. "Weights and Measures." In *The Interpreter's Dictionary of the Bible: An Illustrated Encyclopedia.* Edited by George A. Buttrick. New York: Abingdon, 1962.

The Soncino Books of the Bible. Edited by A. Cohen. 14 vols. London: Soncino, 1947.

Spoto, Donald. *The Hidden Jesus: A New Life.* New York: St. Martin's, 1998.

Strack, Herman L., and Paul Billerbeck. *Kommentar zum Neuen Testament aus Talmud und Midrasch.* 5 vols. Munich: C. H. Beck'sche Verlagsbuchhandlung, 1956.

Sundberg, A. C. "Sadducees." In *The Interpreter's Dictionary of the Bible: An Illustrated Encyclopedia.* Edited by George A. Buttrick. New York: Abingdon, 1962.

Talmage, James E. *Jesus the Christ.* Salt Lake City, Utah: Church of Jesus Christ of Latter-Day Saints, 1962.

Tanakh: The Holy Scriptures. Philadelphia: Jewish Publication Society, 1985.

Urbach, Ephraim E. *The Sages: Their Concepts and Beliefs.* Cambridge, Mass.: Harvard University Press, 1987.

Via, Dan Otto, Jr. *The Parables: Their Literary and Existential Dimension.* Philadelphia: Fortress, 1967.

Wise, Michael, Martin Abegg, and Edward Cook. *The Dead Sea Scrolls: A New Translation.* San Francisco: HarperSanFrancisco, 1996.

The Works of Josephus. Translated by William Whiston. Peabody, Mass.: Hendrickson, 1980.

Index

About the Author

Ordained in 1965, **Dr. Frank Stern** recently celebrated his fortieth anniversary as a congregational rabbi. As executive director of the Board of Rabbis of Greater Philadelphia, he headed an agency that provided chaplains to nursing homes, hospitals, and prisons in Pennsylvania and New Jersey. Dr. Stern has been actively involved in the Central Conference of American Rabbis, and served as president of the Orange County Board of Rabbis (California) and president of the Pacific Association of Reform Rabbis (seven western states). Now retired, he lectures extensively throughout California.

For fifteen years, Dr. Stern taught at California State University in Fullerton in the Departments of Sociology and of Comparative Religion. In addition, he lectures on Judaism, Comparative Religion, and Jewish-Christian Relations and presents at conferences on religious discrimination and diversity in the American workplace. Dr. Stern is the associate director of the Center for the Study of Religion in American Life at Cal State University Fullerton.

Rabbi Stern is married to Joyce Stern. They have five children and seven grandchildren.